The Book of Pheryllt

The Book of Pheryllt

— OR —

"The Body of the Dragon"

The Books of Fferyllt Trilogy :

A Complete Druid Source Book Based on Collected Writings

edited by

JOSHUA FREE

Published by
Kima Global Publishers
50, Clovelly Road
Clovelly
7975
South Africa

First edition August 2018

ISBN 978-1-928234-36-4
Publisher's web site www.kimabooks.com
Author's web site https://mardukite.com/JoshuaFree

Other Books by Joshua Free

Sorcerer's Handbook (writing as Merlyn Stone)
Necronomicon Anunnaki Bible
Arcanum: The Great Magical Arcanum

/|\Y GWIR YN ERBYN BYD\|/

PHERYLLT

THE FIRST SYSTEMATIZERS OF THE ANCIENT CYMRY &

THE PRE-DRUIDIC RELIGION

(from The Blue Book by Llywelyn Sion)

BARD OF THE GLAMORGAN CHAIR

as interpreted for modern purposes by MYRDDIN CERRIG,
12TH CHAIR

"THE BEST CANDLE TO MAN IS REASON."

- Merlyn

Table of Contents

Preface 11
Introduction 13
VOLUME ONE
I
Pheryllt Druidism & the Roll of Tradition 21
II
Origins of Druidism as Celtic Religion 29
III
Eight Fundamental Doctrines of Druidism 34
IV
Three Orders of the Bardic College 46
V
Twenty-One Triads of Pheryllt Philosophy 51
VI
The Wisdom of the Sages 62
VII
Elements of Druid Ritual, Rites & Magic 87
VIII
Hanes Taliesin 103
IX
Pheryllt Magic & Dragon Energy 108
X
The Quatrains of Bran 116
XI
The Gorchan of Maeldrew 125
XII
The Dragon Legacy, Blood & Divine Right 135

Table of Contents

VOLUME TWO

XIII
Cad Godeu (Battle of the Trees) 143

XIV
Coelbren Tradition of the Bards 160

XV
Communing With Nature 165

XVI
Auraicept na n'Eces (Scholar's Primer) 172

XVII
Ogam Alphabet of Ogma Sun-Face 180

XVIII
Ballymote Ogham Scales 188

XIX
Sylva Druieachd (Forest Ogham Tract) 197

XX
The Druid Way - Paths of Encounter 202

XXI
Godform Evocation - The Ogham Pantheon 207

XXII
Dichetal do Chennaib - Hand Ogham 211

XXIII
The Enchanted Forest - Greenwood Magic 213

XXIV
The Wooden Ladder of Authority 216

XXV
Guardians of the Grove 224

XXVI
Magic of Language and Persuasion 228

XXVII
The Great Tree Rite 232

XXVIII
Draughts of Inspiration and Oblivion 236

XXIX
Herbal Pharmacy of Dian Cecht 238

XXX
Oracle of the Trees - Druids Ogham 243

XXXI
The 21 Leaves of Ogma Sun-Face 249

VOLUME THREE

XXXII
Secrets of the Unhewn Dolmen 257
XXXIII
Fire Festivals of Agriculture & Astronomy 269
XXXIV
Astronomy at the Druid Temples of Merlyn. 276
XXXV
Keltic Philosophy & Pheryllt Mysteries 284
XXXVI
Naddred - The Druid's Gem & Snake's Egg. 290
XXXVII
Mysteries of the Book of Taliesin 296
XXXVIII
Preiddeu Annwn - The Spoils of Annwn 300
XXXIX
Book of Taliesin: A Celtic Miscellany. 308
XL
Songs to Trees by Myrddin the Bard 321
XLI
Vita Merlini - The Mystic Life of Merlyn. 325
XLII
Prophetic Dreams with Myrddin the Bard. 358
XLIII
Merlyn & Vortigern - Tale of Two Dragons 368
XLIV
The Prophecies of Merlyn 374
XLV
Stanzas of the Graves - Englynion y Beddau 385
XLVI
Rites of Awen - High Magic of the Pheryllt 388
XLVII
The Truth Against The World. 392
Bibliography 396
Index 399
About the Author 401

The Gorsedd Prayer of the Druids

Grant, O God, Thy Protection;
And in Protection, Strength;
And in Strength, Understanding;
And in Understanding, Knowledge;
And in Knowledge, Justice;
And in Justice, the Love of it;
And in that Love, the Love of All Existence;
And in the Love of All Existence, Love of God;
God and All Goodness.

Preface

WHEN THE FINAL VOLUME of my Merlyn Trilogy was completed, I made myself a personal vow not to publish another word thereafter— that I had said all I cared to say. Then the extraordinary efforts of Joshua Free entered the picture, and my reality shifted once again. Never say never.

OUR PATHS FIRST CROSSED back around 1995. I was teaching university abroad, and there received an email from one Merlyn Stone, a teenage aspiring writer with a headful of penetrating ideas which he confessed the *21 Lessons of Merlyn* had someway triggered. I recall being astounded at the depth of that letter, and was soon to learn that Merlyn Stone was actually the pen name of Joshua Free – the same author whose new work, *The Book of Pheryllt,* has caused me to quite willingly break my vow.

THROUGH THE INTERVENING YEARS I have watched as Joshua has matured into a fine writer – and an even better scholar, whose prodigious output of books cover a wide range of esoteric topics and philosophies, well-worth exploring via his website or on Amazon.com. In my opinion, Joshua's genius lies in his ability to compile, categorize and connect vast stockpiles of lore, ancient to modern, and which has, over the last decade, culminated in a truly impressive contribution to world metaphysics. In time, I believe his work will receive more of the serious recognition it deserves.

SO NOW LET US TURN ATTENTION back to what currently concerns us, the author's unique treatment of the literary remnants of the Pheryllt: that much-overlooked Megalithic culture, whose spiritual remnants– expressed through a system of massive stonework based on advanced astronomy & mathematics – are still clearly visible across the face of Europe to this day. Their language was not the written word, but instead titan stone, and thereby nothing in the literature survives first-hand, save the Bardo-Druidic echoes of consequent folklore. Fortunately, however, several early writers whose cultural roots stemmed from Pheryllt stock, did leave enticing references. And even more importantly perhaps, a handful of later writers who, in fact, contributed published (albeit scattered) accounts of Pheryllt milestones, most notably in editions dating from 1585, 1588,

1676 and 1874; as well as modern scholars ranging from Dr. Thomas Williams to H.M. Evans, T.D. Kendrick, D.W. Nash, Edward Davies and Lewis Spence.

Enter Joshua Free's, *The Book of Pheryllt,* an ambitious venture which seeks to join the virtually un-joinable. Its goal, to reassemble elusive Pheryllt fragments scattered across time back into a coherent framework. And through an effort of solid scholarship combined with far-reaching imagination, the author has accomplished just that.

ICONIC NOVELIST William Styron once commented, "We as writers have a responsibility to reflect upon history, and bring illumination through imagination." Throughout my own writing career, I have always embraced this approach as a guiding light, the most personal and impactful route. But not an easy route; imagination is a personal affair, and when combined with historic interpretation, lays one open to 'The World' ever-ready to tear ones efforts to shreds. Yet this in no way detracts from the validity of the approach, nor the unique Spirit it engenders

AND IT IS IN JUST THIS SAME SPIRIT that Joshua Free has crafted the wondrous reconstruction of Pheryllt wisdom and philosophy now in your hands— a volume which not only the Lady Cerridwen, but the ghostly writers of her ancient tome, would have admired. Such a pride is shared by myself as well, with sincere gratitude that this unique 'Pheryllt element' of our life's work, has converged at this one key point in time.

IT IS INCREASINGLY UNDERSTOOD AS FACT, that all existence is inter-connected on the deepest levels, and thereby nothing truly happens without reason or consequence. I therefore believe that the emergence of Joshua's work in 2018, augurs well towards the fulfillment of that Pheryllt-inspired axiom, "The Truth Against the World..." the idea that true enlightenment, by nature, will ever-defy the norms of establishment. May this new tome reach the destined hands!

Douglas Monroe

New Forest Centre, NY

Lugnassadh, 2018

Introduction

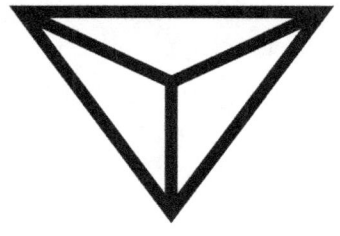

With my Golden Charm – set in gold

I am offered royalty

I am the Feat of Splendour

Born from the Crafts of the Fferyllt.

– Cad Goddeu

In ancient Keltia, the Druid Order consisted of learned ones, those educated in Bardic Arts: cosmology and spirituality, natural-native history and geology, legendary history of heroes and mythology, healing and botanical medicine, astronomy and astrology, and of course 'magic' – all of which are hidden in lines of Bardic verse and the researches of those who study them. As primary preservers of Celtic and Druid Mysteries, it is no wonder that Bardic Druids were considered the transmitter or catalyst of *-awen-* the essence, Divine Spark or spirit of inspiration that the Greeks termed 'gnosis'. It is to the 'ebb and flow' of the *-awen field-* that the magical and poetic genius of the Bard is attributed.

Preservation of ancient knowledge is key among all elite orders of the ages. This Ancient Mystery School is timeless and spans all places on Earth. Past mystical cultures often relied on elite orders of scribe-priests and poet-magicians to bridge ancestral roots and traditions with the future – orders rooted in 'languages', 'communication', and above all the written word. The poetic genius of *awen* – the Divine Spark of Creation –

manifests throughout all creative arts and as the spirit of 'prophecy', an ability to observe experiences with a heightened awareness and communicate it in the World of Form. Druidism is, therefore, an echo of this 'poetic genius', an amalgamation of collected knowledge preserved by the ancient elite, including a mystical and scientific understanding of the world that eluded the perceptual range of 'common' folk.

A unique metaphysical apprenticeship combining diverse facets of knowledge - from practical magic, to Welsh Bardic tradition, to Celtic history, or even foreign philosophies assimilated by the Druids - all appear in Douglas Monroe's classic Merlyn Trilogy under a premise of being derived from the *Book of Pheryllt* (or *Books of Fferyllt*); a collective body of Druidic wisdom also called the *Body of the Dragon.* As such, a wide array of sources and subjects were required to develop an allegorical facsimile (but legitimately authentic) manifestation of the *Book of Pheryllt* consistent with the mysterious manner in which Bards and Druids conceal and reveal the secret tradition. Considering the sheer variety of citations and scattered references in Monroes work, meeting justifiably high requirements and expectations for the 'Body of the Dragon' would require more than one volume to be complete and follow protocols - actually three volumes: a TRIAD interwoven as ONE.

"The Druids believed in books more ancient than the flood called the Books of Pheryllt."

– Ignatius Donnelly, Atlantis

Many antiquated scholarly references to the "Books of Fferyllt" or the "Pheryllt" themselves may be found (included or paraphrased in the current Book of Pheryllt facsmile). Whatever bits trickle down from classical literature and antiquarian druidism to satisfy a modern thirst for the 'pheryllt paradigm' have been collected together in one place - a sacred book once thirded and now made whole - forming a complete sourcebook of undefiled lore. Whatever name, guise, or title we might attribute to the Body of the Dragon - and we have chosen Pheryllt - this same lore (originally accessible to few) serves as basis for the majority of Celtic and neo-Druidic revival of the past few centuries; whether or not it has been given due credit as such.

Several different cycles of important Celtic and Welsh literature and lore - *Hanes Taliesin, Cad Goddeu,* the *Gwarchans, Cymric Triads,* the books of *Aneurin, Taliesin, Myrddin...* - are all found in the *Iolo Manuscripts* including the *Myvyrian Archaeology* anthology and *Barddas.* In fact, we can essentially trace the abundant wealth of surviving Welsh MS. - including the *Mabinogion* - back to "Iolo Morganwg" (Edward Williams) and manuscripts ascribed to "Llywelyn Sion." Where a thick scholarly aura accumulated from years of controversy may surround the 'authenticity' of some of these manuscripts, valid substitution shortages have bound the modern revival specifically to these available texts and the tradition gleaned from them.

A *Welsh Charm of Making* is found frequently in magical rites of Monroe's *Pheryllt Druidism* - an incantation spoken by magician-wizards to cause manifestation or change in reality. *The Charm* appears in the 1982 movie *Excalibur* for summoning the powers of the Dragon - a motif paramount to the Pheryllt paradigm. Positive recommendation for its use can also be found in Rhiannon Ryall's work and in *Ancient Magicks for a New Age* by Richardson & Hughes; but most importantly in the *Druid Histories* compiled by Lewis Spence, a reputable scholar learned in occultism, Celtic Mysteries and the Druids. He writes:

"Even some of the old Druidical cabbalistic expressions used in evoking, or calling up, the spirit of divination, still exist; for instance:

"anail nathrock uthvass
bethudd, dochiel dienve"

These words seem to be a sort of barbarous Irish form of an ancient Celtic expression, and are among the oldest surviving fragments of prehistoric verse to be recovered from Ogham inscriptions."

The Charm is usually written phonetically (as seen above), a puzzle that made literal translation exceptionally difficult in 2008, when members of the Mardukite Research Organization worked it out to mean:

DRAGON'S BREATH

SPELL OF LIFE AND DEATH

THY CHARM OF MAKING

Anail Nathrach

(anail nathair) {breath} {serpent}

Orth'bhais's Bethad

(ortha bhais-is beatha) {spell} {life} {death}

Do Chel Denmha

(do cheal deanaimh) {thy} {charm} {making}

Trees are an inseparable icon to the Druidic archetype. Supplementing a wealth of "Welsh Bardic Druidism" found within the *corpus draconis* of Pheryllt materials, the Seeker is also led into deep forests of woodland mystery within these pages where lies the *Great Magical Arcanum* – initiation to Divine Secrets of the Universe hidden within runic glyphs representing twenty-one keys – the Ogham – the secret alphabet and language of the trees. Druids adopted the Ogham as a mnemonic system among scribe-magician-priests to classify and under- stand the world. True initiates will discover an incredible "Druid Database" – the original mainframe – of knowledge and wisdom that unified Keltia for at least a millennium and forever shaped the consciousness of the planet thereafter.

Barddas describes the Bardic tradition of *Coelbreni,* "wood of credibility" or "omen sticks" cut with *Ogham* letters. Diviners would ceremonially cast them upon the ground making predictions from the way they fell. This was sometimes called "Crane Knowledge" because the birds would make "letter patterns" in the sky as they flew. These too, were observed and interpreted as omens. Other literary sources for the *Ogham Tree Alphabet* include the *Ogham Tract* and 14th Century *Book of Ballymote* transcribed by George Calder as *Auraicept na n'Eces* –

named after the opening line: "primer of the poets" or "beginning of the lessons." All modern "Ogham Tree" systems revived for New Age practices actually derive from this *Scholar's Primer.* The Ogham origins, however, are from the "Tower of Babel" (Babylon) and attributed to the god "Ogma Sun-Face," Patron to Bardic Druids (poets, writers, scribes, and artists) and the "Mercurial" (messenger) archetypal current appearing elsewhere with *Merlyn, Nabu, Thoth, Hermes,* and so forth. Authorship is attributed to "Ogma" directly, as in the infamous passage:

"Ogma, a man skilled in speech and poetry, invented the Ogham. The cause of its invention, as proof of his ingenuity, that this speech should belong to the learned alone, to the exclusion of rustics and herdsmen."

– Auraicept na n'Eces

Merlyn... Since the most ancient times – when technology and magic of gods coexisted with the Realm of Men – there has been no other Western World figure more strongly resonating with the true and sacred Hermetic mysteries than the archetypal Druidic wizard-magician Merlyn. Accounts of his mystic life – whether historical or legendary – reflect personal initiation to all paths found on the Tree of Life and a direct connection to all archetypes of the Tarot. These matters are no convoluted mystery to esoteric scholars and may be gleaned from the *Myrddin* writings – and also the allegorical *Vita Merlini* – included in the third part of this work.

The Pheryllt trilogy of volumes I have edited from 2014 through 2018, using the files from (and my two decades of experience with) Douglas Monroe's New Forest (now collected together in one volume as *The Book of Pheryllt* -or- *Body of the Dragon* anthology) is a realization of the legendary tome collecting wisdom passed down from an equally legendary 'priesthood' known in the histories of the Druids as the Pheryllt (pronounced FAIR-ee-llt or VAIR-ult) – those who resided in the ancient Snowdonian mountains of northern Wales. There, they inhabited an 'ambrosial city' named for its mysterious founder, Pharaon (FAR-ah-on), meaning 'higher powers' and possibly alluding to the celestial authority of a "Pharaoh." Perhaps it is the practice of "Druid Craft" to call down 'higher powers' to conjure inspiration and magic in the world - perhaps that is what Ceridwen is doing where Taliesin the Bard writes:

"She took to the crafts of the Books of Fferyllt to boil a cauldron of awen."

According to our modern Neo-Pheryllt tradition, a manuscript known as the *Book of Pheryllt* exists from the 16th Century collection attributed to Llywelyn Sion of Glamorgan Wales. Along with its companion volume, *Barddas,* also purportedly by Llywelyn Sion, the manuscripts moved from the library of Owen Morgan ("Morian") to the private collection of the Albion Lodge of the United Ancient Order of Druids in Oxford - an ancient stronghold of the Pheryllt Order noted by many antiquarian scholars and even Ralph Waldo Emerson.

"Oxford is old, even in England... its foundations date from Alfred, and even from King Arthur, if, as is alleged, the Pheryllt of the Druids had a seminary there."

- Ralph Waldo Emerson

Representing a classic archetype of "The Book" ...of secrets, power and/or magic for the Druid Tradition, the archetypal *Books of Fferyllt* exist both immaterially in spirit and as a body ("corpus") of literary work solidified in modern times from surviving fragments of ancient Druidry. It comes as no surprise to those familiar with my other work that I would feel the calling to this task - not only because of my involvement with Douglas Monroe's New Forest, but also that I possess a great experiential affinity for this archetype of legendary mystic tomes of epic proportion - having previously done this elsewhere with the oldest surviving Mesopotamian (Sumerian and Babylonian) texts collected together under the banner name of the *Necronomicon Anunnaki Bible.* And now, for the first time, this completion of the *Pheryllt* Trilogy permits all seekers full access to the *Body of the Dragon,* intended to compliment any personal journey into Celtic and Druidic mysteries.

"In the Darkness of the Oak Hidden in the Forest of Ffaraon"

- JOSHUA FREE / | \

"Merlyn Stone" (Myrddin Cerrig)

New Forest Bard of the Twelfth Chair

Volume One

Chapter 1

Pheryllt Druidism & the Role of Tradition

Translated by Llywelyn Sion

Bard of the Glamorgan Chair.

Transliterated by Meyryg Davydd

From the Library of Raglan Castle.

Selections Introduced & Relayed by J. Williams ab Ithel.

The Pursuit of Druidism

It is sad and strange that, in matters connected with our early history, men of learning and intelligence should despise our own native traditions, and seek for information from foreign sources. In Caesar's time it was currently reported that Druidism had originated in Britain; and it was a fact, that such as were not well acquainted with the system on the continent, used to repair hither for the purpose of acquiring a more perfect knowledge of it. As we have traditions on the subject, and, moreover, as there exists among us an order of men who profess to form a link of the chain which communicates with prehistoric times, and to be in possession of the views and doctrines of Druidism, as they were taught of old, it is but meet and proper that we should attend first to what they have to say, especially on the subject of the stone circles...

Stone Circles of the Bards

In the "Voice Conventional of the Bards of the Island of Britain" - an account of the rights and usages of the Bards of the Island of Britain, as exercised in the times of the primitive Bards and Princes of the Cymry - we have the following description of the situation and form of the circle:

A *gorsedd* of the Bards of the Island of Britain must be held in a conspicuous place, in full view and hearing of country and aristocracy, and in the face of the sun and the eye of light; it being unlawful to hold such meetings either under cover, at night, or under any circumstance, otherwise than while the sun shall be visible in the sky; or, as otherwise expressed, a chair and *gorsedd* of the British Bards shall be held conspicuously, in the face of the sun, in the eye of light, and under the expansive freedom of the sky, that all may see and hear.

It is an institutional usage to form a conventional circle of stones, on the summit of some conspicuous ground, so as to inclose any requisite area of greensward; the stones being so placed as to allow sufficient space for a man to stand between each two of them; except that the two stones of the circle, which most directly confront the eastern sun, should be sufficiently apart to allow at least ample space for three men between them; thus affording an easy ingress to the circle.

This larger space is called the entrance, or portal; in front of which, at the distance either of three fathoms, or of three times three fathoms, a stone, called station stone, should be so placed as to indicate the eastern cardinal point; to the north of which another stone should be placed, so as to face the eye of the rising sun at the longest summer's day; and to the south of it, an additional one, pointing to the position of the rising sun at the shortest winter's day. These three are called station stones; but, in the centre of the circle, a stone larger than the others should be so placed, that diverging lines, drawn from its middle to the three station stones, may point, severally and directly, to the three particular positions of the rising sun, which they indicate.

The stones of the circle are called sacred stones, and stones of testimony (*crair*); and the centre stone is variously called the stone of presidency, the altar (*crair*) of gorsedd, the stone of compact (*hog*), and the stone of perfection (*armerth*). The whole circle, formed as described, is called the greensward enclosing circle (*cylch ambawr*), the circle of presidency, and the circle of sacred refuge (*gwyngil*); but it is called *trwn* (circle) in some countries. The bards assemble in convention within this circle; and it accords neither with usage nor decency for any other person to enter it, unless desired to do so by a bard.

Here we have a detailed plan of the Druidic circle, but still we are left in ignorance of the meaning of the whole, further than what may be inferred from the names assigned to its several parts. Some time ago the writer of this paper hazarded the opinion that the three radiating lines had some reference to the bardic memorial of the creation, which is to the following effect:

The Divine Name

God, in vocalizing His name, said / | \ , and with the Word all worlds and animations sprang co-instantaneously to being and life from their non-existence, shouting in ecstasy of joy – / | \ – and thus repeating the name of the Deity.

God, when there was in life and existence none but Himself, pronounced His name, and co instantaneously with the Word, all being and animation gave a shout of joy in the most perfect and melodious manner that ever was heard in the strain of that vocalization. And co-instantaneously with the sound was Light, and in the Light the form of the name, in three voices thrice uttered, pronounced together at the same instant; and in the vision were three forms, and they were the hue and form of Light; and united with the sound and hue and form of that utterance were the three first letters, and from a combination of their three sounds were formed all other sounds of letters.

And it was *Menw Hen ap y Teirgwaedd* that heard the sound, and first reduced into form the vocalization of God's name; but others affirm that it was Einigan Gawr who first made a letter, and that it was the form of the name of God, when he found himself alive and existing co-simultaneously and co-instantaneously with the utterance.

It now appears that such an opinion was correct. The sacred name turns out to be the very basis of Druidism, and the spirit that regulates all its doctrines and ceremonies.

Welsh bards and bardism

It must be premised that the Bards are strictly enjoined by the rules of their order to preserve and hand down intact all the memorials of their ancestors. The most abstruse questions

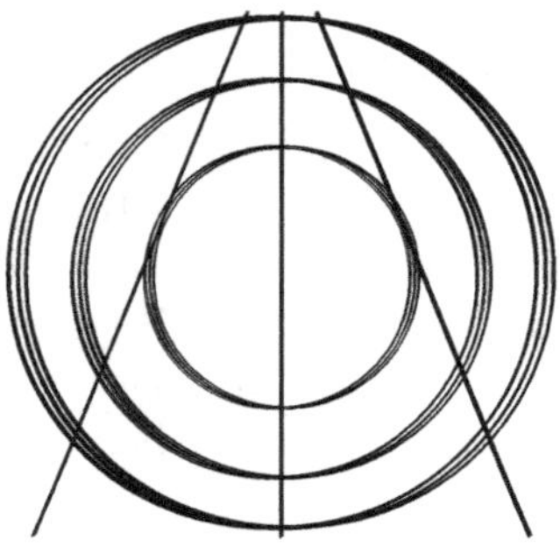

connected with their system are committed exclusively to their care, professedly lest a too vulgar handling of them should cause them to be misunderstood and corrupted. Whether such a pretext would hold good in the present day may fairly be doubted; and it were well for the *Glamorgan Bards,* the sole deposits of these secrets, to consider whether they would not be better preserved, and withal prove more practically valuable, if committed to print, than left to the oral care of a few individuals, who, however faithful themselves, may not have successors of equal trustworthiness.

We are convinced that there is nothing in the fundamental principles of Bardism that requires a perpetual reserve. There are several things already published, which were once looked upon as bardic secrets...

The Druid's Cabala

Myvyr Morganwg, a profound, well-read man, and a genuine representative of the ancient Bards, is in possession of a vast store of these mysteries; and, though he is reluctant to give publicity to the whole, he has undertaken to make revelations of an astonishing character; and, indeed, he has already allowed enough to escape in reference to the mystical / | \, to furnish us with a key to the proper understanding of the religious system of the whole Gentile world.

From the "Mysteries", as explained by him, we learn that the Bards considered the sun as the most lively representation of the deity. When God pronounced His name, and said / | \, the cause of all animation, the form took in the whole light of the sun, as it were, from the summer solstice to the winter solstice, these points being indicated by the outer lines respectively; the middle line represented the sun at the equinoxes. These radii, according to the influence of the sun upon nature at the several *albanau,* which they indicated, were regarded as emblematical of His great attributes. That of *Alban Hevin,* or the summer solstice, represented Him as a creator, the middle one, or that of the equinoxes, as an upholder, and that of *Alban Arthan,* as a withholder, or a destroyer.

In the bardic account of the creation, it is said that all letters and sciences were formed from / | \, and it is observable that the three lines contain the elements of the British alphabet, every character of it being formed from one or more. Again, the *name,* in different aspects, was made to educe doctrines, religious and philosophical, in endless varieties; for instance, the space between the two outer lines was divided into seven portions - seven forces - represented by the seven days of the week; the middle ray, along which the presiding Bard always looked, ran through Woden's day *(Mercury)*, i.e. *dydd Gwyddon,* the Druid's primitive name.

The British Bards seem to have been always very jealous of the honor of the true God. The proclamation of His name they considered as the manifestation of Him in His works; and, as they regarded the visible creation as being brought into order chiefly through the agency of the sun, they looked upon Him as pronouncing and giving form to His name by means of the triple ray, which embraced the whole extent of the sun's influence.

The Divine Logos and Gorsedd

The danger seems to have been that men, not properly understanding the *name,* would deify the form, which, we are told, they did at a very early period. This mistake would appear to have been at the bottom of most of the idolatry of the heathen world.

There is something in the "Mysteries" remarkably corroborative of the age of the world, according to common computation, as well as of the great antiquity usually assigned to the bardic system. They give us to understand that the gorsedd was in operation, when the sun of the vernal (spring) equinox was being conveyed over the point of liberty, or the equinoctial line, from the celestial *annwn* of the Druids into heaven, exactly on the points of the bull's horns, which, calculating by the precession of the equinoxes, could not have been less than 5,800 years ago!

Whilst / | \, the great seal of the *gorsedd,* symbolized the triune God in His several attributes, so there was exhibited in connection with it most remarkable antetypes of the future manifestation of the second Person.

The Bard, standing on the central stone, at the concentration of the rays, in the eye of light, was considered as the sun of the moral world; looking due east, along the two-fold middle ray, which proceeded from the signs of the ram and of the virgin, he was regarded as the son or lamb of God, born of a virgin. He was considered as the son of God, because he stood at the conjunction of the triple symbol of the name of God, and was a living and corporeal representation of the / | \, the Logos, by which the world was made. He was thus looked upon as God in the flesh.

As the Druids believed that the world was gradually advancing towards perfection, which was being brought about through the instrumentality of these moral teachers, the Bards, figuratively sons of God and born of a virgin, they were well disciplined to follow the "Great Bard" (with reverence be it said), who was really the Son and Lamb of God, really virgin-born, the Prince of Peace, author of the "Glorious Liberty", the Truth, those three great ends to which the Bards aspired; He, who was the Word, "by Whom all things were made;" the "True Light, which lights every man that comes into the world;" whose "sign" – the starry cross – the development of / | \, shall appear resplendent in the heavens at the renovation of all things.

The Sun - Solar Logos

There is one philosophical doctrine connected with the sun, as held by the Druids, which is in a peculiar manner figurative of an event in the history of the redemption.

The sun, emblem of the Deity, was considered, when on the vigil of Alhan Arthan, as dying and descending into *annwn;* he was supposed to remain there during the whole of the next day, the short black Saturday; but on the morning of the third day, the Festival of the Alban, he was regarded as born again, and arising from his grave, victorious over all the dragons and monsters of *annwn.*

Is not this a lively picture of death, burial, and resurrection for the "Sun of Righteousness?" There is something that fills the mind with astonishment, when we contemplate the dispensation of God in thus guiding or instructing our forefathers to have constantly before their eyes, whilst engaged in the act of public worship, such anticipatory tokens of better things.

The primitive fathers believed that the "sign of the Son of Man," which should appear in the heavens at the last day, was the cross. "That is the cross," says St. Chrysostom, "more bright than the sun, if the sun is darkened and the cross appears; for it would not appear, if it were not brighter than the sun's rays."

It would appear that the bards believed that a manifestation, similar to that which took place at the creation, would be repeated at the renovation of the world, for in the "Roll of Tradition," after having spoken of the former, it is added; "Still and small was that melodiously sounding voice (i.e. the Divine utterance), which will never be equaled again until God shall renovate every pre-existence from the mortality entailed on it by sin, by *revocalizing that name.*"

Mottos of the Chairs of the Island of Britain

The Chair of the Bards of the Island of Britain—"Truth against the World."

- Glamorgan or Siluria—"God and all goodness."

- The Round Table of Arthur, of Taliesin, and of Tir Iarll (EarFs Land)—"Nothing is truly good that may be excelled."
- Powis—"Who slays shall be slain."
- Deheubarth (South Wales)—"Heart to heart."
- Bryn Gwyddon—"Hearing is believing; seeing is truth."
- Dyvnaint (Devon) in the Chair of Beisgawen—"Nothing is forever that is not for ever and ever."
- Urien Rheged, at Aberllychwr (Loughor), under the Presidency of Taliesin—"Truth will have its place."
- Rhaglan Castle, under the Patronage of Lord William Herbert—"Awake! It is day."

Chapter II The Origins of Druidism as Celtic Religion

Illuminated by W. Winwood Reade

in Mysteries of the Druids, Book III,

Selections Adapted by Myrddin Cerrig

The Druids - Origins

Although the term Druid is local, their religion was of deep root, and a distant origin. It was of equal antiquity with those of the Persian Magi, the Chaldees of Assyria, and the Brachmans of Hindostan. It resembled them so closely in its sublime precepts, in its consoling promises, as to leave no doubt that these nations, living so widely apart, were all of the same stock and the same religion – that of Noah, and the children of men before the flood. They worshiped but one God, and erected to him altars of earth, or unhewn stone, and prayed to him in the open air; and believed in a heaven, in a hell, and in the immortality of the soul. It is strange that these offspring of the patriarchs should also be corrupted from the same sources, and should thus still preserve a resemblance to one another in the minor tenets of their polluted creeds.

Those pupils of the Egyptian priests, the Phoenicians, or Canaanites, who had taught the Israelites to sacrifice human beings, and to pass their children through the fire to Moloch, infused the same bloodthirsty precepts among the Druids. As the Indian wife was burnt upon her husband's pyre, so, on the corpses of the Celtic lords, were consumed their children, their slaves, and their horses. And, like the other nations of antiquity, as I shall presently prove, the Druids worshiped the heavenly bodies, and also trees, and water, and mountains, and the signs of the serpent, the bull and the cross.

The doctrine of the transmigration of souls which formed a leading theory on the system of the Brachmans, of the Druids, and afterward of the Pythagoreans was obtained, through the Phoenicians, from Egypt, the fatherland of heathen mythology. It cannot be denied that they also honored inferior deities, to whom they gave the names of Hu and Ceridwen, Hesus Taranis, Belenus, Ogmius, and the attributes of Osiris and Isis (or Zeus and Venus) Bacchus, Mercury and Apollo.

As the Chaldeans, who were astronomers, made Hercules an astronomer; and as the Greeks and Romans, who were warriors, made him a hero of battles; so the Druids, who were orators, named him Ogmius, or the Power of Eloquence, and represented him as an old man followed by a multitude, whom he led by slender and almost invisible golden chains fastened from his lips to their ears.

As far as we can learn, however, the Druids paid honors, rather than adoration to their deities, as the Jews revered their arch-angels, but reserved their worship for Jehovah. And, like the God of the Jews, of the Chaldees, of the Hindoos, and of the Christians, this Deity of the Druids had three attributes within himself, and each attribute was a god. Let those learn who cavil at the mysterious doctrine of the Trinity, that it was not invented by the Christians, but only by them restored from times of the holiest antiquity into which it had descended from heaven itself.

Although the Druids performed idolatrous ceremonies to the stars, to the elements, to hills, and to trees, there is a maxim still preserved among the Welsh mountaineers, which shows that in Britain the Supreme Being was never so thoroughly forgotten and degraded as he had been in those lands to which he first gave life. It is one of those sublime expressions which can be but faintly rendered in a foreign language --

"Nid dim oxd duw: nid duw ond dim."

God cannot be matter; what is not matter must be God.

The Druids - Power

This priesthood flourished in Gaul and in Britain, and in the islands which encircled them. In whichever country they may first have struck root we at least know that the British Druids were the most famous, and that it was a custom in the time of Julius Cæsar for the Gallic students to cross the British channel to study in the seminaries of the sister island. But by that time, Druidism had begun to wane in Gaul, and to be deprived of many of its privileges by the growing intelligence of the secular power.

The Druids possessed remarkable powers and immunities. Like the Levites, the Hebrews, and the Egyptian priests they were exempted from taxes and from military service. They also annually elected the magistrates of cities: they educated all children of whatever station, not permitting their parents to receive them till they were fourteen years of age. Thus the Druids were regarded as the real fathers of the people. The Persian Magi were entrusted with the education of their sovereign; but in Britain the kings were not only brought up by the Druids, but also relieved. by them of all but the odium and ceremonies of sovereignty.

These terrible priests formed the councils of the state, and declared peace or war as they pleased. The poor slave whom they seated on a throne, and whom they permitted to wear robes more gorgeous even than their own was surrounded, not by his noblemen, but by Druids. He was a prisoner in his court, and his jailors were inexorable, for they were priests. There was a Chief Druid to advise him, a bard to sing to him, a *sennechai,* or chronicler, to register his action in the Greek character, and a physician to attend to his health, and to cure or kill him as the state required.

All the priests in Britain and all the physicians, all the judges and all the learned men, all the pleaders in courts of law and all the musicians belonged to the order of the Druids. It can easily be conceived then that their power was not only vast but absolute.

In all things, therefore, they endeavored to draw a line between themselves and the mass. In their habits, in their demeanor, in their very dress. They wore long robes which descended to the heel, while that of others came only to the knee; their hair was short and their beards long, while the Britons wore but mustaches on their upper lips, and their hair generally long. Instead of sandals they wore wooden shoes of a pentagonal shape, and carried in their hands a white wand called *slatan drui' eachd,* or magic wand, and certain mystical ornaments around their necks and upon their breasts.

It was seldom that anyone was found hardy enough to rebel against their power. For such was reserve a terrible punishment. It was called Excommunication. Originating among the Hebrews, and descending from the Druids into the Roman Catholic Church. It was one of the most horrible that it is possible to conceive. At the dead of night, the unhappy culprit was seized and dragged before a solemn tribunal, while torches, painted black, gave a ghastly light, and a low hymn, like a solemn murmur, was chanted as he approached.

Clad in a white robe, the Arch-Druid would rise, and before the assembly of brother-Druids and awestricken warriors would pronounce a curse, frightful as a death warrant, upon the trembling sinner. Then they would strip his feet, and he must walk with them bare for the remainder of his days; and would clothe him in black and mournful garments, which he must never change.

Then the poor wretch would wander through the woods, feeding on berries and the roots of trees, shunned by all as if he had been tainted by the plague, and looking to death as a salvation from such cruel miseries. And when he died, none dared to weep for him; they buried him only that they might trample on his grave. Even after death, so sang the sacred bards, his torments were not ended; he was borne to those regions of eternal darkness, frost, and snow, which, infested with lions, wolves, and serpents, formed the Celtic underworld, or *Ifurin.*

Although all comprehended under the one term Druid, there were, in reality, three distinct sects comprised within the order.

First, the Druids or *Derwydd,* properly so called. These were the sublime and intellectual philosophers who directed the machineries of the state and the priesthood, and presided over the dark mysteries of the consecrated groves. Their name was derived from *derw* (pronounced derroo) Celtic for oak, and *ydd*, a common termination of nouns in that language, equivalent to the 'or' or 'er' in governor, reader, etc., in ours.

The Bards or *Bardd* from *Bar*, a branch, or the top. It was their province to sing the praises of horses in the warrior's feasts, to chant the sacred hymns like the musicians among the Levites, and to register genealogies and historical events.

The Ovades or *Ovydd*, (derived from ov, raw, pure, and ydd, above explained) were the noviciates, who, under the supervision of the Druids, studied the properties of nature, and offered up the sacrifices upon the altar.

Thus it appears that Derwydd, Bardd, and Ovydd, were emblematic names of the three orders of Druidism. The Derwydd was the trunk and support of the whole; the Bardd the ramification from that trunk arranged in beautiful foliage; and the Ovydd was the young shoot, which, growing up, ensured a prospect of permanency to the sacred grove. The whole body was ruled by an Arch-Druid elected by lot from those senior brethren who were the most learned and the best born.

Chapter III The Eight Fundamental Doctrines of Druidism

Illuminated by Myrddin Cerrig

Bard of the Twelfth Chair

1. Doctrine of Separations

Energetically, a destructive interference is likely to occur in mixed genders - specifically concerning energy flow between individuals. The sexes are programmed to operate (attuned) to different vibrations. This makes it difficult for a 'complete circuit' (circulation) of energy to take place.

Children trained with Druids (or in Druidism) are schooled in like-gender environments with curriculum designed specific to the learning style of that gender. Druids educate males and females separately - each sent to a Druidic school in a remote location, independent of one another and free from gender-based distraction. Some male schools were found on Anglessey, Iona and Ynys Wyth (Isle of Wight), and the most famous of female colleges was in Avalon - now Glastonbury.

"New Age" metaphysical teachings acknowledge that each gender operates on different polarity of energy (in our dualistic universe experience), sending out (projecting) and receiving energy based on the structure or programmed nature of the respective polarity. As such, 'polarity' can be seen as a metaphysical 'filter' to the experience of constant projection and receipt of energy.

Energetic transference, exchange or communication of forces is what constitutes "reality" on the part of the "Observer". It is how we 'perceive' or 'internalize' our objective experience, or rather how we interact and relate to encounters with external energies and forces. Consider the following 'energy flow equation':

(x) → [+/-] → {EGO} → [+/-] → (y)

(x) = energy received

(y) = energy projected

{EGO} = "I" of the Observer

From a relatively 'higher perspective' these polarities – as well as polar dualism in general – do not actually exist and are only illusions or glamours fueling relative movement of the 3-D physical expression of the universe. This truth is found hidden within this doctrine, revealing a subsequent Doctrine of Like-Aspects, where we see the separation of like-energies in Druid magic as a means of maintaining or preserving a more highly concentrated flow of specific unadulterated energy. By keeping polarity isolated, a stronger bond with a specific energy current could be achieved.

Pythagorean-styled Druids and others with an ancient interest in mathematics came to discover another unique quality concerning the unity of polar opposites. If one sought to unite them as a balanced force, they would, in turn, cancel each other out. This later resulted in the Doctrine of Imbalances, which explains that perfectly balanced oppositional forces will allow for the net sum of zero. Consider a polar line:

(–3), (–2), (–1), (0), (+1), (+2), (+3)

Consider the following mathematical example:

(–4) + (+4) = 0

2. Doctrine of Authority

A true quest of mastery is of the self, and in that self-honest discipline, cumulative mastery of what is perceived as apart from or external to self. True authority is achieved only in discipline, meaning self-discipline. Psychological authority requires psychological discipline.

To ensure the logic of this sentiment, the deeply hidden Doctrine of Like-Aspects appears to depict how like-forces will (at their highest level) attract other like-forces. Positive movement and true growth exists through a combination of like-terms, which we can illustrate (again) using mathematical models. Allowing (+) to be any positive integer (or number) and (–) to be any negative integer, the resulting sum (or product) of these combinatorial equations will always be positive.

(+) + (+) = +	(–) + (–) = +
(+) x (+) = +	(–) x (–) = +

These cases always apply – the other operations are unimportant because they do not seek to increase the value of the whole. Changing these equations with a union of polar opposites will result in a negative sum (or product) or decline/decrease. The application of this principle is not exclusive to only mathematics.

Thoughts produce like-manifestations, energy from the internal mind is projected into the outer environment – this is only natural since on the highest level the two are not separate. Individual expectations, emotional charges and even physical behaviors all contribute to the energetic flow (which people call "vibrations").

Experiential knowledge is a result or product of some existing factor for it to have meaning. You could not build a "house" without first internalizing the concept of "house" in your mind's eye. If you had no frame of reference for such a semantic or concept, then the whole idea of "house" would be non-existent to you – not within your *realm;* or *reality.*

The more examples of "house" you witness, the greater your experience becomes with the concept and the greater number of possible pictures held in the mind. This does not dismiss the idea of creating new things – though many innovations are really enhancements or alterations of an existing archetype. Consider how these principles would apply to the Druidic method of instruction directly. The (a) value will, for our purposes, be a singular Bardic lesson.

$(a1) \rightarrow \{EGO\} \rightarrow (a2)$

(a1) = lesson given from teacher to student

(a2) = lesson reinterpreted from student

{EGO} = student formula is calculated for

The instructor observes the student's learning process until the introduced variable (a) has been completely internalized and reproduced (given the personalization of the student) to a satisfactory standard. The variable (a) must be completed (as a cycle) before a new variable of supplemental learning will be introduced.

Cumulative education programs are designed to supplement preexisting knowledge rather than replace it or consistently change focus. In unstructured modes of academia, new learning often interferes with the recall and use of old learning. The total sum of the parts [a + b + c] is impossible to figure until we have the value for each variable separately. This is how a Mystery School is gauged.

3. Doctrine of Instruction

The curriculum, to be effective, must always be personalized to the individual student. Close monitoring of an initiate's process is critical. The subsequent grades (for example, b), shall not be administered until aptitude is proven in a current level of learning (a). There is also a strict enforcement in Mystery Schools concerning the communication of subsequent knowledge (b) among students (or other initiates) who are not yet officially being administered that (b) grade.

In some Druid schools this philosophy is a part of the Doctrine of Critical Periods, wherein children are acknowledged as possessing unique learning abilities generally disappearing with age. Thus, Druids would closely watch children of the Celts, taking special interest in those who seemed to "shine." Gifted youth were usually spirited away into seclusion at Druid Colleges or given private instruction in the wild - outside the reach of townspeople - in small huts and forest groves. In such places, the high minds among the Celts were reared separately and installed into positions of power and authority within Celtic civilization. For this reason, some classical renderings have attributed to Druids the title *Father of the Celts*.

In accordance with the laws of apprenticeship, a master could only have one (a) student and one (b) student at any given time. The (c) curriculum (that which was possessed by the master) was typically only administered at the Druidic Colleges (located on islands or within dense forests). The concept of [a + b + c] can easily be used for our purposes to reflect the three traditional degrees of *Druidry* – the Ovate, Bard and Derwydd (Druid) respectively. However, since the lessons of each are actually cumulative, it would be more accurate to illustrate the academic development in the following formula:

[a] → [a(b)] → [ab(c)] = [abc]

4. Doctrine of Mnemonics

That lore and wisdom that is attained through *Druidry* is better experienced, internalized and committed to memory rather than to be profaned through writing. Knowledge is to be accessed by direct experience and used by intuition prior to being intellectualized and analyzed in text. Without direct experience, many limitations exist in sole relay of language and semantic terminology to fully encompass the essence of Druidic lessons learned in Nature.

It is significant that the Druids recognized this limitation in language and the semantics (meanings) attached or associated with vocabulary and terminology. Such limits the relay of an experience either in verbal or written expressions that rely on words. Some sensations and experiences are difficult to grasp in any language, simply by nature.

5. Doctrine of Imbalances

From the point of greatest imbalance comes the point of greatest stability. The continuous development in what is considered the weakest point will provide for a steady and well-balanced growth pattern. This philosophy is established to assist the initiate in succeeding in each of the Liberal Arts grades in addition to personal development. The purpose of the pursuit in *Druidry* is for self-actualization. When you have two areas of focus where one is accelerated and one is weaker, the focus on the weaker will help to balance the forces (or knowledge) combined between the two.

Imagine building a brick wall. If you allowed one side of the wall to be built up too much quicker than the other side, then building up the lower side becomes more difficult (or almost impossible) later. Further still, imagine being instructed to jump from one pillar to another right beside it and both are continually moving apart from one another. The challenge level of the encounter increases drastically as the perceived difference of the distance between the two platforms increases - one significantly higher than the other.

6. Doctrine of Mystery Schools

By heavily guarding the secrets of the universe from the naïve population, the Absolute Truth of the Mystery School can be maintained. Through the existence of a 'fellowship' or 'school' formed of those who are working together to protect these mysteries, Absolute Truth can be shared amongst a segment of the masses. By sharing Absolute Truth within the confines of a Mystery School, one can work toward these pursuits safely and without fear of reproach by the larger segment of society that is not made aware of the wisdom from the Mystery School.

Since the beginning of human civilization there have always been a unique and almost 'elite' percentage of individuals that are considered "those who know". Many of these enlightened individuals have brought their identities public - because those who do are often the subject of intensive criticisms or worse fates. Therefore, the 'underground cabals' and 'secret societies' have existed in nearly all times and places. Even in aboriginal and tribal communities, the secrets of the *shaman* are those that only the *shaman* (and perhaps also someone who is apprenticed to the shaman) knows.

7. Doctrine of the Enlightened

When a child is visibly prodigious beyond their years, the knowledge and intuition can give way to wisdom at an early age. When a child pursues wisdom via the Quest for Absolute Truth, then the real wisdom will be more likely to remain into adulthood. When the focus of a youth concerns worldly matters, then such a focus will usually remain fixed into adulthood.

This doctrine might also go forth to explain the concept of the mid-life crisis. Consider one who realized that half (or more) of their life, their prime and able years, is behind them and they begin to reflect about what true advancement they have achieved during this lifetime (including spiritual and intellectual ideals). True spirituality, in this way, is not concerned with "religion", but is instead representative of one's own personal relationship with the Source of All Being and Creation, however the individual has come to see this force. It is by following the spiral, returning to the Source, that true wisdom is eternally maintained. The Doctrine of the Enlightened Child corresponds with the Doctrine of Critical Periods and the clean-slate theory of contemporary psychology.

Before being exposed to all of the available 'worldly' stimuli, the young Druid initiate is trained and strengthened on a personal and individual level, then given unhindered means to reach their highest potential - and then only *after* this are they permitted to go an express this individuality out in the greater world. It is much easier to be allowed the chance for self-discovery prior to being put into various social conditions, particularly in a world where many masks and facades must be created and worn in order to survive.

We know now that there are indeed critical periods of learning in the human being. A child is much more capable, for example, of learning multiple languages with ease than an adult who has become more fixed in their wiring. One gets accustomed to seeing the world through a specific lens of truth.

Consider "magic". Magic is a 'mind-set' - one that is not particularly understood by the general population and is thus considered mysterious and esoteric (see the Doctrine of the Mystery Schools). Much of what separates a magical classification of reality, versus what is perceived by the norm, is mainly concerned with semantics, vocabulary and language. But there is a hidden irony at play here: all of the same matters explored in conventional sciences and philosophies are also deal with in the occult realm, simply by using different semantics to apply to a greater world-view experienced mystically all-as-one

- the ability to see the all-encompassing connection and unity of all forces in the cosmos.

Critical thinking and the ability to be creative are the products of an enlightened child. It appears that these things, when nurtured, will significantly aid the individual through adulthood where they are more difficult to attain (and maintain) if previously non-existent.

The question still remains as to whether this is an ability that all humans innately possess - raising the question of the human being is a produce of nature or environment. The position taken from the lore of the Druids suggests that they would view the human being as traveling through a combination of the two factors - who they are genetically and who they are spiritually. For example, a child being enlightened from birth, but strengthened by proper environment. Naturally this can work against the person as well, with a unrecognized prodigious child being thwarted in their advancement due to environment.

8. Doctrine of the Spheres

The Universe, both the visible and unseen parts of the continuous spectrum (considered dimensions), operates according to the Doctrine of the Spheres. The three primary spheres cohabit the same points in space as we understand it, though they exist at levels perceived as above and below the range of the spectrum as the geographic or physical points that the human 3-D being is wired or programmed to receive awareness from. Thus, they are considered semantically to be spheres existing at a different vibration or frequency.

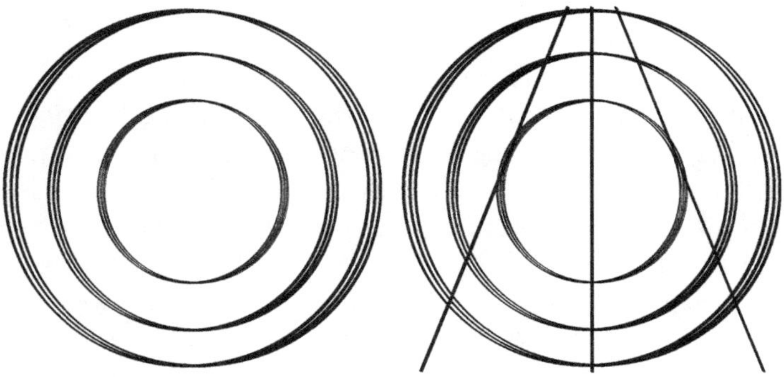

Although the literal existence of the dimensions are perceived as independent, they are actually all connected *all-as-one* - and the energies from one level can and will affect another level by either a seemingly unobserved means, or else by a medium that is considered to be something other (on the plane it is experienced on) than it actually is (as manifest on a different plane). This is called *perturbation*.

The Three Spheres model of the Druids (made popular in an antiquarian work entitled *Barddas*) is often considered the "Druid's Cabala" because of its similarity in nature to the Semitic Kabbalah. The spheres or Circles of Existence are usually depicted as a series of three concentric rings. They are defined (from the inside, out) as *Abred, Gwynedd* and *Ceugent*.

The First Sphere - Abred

Abred is the smallest circle or sphere of existence as plotted on the Druid's Cabala. It envelops the Cauldrons of Annwn (pronounced *ah-noon*), the "pool" or realm of elementary minerals, atoms and particulates (the basic requirements for physical existence). The Middle Earth (as humans understand it), is the circle of Abred, the Realm of Matter, home of the animal, plant/tree and human kingdoms.

The sphere of Abred is the smallest because the part of the continuous spectrum that is experienced at this level is more refined and fragmented - restricted to the most condensed of existences. According to the Druidic Tradition, a genetic entity can spend incarnations (rebirths) in Abred, even existing in forms that are other than human in order to learn (experience) different lessons that are contributory toward a permanent transition (or ascension) into *Gwynedd*.

A being residing on Abred first emerges from the Cauldron of Annwn and must first master the harsh Law of the Jungle in the animal kingdom. When lessons are not being mastered, a person can find themselves entangled in one of life's many viscous cycles. The *Barddas* material does not glorify existence in the physical world of Abred *(cylch yr Abred)* because the dependencies and pitfalls that distract spiritual progress are more numerous in Abred than anywhere else in creation. But if the freedom to pursue one's own destiny (program) and the resources (environment) are permitting, a spiritually-governed entity (human or otherwise) has a naturally tendency (or inclination) to return to the Source.

The teachings of the Bardic Tradition describe the pools of Annwn as a dark swirling Abyss; a cauldron; a melting pot of primordial elements swirling about. . . It is not, however, portrayed as an Underworld or Land of the Dead - such as we might find in other cosmological models. Rather, the *Primordial Abyss* or Cauldron is a place of origins - a world of birth and renewal, recycling the energy that has come from the Source - a White Hole. It is not a destination after death, but a place where fragmented beings are formed an the magnetic or gravitational pull of *Abred* keeps the physical incarnation solid in place once it is born (and it is the destiny for such beings to eventually es-cape the pull down to the realm of *Abred* - for when the bonds to the mundane are not broken, you spiral back to a mutual starting point; reset).

The purpose of any spiritual being is to successfully navigate the labyrinth of dimensions, and the lessons found in each, to seek an avenue that returns to the Source. The Realm of Abred is essentially where you are materializing your conscious existence at this very moment. Many spiritual beings and Ascended Masters have visited, learned and contributed to this Earth School throughout the ages. But most have given in to the Once-born Animus mentality and become slaves to the senses and the limited perception or range of physical existence.

The Second Sphere - Gwynedd

Gwynedd (pronounced *gweneth*) is the middle sphere or second circle of existence - not to be confused with Middle-Earth (mid-Branch), which is *Abred*. Unlike a more contemporary worldview held in orthodox traditions today, the Druid's Cabala does not depict Gwynedd as a permanent resting place after death in this (Abred) life. Rather, *Gwynedd* is a transitional place during the progressive journey of a spiritual being who has escaped the hold of the material realm. The Bardic lore suggests that the *cylch y Gwynedd* is equated with the spirit realm, Otherworld, astral plane and even elemental kingdoms.

By whatever title it is given, the Sphere of Gwynedd exists at a perceived degree of vibration that is beyond the 3-D range of creation, but it is not the highest plane. In *Gwynedd,* the spirit-soul is still a singular fragmented identity with the ability to continue learning new lessons to compliment those uncovered in their prior experiences in Abred - but now they are able to be mastered in a new environment.

The memories, or more correctly imprints, on the consciousness of a being are carried (transitioned) to other successive levels of existence. Only those beings attaining perfection in *Gwynedd* can rise above (ascend) to the Sphere of *Ceugent* - Infinity. Mental faculties and a combination of spiritual and genetic memory are the seeker's main tools when working in *Gwynedd.* This psychologically oriented domain also holds the "Hall of Records", what those in the "New Age" community have also referred to as the "Akashic Records" (or library).

The Bardic Tradition describes *Gwynedd* as "free of evil, desire and death", which makes it ideal for devoting an existence to personal spiritual development. As the second of three main divisions seen within the Druid's Cabala, *Gwynedd* is another school (like what we experience in *Abred*), but one intended to perfect the spirit (being) so that its form resonates (is synchronous) with the vibration (frequency range) of *Ceugent.* Only a Perfected being is capable of beholding Ceugent and so the Otherworld provides that necessary opportunity. The goals or virtues of *Gwynedd* (listed in the *Barddas*) are perfect love, perfect peace and perfect knowledge. That which is perfect, ineffable and absolute, by logic and definition, will lead to the Source.

The Third Sphere - Ceugent

Ceugent is the "infinite" realm, that which extends in all spatial dimensions and times simultaneously and envelops all presences in the lower realms, entangling and interconnecting all existences at the highest level of creation. In the Druid's Cabala *cylch y Ceugent* is the very domain of the Source of All-Being and Creation - the place where all beings ascend to reunite with the Source. This energy is funneled back via the infinite spiral to the Cauldron of Annwn to be recycled into new forms of existence; manifestations of expression.

As each plane of existence vibrates or exists at a particular frequency (a range or parameter within the continuous spectrum), a spiritual being must achieve spiritual perfection in *Gwynedd* in order to return to the Source via *Ceugent* – a zone that only resonates the spiritual perfection of creation, a unified field or state of awareness whereby all existence is connected to all other existence.

As depicted on the model, the *Sphere of Ceugen*t is the largest outer ring - demonstrating its nature as an all-encompassing force; big energy in small places (by our perception of space-time). The energetic potential of matter is astronomical. The energetic potential of *Ceugent* is infinity.

Chapter IV
The Three Orders of the Bardic College

Translated by Llywelyn Sion

Bard of the Glamorgan Chair.

Adapted by Meyryg Davydd

From the Library of Raglan Castle.

The Voice Conventional

The Bards of the island of Britain are divided into three kindred orders, according to the rights of primitive Bards; and every member of those three distinctive classes is called a primitive Bard, being so by common origin, according to the ordinance, usage, and rights of the primordial *Gorsedd* of the Bards of Britain in the time of *Prydain*, the son of Aedd the Great.

The first order is that of poets, or primitive Bards positive, called also—Primitive Bards according to the original institution; a distinction which no one can attain but a poet of innate and scientific genius, and of progression; and the duties incumbent on this class are—to compose poetry, to perpetuate the traditions of rights and usages, and to rescue Bardism from corruption and oblivion.

The second order is that of Ovates, who are not expected to have undergone progressive discipline, but depend on prospective graduation at *Gorsedd*: for an Ovate is simply a person of innate genius, application, and chance; and his duties are—to improve and enlarge knowledge, and to submit his performance to the judgment of *Gorsedd*, until declared efficient in authority.

The third order is that of Druids (*Derwydd*), which must be appointed either from the class of poets or that of Ovates, by the verdict and judgment of *Gorsedd*. A Druid acts in accordance with reason, circumstance, and necessity, and his duties are—to instruct, hold subordinate chairs and conventions, and keep up divine worship at the quarterly lunar holy-days. It is incumbent on him, also, to initiate persons into the secrets of Bardism, and to inculcate godliness, wisdom, and good morals.

The Bardic Grade

The rights and appellation of primitive Bard appertain to every member of each of the said three orders; the whole of them being coequal in privileges and dignity. The course pursued in graduating an ovate is—first, to place him under the examination of a chief of song, that is, of a primitive conventional Bard, who shall testify, upon his word and conscience, that he possesses the qualities requisite for a Bard; he, then, must seek the verdict and judgment of *Gorsedd*, and if pronounced efficient, will thereby attain the rights of a primordial bard, and be qualified to exercise in *Gorsedd* the functions of a progressively instituted primitive bard of that order.

Aspiring Ovates

A primordial Bard may assume the grade and rights of an Ovate, by virtue of the extent of knowledge and poetic genius requisite for a primitive ovate which he may display before a *Gorsedd*, with no other protective ceremony than that of greeting; and those qualifications imply the improvement and extension of learning.

A primitive Bard is entitled to an Ovate's degree, who shall, upon his word and conscience, recommend any one as a person duly qualified to be a Bard, if the person so recommended obtain, in consequence, the affirming judgment and protection of a *Gorsedd*; for it is considered, that whoever shall form a just estimate of the poetic genius and science of any person, and have that opinion conventionally confirmed, must fully understand such attainments, and know to what extent they are calculated to qualify their possessor for graduation and privileges.

The Ovate Grade

There are two classes of Ovates, namely, the primitive Ovate, and the Ovate by privilege, that is, a primitive Bard either of the order of poets or of Druids, who may have obtained an Ovate degree in *Gorsedd,* by virtue of his exertions in favor of an aspirant, who had, thereupon, been legally constituted a primitive Ovate in *Gorsedd.*

A primitive Ovate is entitled to exercise in *Gorsedd* the functions of a primitive Bard of the original order, if no poet either by progression, or by the claim and the privileges of efficiency, be present there.

When a Bard of the order of primitive Ovates becomes a primitive Bard, he is designated a primitive Bard by privilege, and not a primitive Bard of the original order; but to obtain the latter grade, it will only be requisite for him to submit his own composition to the judgment of a *Gorsedd* of vocal song, so as to ascertain whether it be deemed worthy of conventional sanction or not; if adopted thereby, he will be pronounced a poet, and be entitled to the privileges and office of a primitive Bard.

When a Bard of the original Ovate order takes a chair in *Gorsedd,* in the absence of a primitive Bard of the original order, and exercises the functions and privileges of that grade, if his proceedings on that occasion be sanctioned by another *Gorsedd,* according to rights and privileges, and finally confirmed in efficiency, he shall be entitled to claim and exercise the functions of a primitive Bard or poet:—and some say, that none but persons of this particular class are justly entitled to the appellation of graduates by privilege, and that they should not be denominated graduates of the original order,—a designation that appertains solely to primitive Bards of the order of poets by progression.

The Druid Grade

A Druid is graduated by conventional suffrage and judgment; but, if previously a primitive Bard of the original order, an election by ballot only will be requisite to substantiate his efficiency ; for every conventional transaction effected either by, or on account of, a chair-bard in *Gorsedd,* shall be deemed efficient, without the preparatory steps of greeting and claim; such Bard being already a person by claim, and acting under the protection of that privilege.

A primitive Ovate may be made a Druid by conventional suffrage;— a proceeding that would establish his efficiency. Some have asserted, that a disciple by progression in poetry may be graduated a Druid, and that, thence, he would become one of the primitive order of that grade; but it is an erroneous opinion, for a disciple, by progression, in poetry must, to be so, possess the genius of vocal song; and, consequently, be a poet, according to the protection and claim of the Bards of Britain; therefore, he cannot, in accordance with inherent distinction and usage, receive any other degree than that of poet, or primitive Bard of the original order: for when any person of progressive discipline in vocal song obtains a degree by the verdict and judgment of *Gorsedd*, the distinction so conferred must be that of primitive Bard of the original order, notwithstanding any thing that may possibly be said, conceived, or urged to the contrary: but it is also very certain, that the person so graduated may, immediately after, and, as it were by the same breath, be also constituted a Druid.

Of what grade soever a Druid may be,—or (if by progression) were he but an endowed disciple by protection,—if he assume, in chair or *Gorsedd*, the office or functions of any other grade, provided that such proceedings be sanctioned by a subsequent *Gorsedd* or chair, he shall, under the conventional rights of claim, acknowledgment, and protection, be considered a graduate of the dignity which he assumed, upon the very same principle that a person may become a primitive bard by attesting such truths in *Gorsedd*, upon his word and conscience, as shall obtain conventional graduation for an Ovate;—for he will be considered, in adopting such a course, as merely submitting to reason and circumstance, under the law of necessity and conviction, that made it imperative on him to exercise the functions of a Druid;—for nothing can be efficiently carried into effect, that is not well understood; and such a thorough comprehension will be inferred, if the extraordinary transaction, arising from the causes stated, obtain the protection and affirming judgment of another *Gorsedd*.

Such are the reasons that entitle a person to a degree, by privilege, in the order that he assumed and explained 'so well, without any progressive step, beyond that of proclamation and notice in *Gorsedd*. An Ovate, exercising the functions of a Bard, will be entitled to similar privileges, if his proceedings be likewise affirmed by a subsequent *Gorsedd*. By the functions of a Bard, are meant—the composition of poetry, and the perpetuation of oral tradition. But if an Ovate exercises assumed functions, under the control of reason, circumstance, and necessity, and obtain conventional protection for such a course, he will thereupon become a Druid, and be consequently entitled, by privilege, to perform religious duties, and to hold inferior chairs and subordinate conventions, at the usual and legally prescribed periods.

Chapter V
The Twenty-One Triads of Pheryllt Philosophy

Illuminated by Myrddin Cerrig,

The Bard of the Twelfth Chair

1. The 3 Quests of Mastery

a.) mastery of the self

b.) mastery of the physical

c.) mastery of the unknown

The first is a chronological triad in which successive stages of development are plotted out in an: a, then b, then c, schema. Though not all triads can be broken down into this energetic formula of accumulation, this one works nicely for this.

[abc] = [a] → [a(b)] → [ab(c)]

Consider that Mastery of the Unknown requires Mmastery of the Physical; and Mastery of the Physical is dependent on a Mastery of the Self. In this triad we can easily see a direct relationship between the parts. Each of the parts of the triad can be further broken down for comprehension.

a.) Authority in self-discipline, possession of true self-knowledge (self-honesty), the proper use of willpower, and exercising the influential power of the mind.

b.) Authority over one's personal environment, enlightenment through True-knowledge, the power of the psyche as an extension of the Universe or Cosmic Consciousness.

c.) Authority over the forces of the Universe, creating and maintaining an energetic communicative link with the *Other* (or the Source), and finally the realization and manifestation of the Godhead within.

II. The 3 Virtues of Wisdom

a.) to be aware of all things

b.) to experience all things

c.) to be removed from all things

III. The 3 Keys to Transcendence

a.) see all

b.) study all

c.) experience all

Although expressing the same ideal, the previous triads come down from different schools of *Druidry* and two keywords expressed ("Wisdom" versus "Transcendence") carry different meaning. The triads explain the need to be an Observer, to be witness to all but to remain separate and be able to glean the True-knowledge from all experience in an objective way.

From the combination of parts, we can deduce the following:

wisdom = {true-knowledge} x {experience} x {objectivity}

The triad expresses the need for detachment from what is being observed, for without this there really is no truly objective view. Just as we see with contemporary sciences, the Druid method of interpreting natural phenomenon also resulted from empirical observation.

IV. The 3 Keys to Druidic Mastery

a.) to know

b.) to dare

c.) to remain silent

To *know* is to learn and take initiative toward comprehension. To *dare* is to use the knowledge that is learned and the utilization of True-knowledge can result in wisdom. Wisdom will aid one in identifying the "Right Way."

This triad warns the initiate to remain silent about the work and study being conducted (also in regard to the Druidic Tradition being presented as a Mystery School). It is also important to note, concerning ritual magic and low magic (spellcraft) that the informing of other non-related persons can deter the purity of the energetic link being maintained between the magical operator and the goal.

Going about your (Druidic) work quietly will have many benefits for you. Keeping the magical things that happen to you to yourself will help them remain more magical and enchanting to you; more personal and powerful. The enthusiasm and energy related to any experience can be emotionally taken away by others if you allow it. The disbelief that many magical practitioners face from others is a perfect example of this.

V. The 3 Requirements for Druid Apprenticeship

a.) eyes that can truly see Nature

b.) a heart that can truly feel Nature

c.) clarity that can truly understand Nature

Druidry is Nature-oriented - often considered a natural philosophy more than an occult tradition. Appreciation and empathy for the world of Nature is essential - evident in art, prose and traditions of Druids and Celts, the green world of Nature played a significant role in their understanding of life and their interaction with creation. Druids concluded inspiration from Nature was of the highest order and utmost significance to all humanity, especially the Druidic initiate.

The clarity or resolution of the Matrix Screen - of which one views the world - must be open and attuned to follow the essence of what Nature (the Universe) *actually* is - in its state that we observer every day, but also in its timeless and formless essence.

VI. The 3 Objectives of Bardcraft

a.) to reform society

b.) to ensure peace in the land

c.) to preserve the excellence of the earth

Druids pride themselves on their abilities to manifest energetic change in an external environment - seeking to maintain peace and harmony (balance) between people and the land throughout ancient *Keltia.* Bards and Druids were able to come between rivaling tribes and prevent war. After the battle ceased, Bards would come with musical instruments and voice to create an air of tranquility while the Druids administered logical counsel to the leaders and soldiers. Druids seek, revere and maintain all that is beautiful, good and true on earth.

VII. The 3 Laws of Apprenticeship

a.) a master may take only one per degree at a time

b.) a master must instruct the degrees separately

c.) apprentices may not take apprentices of their own

By limiting classroom size, Druids ensured that initiates would not slip through the academic process; rather, they would experience a significant amount of personal attention. The Druids restricted the number of possible apprentices a master could keep at once to two: a *Bardd* and an *Ovydd*. When ready, the *Ovydd* is permitted to the Druidic College and eventually the *Bardd* progresses to *Ovydd* grade.

During *Ovydd* grade, the initiate spends a great deal of time in seclusion - taking their lessons deep into forests and wilderness in order to exercise them. This also frees up the daily attention of the instructor (*Derwydd* - master) to dispense the elementary lessons (called *gwers / gwersu* plural) to a Bardic student. This triad law prevents *Bardd* and *Ovydd* initiates from taking on apprentices of their own - though they might be instructed to mentor or tutor a peer. A *Bardd* might be permitted to receive assistance by a fellow *Bardd* or a higher degree initiate (such as an *Ovydd*).

VIII. The 3 Foundations of the High Council

a.) truth in our hearts

b.) strength in our hands

c.) consistency in our tongues

IX. The 3 Conditions for Losing a Chair on the Council

a.) performing murder or warfare

b.) telling a falsehood in council

c.) divulging the secrets of council

Although corruption inevitably takes over any elite secret society, the tenets put down in these triads shows that the original Druids did everything to prevent such from happening. The first triad example proves that Truth and Sincerity should be the ruling voice in Council and that the social power of the Druids should be tempered with wisdom. This is an element that we do not frequently see with the rulers of ancient cultures.

To possess a unified strength in the Druid community is to have power to carry out whatever necessary to uphold the integrity of the Celtic world. Druids exercised authority with *Utilitarian* elements, executing all judgments with the good of Nature and the greater whole in mind. "The needs of the many outweigh the needs of the few, or the one..." Authentic synergy in Council can only arise from all persons being singular in their vision and the ability to carry out the goals of the organization.

Druids evolved into philosophical pacifists - they trained in combat but did not participate in military warfare. References appaear in lore when they did bless or consecrate the weapons of the armies of the Celts (for example, against the Romans). Druids were neither allowed, nor did they condone in others, the ability to enact violent acts against fellow citizens. Druids valued Truth above all things - one of their secret axioms is: Through True Knowledge, Power. Although there were instances where social manipulation might require the bending of truth, to do such in the company of or toward the Council directly was a grave sin, punishable by excommunication.

X. The 3 Responsibilities of Right Judgment

a.) to listen openly

b.) to answer discreetly

c.) to observe mercy and justice in judgment

Responsibility of social judgment fell upon the Druids of ancient Keltia. Initiates of the Order also served the community as lawyers, physicians, teachers and government officials - all of which are positions of casting some judgment of action on another citizen.

Consider if your physician never listened to what you said, always went around gossiping about your condition to associates and then gave poor treatment. Druids who became lawyers and judges were particularly affected by this triad.

XI. The 3 Rights of a British Druid

a.) have shelter wherever they go

b.) no weapons shall be raised against them

c.) their counsel to be preferred over all others

Aside from the Druidic Colleges and temporary make-shift homes in the forest, it does not appear that the lifestyle of the Druid really allowed for them to take on permanent residences. Most Druids, particularly Bards, would spend much of their life wandering about the Celtic lands collecting and spreading the news and teachings. They were able to travel from village to village freely and know that they would be taken care of and safe.

For many smaller towns and villages, it was an honor to be visited by Druids. Though they frequently made appearances throughout the land, some specialists among most often sought out (such as the healers) were seldom stationed anywhere permanently and so the Celts would take advantage of their blessings on the occasions a Druid *did* appear in their community. Shelter and food were immediately provided, usually by the noblest families in the area.

Although Druids were not necessarily 'priests' in the conventional sense of the word, striking one down on the road would have still been considered in the same light as what we would consider today of someone who killed a priest, a figure that is generally considered to be non-violent and unarmed. Given the way in which the Druids were held in such high regard in Celtic society, a Celt killing a member of the Druidic class would be more like the murder of a government official by a civilian today. For nearly a millennium, the 'weight' of the words from a Druid, their counsel and judgment, dominated the Western World in Europe. Druids had final say in all Celtic matters, public and private.

XII. The 3 Influences of a Person

a.) what they believe themselves to be

b.) what others believe them to be

c.) the identity of the Self

This triad depicts Druidic Psychology - a means to understand the personality and motivation of humans. The knowledge assists in developing curriculum for students as well as administering matters of state.

"What a person thinks, they are" regards one's self-esteem and self-image, meaning essentially how you carry yourself in the world and when alone. When we encounter the 'greater' world-at-large, our own reality and energy immediately begins interacting with our environment - both the physical locations and the people that inhabit them. The standards, beliefs, expectations and social norms that are in place at any given moment and locale will, in turn, have an effect on us, whether or not the influence is apparent or not - we have an energetic interaction with the world around us and this contributes to who we are in those situations as we go through life.

When we come to interact with the world, we learn to create masks, personas and facades for different situations and with different people. These masks are a glamour - not generally representative of who we truly are - but some people become attached to them nonetheless and eventually over-identify with and assimilate these personas as "Self" (as a result of increased social interaction outside of self-honesty).

XIII. The 3 Aspects to Always Keep in Check

a.) the hand
b.) the tongue
c.) desire

What you do, what you say and how you feel are often the result of thoughts that seem to come unbidden. The thought discipline and willpower exercises of the Druids all centered around one point: self-control.

XIV. The 3 Avenues of Active Imagination

a.) the way things might be

b.) the way things ought to be

c.) the way things seem to be

This triad teaching is also known by the name of "The 3 Aspects of Wondering Left to the Imagination" - another psychological lesson where we can uncover the nature of mental creativity. Given the creative arts emphasized among the Bards, it is not so surprising to see such a simplified list of analytical inspirations.

XV. The 3 Aspects Avoided by the Wise

a.) fearing the inevitable

b.) expecting the impossible

c.) grieving the irretrievable

Druid psychologists realized the sources of most pain and suffering came from within and are manifested or internalized as "stress," usually from an unnecessary source. As such, this philosophy is similar to Buddhist doctrines on desire and suffering. People are likely to get themselves worked up over non-existent problems, over-complicating simple issues and showing the general inability to manage 'stress' to the point where it will psychosomatically result in physical illness, ailments and obstacles.

We are told not to stress about what is likely to happen, not to expect what could never happen and not to fret endlessly over things that cannot be changed. The most logical way to avoid stress is discovering sequences or patterns producing high stress levels or stressful situations and then avoid these behaviors triggers. It would seem commonsense for an organism to discontinue behaviors resulting in negative consequences but such is not the case - as we can clearly see with the human population.

XVI. The 3 Ways by which a Person is Measured

a.) by their hopes and ideals

b.) by their fears and issues

c.) by their neutrality and indifference

The term "measured" is not meant to denote competition but rather continues the ideals of Druidic Psychology in being able to figure a person out to almost quantitative accuracy. Of course, in this triad, we are not given any values for the variables and so this must be taken as conceptual only.

In the first part, we are told Hopes and Ideals, which is actually given as Gods and Ideals in some versions, indicating what a person strives for or models after; their Crown. This is also an indication of what they value in the world and about life and existence. Fears and issues carry with a person in their psyche and contribute to their behavioral makeup. Some translations of this triad given the second part as Demons and Fears, which contemporary folk would see as baggage - the perceptibly negative energies that are carried around with a person during their life.

XVII. The 3 Distractions Laden with Trouble

a.) hunting

b.) war

c.) love for a woman

While this is not an exceptionally deep spiritual triad it illustrates the Druidic attitude toward such activities; an ideal we should expect to find catalogued in the codes of a class of Nature-priests. They did not find killing to be rewarding or sportsman-like, and the highest class of Druids were quite stoic and weary of engaging in interpersonal-sexual and emotionally taxing relationships.

XVIII. The 3 Aspects Beyond Societal Control

a.) time

b.) space

c.) truth

In one of its versions, this triad is presented as "The 3 Absolutes Which Appear Relative in the Physical World" - indicating that Druids possessed an understanding of space-time relativity thousands of years before Albert Einstein. In this other translation, the three aspects are given as Absolute Time, Absolute Space and Absolute Truth. So, what is an Absolute?

Ab-so-lute: a value or principle regarded as universally valid, viewed without relation to other things.

The Absolute is the Real hidden behind the glamour and illusion of perception. If you were to take the concept of time and shred it of all the subjective human misconceptions about it, you would be left with Absolute Time, which is ironically the name of the fourth spatial dimension (by modern classifications).

If you take all that is known of spatial physics and rid them of all the misconceptions that apply only to the physical range of perception that humans understand, you are left with absolute space; the fifth spatial dimension.

XIX. The 3 Foundations of Innovation

a.) bold design

b.) frequent practice

c.) frequent mistakes

Innovation in society and creativity in invention and design is one of the primary motivations for existence, whether it be the movement of the cosmos or the artists hand holding the brush against the canvas. This triad is essentially synchronous with what contemporary academicians call the scientific method - one makes a hypothesis, tests the hypothesis, sees what works and what doesn't, then re-investigates the original hypothesis, revising it (or not). You make a plan; you try it, noting the results; you take those results in-to consideration when you go about trying the situation again. Pretty simple, right?

XX. The 3 Causes of Personal Stagnation and Reincarnation

a.) failure to obtain wisdom

b.) failure to attain independence

c.) failure to separate from the lower self

In some translations, this triad is presented by the name: "The 3 Things That Make Rebirth Necessary for a Person". In essence, these are the reasons that we do not grow and evolve as individual spirits during our human experience - these are the reasons we really get frustrated; reasons we bring unnecessary stress into our lives; and even the reason we suffer physical ailments while occupying an overstressed body.

XXI. The 3 Grand Purposes of Life

a.) to attain happiness

b.) to spread positivity

c.) to manifest positive innovation

This one should require no explanation...

Chapter VI
The Wisdom of the Sages

Translated by Llywelyn Sion

Bard of the Glamorgan Chair.

From the Iolo Morganwg MS.

The Sayings of the Wise

1

Hast thou heard the saying of Ciwg,
The truly wise bard of Gwynhylwg?
The owner of discretion is far sighted.

2

Hast thou heard the saying of Cadeiriaith,
A bard of highly inspired speech?
The first step is half the journey.

3

Hast thou heard the saying of Cynrain,
The chief counsellor of the Island of Britain?
Better to keep than to pursue.

4

Hast thou heard the saving of old Idloes,
A mild man of respected life?
The best quality is that of maintaining morals.

5

Hast thou heard the saying of Meigant,
At parting from his foes?
The children of the wicked are evil spoken of.

6

Hast thou heard the saying of Cattwg
The Wise, the son of Gwynllyw of Essyllwg?
Let the heart be where the appearance is.

7

Has thou heard the saying of Cyngar,
To those who derided him?
Longer endures anger than sorrow.

8

Hast thou heard the saying of Gildas
Of the Golden Grove, a man of great dignity?
Rome will not confer prosperity upon the vile.

9

Hast thou heard the saying of Stephen,
The hard of Teilaw, of quick answer?
Man desires, God confers.

10

Hast thou heard the saying of Madoc,
Son of Idwal, the amiable poet?
There is no success to the coward.

11

Hast thou heard the saying of Oynllwg,
The venerable bard of wide observation?
He has received good who has not received evil.

12

Hast thou heard the saying of ancient time,
Of worthy clearest utterance?
The fool will laugh when drowning.

13

Hast thou heard the saying of St. Cynog,
Chief of the land of Brecknock?
The one half of learning is [already] in the head.

14

Hast thou heard the saying of Illtyd,
The studious golden-chained knight?
Whoso does evil, evil betide him.

15

Hast thou heard the saying of the Car Cu,
After defeating the army?
It is no disgrace to amend.

16

Hast thou heard the saying of Urien,
—And who has gain said it?
God can make the afflicted joyful.

17

Hast thou heard the saying of Heinin
The Bard, of the choir of Llanveithin?
The brave will not be cruel.

18

Hast thou heard the saying of Ceinddar
To the inhospitable?
Christ loves not those who mocked him.

19

Hast thou heard the saying of Cynvarch,
The bold and active warrior?
"Whoso respects thee not, respect not him."

20

Hast thou heard the saying of Oadgyfro
The Aged, whilst reading the book of Cato?
He is not a good man who is not a Welshman.

21

Has thou heard the saying of St. David,
The venerable man of extended honor?
The best usage is goodness.

22

Hast thou heard the saying of Ystudvach,
Whilst carousing with his bards?
A cheerful countenance, a sound heart.

23

Hast thou heard the saying of Kibddar,
To those he saw brutish?
It avails not to whisper to the deaf.

24

Hast thou heard the saying of Bedwini,
Who was a Bishop, good and void of vanity?
Consider thy word before uttering it.

25

Hast thou heard the saying of the Cwtta
Cyvarwydd, by gathering fire-wood?
The wicked will not perceive his good.

26

Hast thou heard the saying of Dwynwen
The Saint, the fair daughter of Brychan the Aged?
None so amiable as the cheerful.

27

Hast thou heard the saying of Huail,
The son of Caw, of the discreet argument?
Often will the curse drop from the bosom.

28

Hast thou heard the saying of Cawrdaf,
Son of Caradawc Vreichvras, the chieftain?
The promoter of work is the cautious hand.

29

Hast thou heard the saying of the Wise Man,
Counseling the servant of another?
Who does mischief, let him expect its fellow.

30

Hast thou heard the saying of Lleynawg,
The honored and exalted warrior?
Better a grave than a needy life.

31

Hast thou heard the saying of Cynan
Wledig, a Saint of good disposition?
Every rash person injures his portion.

32

Hast thou heard the saying of Gwrgi,
Counseling on the Sunday?
The lucky needs only to be born.

33

Hast thou heard the saying of Cynon,
When avoiding the drunken?
Good ale is the key of the heart.

34

Hast thou heard the saying of Hylwydd,
Who was a wise and experienced sage?
The favor of a lord is no inheritance.

35

Hast thou heard the saying of Hu Arddar,
Whilst conversing with his friend?
Happy is he who sees those who love him.

36

Hast thou heard the saying of Rheged,
Who was faithful, and upright in his creed?
Who does evil, let him beware.

37

Hast thou heard the saying of the Counselor,
Whilst conversing with the color of the dawn?
Beauty lasts but an hour.

38

Hast thou heard the saying of Ivor Hael,
Of the open hall-portals?
Woe to the aged who shall lose his shelter.

39

Hast thou heard the saying of the bold man?
Let every one be cheerful in his house;
The rueful visage, ill betide it.

40

Hast thou heard the saying of Llywarch,
That bold and intrepid old man?
Though not intimate, yet offer greeting.

41

Hast thou heard the saying of Dingad,
When rebuking the son of a wicked father?
Soon will the duck's son learn to swim.

42

Hast thou heard the saying of Mordav,
Who one of the three most generous men?
Of evils, best is the smallest.

43

Hast thou heard the saying of Dynolwas,
The best man in society?
The orderly will long he loved.

44

Hast thou heard the saying of Avaon,
Son of Taliesin of recording verse?
The cheek will not conceal the anguish of the heart.

45

Hast thou heard the saying of Morgan
Mwynvawr, of gentle nature?
He is not wise who does not conceal his intentions.

46

Hast thou heard the saying of the nurse,
Counseling her foster son?
Let the skilful conceal his purpose.

47

Hast thou heard the saying of Ysgavneil,
Son of Dysgyvundawd Gradgymmell?
The poor will not receive presents from a distance.

48

Hast thou heard the saying of Caw?
Though it easy to un-freeze frost,
It is not easy to un-sort sort.

49

Hast thou heard the saying of Ysperir,
While conversing with Menw Hir?
The true friend is seen in adversity.

50

Hast thou heard the saying of Ivan,
Brother in the Faith to Cattwg of Llancarvan?
The grain of sand has his portion of the beach.

51

Hast thou heard the saying of Heledd,
The daughter of Cyndrwyn, of extensive wealth?
Prosperity cannot come of pride.

52

Hast thou heard the saying of Eleri,
Where there was not a bestowing hand?
It is not almsgiving that causes poverty.

53

Hast thou heard the saying of St. Cewydd,
To his numerous relatives?
There is no true friend but the Almighty.

54

Hast thou heard the saying of Endigant,
The Bard, where his audience was illustrious?
Bad words will not be recalled.

55

Hast thou heard the saying of Cadwgi
The Little, who overcame giants?
There is no sickness but sloth.

56

Hast thou heard the saying of Haearnwedd
Vradawg, the warrior of kings?
Stronger is force than justice where there is hatred.

57

Hast thou heard the saying of Bleddyn,
When speaking to his enemy?
Truth is no truth without following it.

58

Hast thou heard the saying of Eildderw,
The amiable and magnanimous knight?
Long will a bitter bit be chewed.

59

Hast thou heard the saying of Caractacus,
The exalted son of the noble Bran?
Robbery long continued will come to the gallows.

60

Hast thou heard the saying of Cenydd,
Son of Aneurin, the skilful Bard?
None is void of care but the religious.

61

Hast thou heard the saying of Follwch,
When doing penance?
Frequent after running comes standing still.

62

Hast thou heard the saying of Hugyvlwydd,
When counseling against offense?
Often after waste comes distress.

63

Hast thou heard the saying of Geraint,
Son of Erbin, the just and experienced?
Short lived is the hated of the Saints.

64

Hast thou heard the saying of Andras,
Who suffered on the extended cross?
Whoso distributed to religion obtained heaven.

65

Hast thou heard the saying of Hywydd,
Who was possessed of office?
Frequent after excess comes offense.

66

Hast thou heard the saying of Padarn,
The upright and powerful preacher?
What man does, God will judge.

67

Hast thou heard the saying of Rhydderch,
The third generous one, throned and amiable?
Frequent is seen extreme hatred after extreme love.

68

Hast thou heard the saying of Mygotwas,
Of great knowledge in Bardism?
Ill will the devil protect his servant.

69

Hast thou heard the saying of Anarawd,
The wise and wealthy prince?
With the impatient, patience is needful.

70

Hast thou heard the saying of Pengwlad,
Whilst warning all lawlessness?
It is easier to burn than to build a house.

71

Hast thou heard the saying of Mabon,
Whilst giving instruction to his sons?
Except God there is no searcher of the heart.

72

Hast thou heard the saying of Sandde
Bryd Angel, in time of separation?
There is nothing so strong as combination.

73

Hast thou heard the saying of Orallo,
When there was nothing stirring?
It is easy to make the wry-mouthed weep.

74

Hast thou heard the saying of Marthin,
The exalted saint, to the public?
Except God there is no sovereign.

75

Hast thou heard the saying of Vortimer
The Blessed, of wise import?
A string too tight is easily broken.

76

Has thou heard the saying of Gwrhir,
The servant of Teilaw, a Bard of truthful language?
Whoso deceives shall be deceived.

77

Hast thou heard the saying of Teilaw,
While doing penance?
It is not wise to contend with God.

78

Hast thou heard the saying of Rhioged,
After obtaining tribute?
God will not sleep when he will give deliverance.

79

Hast thou heard the saying of Dyvan
The Martyr, in the day of slaughter?
God is superior to ill foreboding.

80

Hast thou heard the saying of St. Hid,
One come of the race of Israel?
There is no madness like extreme anger.

81

Hast thou heard the saying of Gwynlliw,
In mutual upbraiding?
It avails not to reason with a madman.

82

Hast thou heard the saying of Arthur
The Emperor, the mighty sovereign?
There is no devastation like a deceiver.

83

Hast thou heard the saying of Bran
The Blessed, to the renowned?
There is none good save God alone.

84

Hast thou heard the saying of Angar,
Son of Caw, the celebrated warrior?
The heart will break with grief.

85

Hast thou heard the saying of St. Tyvodwg,
Of the uplands of Morganwg?
No good will come of wantonness.

86

Hast thou heard the saying of Penwyn,
When refusing the yellow mead?
There is no monstrosity like the drunkard.

87

Hast thou heard the saying of St. Bleiddan,
Of the land of Glamorgan?
Possession of reason is possession of all things.

88

Hast thou heard the saying of the Bardd Glâs,
When giving social advice?
Better the dog's love than his hate.

89

Hast thou heard the saying of Hhiwallawn,
Whilst instructing the liberal?
Where there is no learning there will be no genius.

90

Hast thou heard the saying of Gwiawn,
The observer, of accurate sight?
The mighty God will determine every right.

91

Hast thou heard the saying of Taliesin,
While conversing with Merlyn?
Excessive laughter is customary with the fool.

92

Hast thou heard the saying of Golifer
Gosgorddvawr, of the valiant host?
Every truth is hateful where there is no love.

93

Hast thou heard the saying of Beuno,
To all who repaired to him?
From death it avails not to flee.

94

Hast thou heard the saying of Bergam
Of Maelor, to his stepmother?
Slow is the step of her of the dainty morsel.

95

Hast thou heard the saying of Dirynig,
The wise and distinguished warrior?
God will provide good for the lonely.

96

Hast thou heard the saying of Mathavar,
When giving instruction to a kinsman's son?
Long will the dumb remain at the gate of the deaf.

97

Hast thou heard the saying of Fagan,
After showing his declaration?
Where God is silent, it is not wise to speak.

98

Hast thou heard the saying of the Bard of Cwm Llwch,
In his old age and tranquility?
The pious loves giving of praise.

99

Hast thou heard the saying of Clodri,
After oppression and perplexity?
The pious loves giving praise.

100

Hast thou heard the saying of Howel the bent,
To his namesake Howel the bare?
When God strikes, he strikes heavy.

101

Hast thou heard the saying of Eldad,
When counseling his countrymen?
To the pious, God gives grace.

102

Hast thou heard the saying of Gwgan,
After escaping from the turmoil?
Great promise and a small gift.

103

Hast thou heard the saying of Cadwalader,
King of Wales supreme?
The best [£5K] is that of the plough.

104

Hast thou heard the saying of Merlyn Wyllt
contending with his enemy?
The best candle to man is reason.

105

Hast thou heard the saying of Cyminawd,
An eminent man, of fruitful imagination?
Let there be, in speaking, ready deliberation.

106

Hast thou heard the saying of Howel,
A chieftain powerful in war?
Where love exists, it will not be concealed.

107

Hast thou heard the saying of Talhaiarn,
To Arthur of the splintered lance?
Except God there is none strong.

108

Hast thou heard the saying of St. Dathan,
After losing the whole?
God will not portion out unjustly.

109

Hast thou heard the saying of Cadrawd
Calchvynydd, of vast meditation?
The best woman is the one without a tongue.

110

Hast thou heard the saying of the Old Gwrlais,
Where two magpies were chattering?
Every one will seek his like.

111

Hast thou heard the saying of Idwallon,
An aged grey-headed man leaning on his staff?
Argue not with the unwise.

112

Hast thou heard the saying of the learned man,
Counseling against tumult?
Argue not with the uninstructed.

113

Hast thou heard the saying, which no one can find
In it a word of folly?
There is no beauty but in uniformity.

114

Hast thou heard the saying betwixt two,
Sitting in their chimney corners?
The pious will not agree with disputations.

115

Hast thou heard the saying of Gyttyn,
Who knew not which side of the loaf the butter was?
It is either a fox, or a bush of fern.

116

Hast thou heard the saying of an old Author,
Who explored all the recesses of nature?
A sweet apple will not be got from a sour tree.

117

Hast thou heard the saying of the aged man,
To a proud and reprobate lord?
God will limit the intention of man.

118

Hast thou heard the saying of old Oaradoc,
When he lost half a penny?
The full knows not the grief of the needy.

119

Hast thou heard the saying of the old Friar,
Concerning the ready arrangement of art?
There is no summing up like explanation.

120

Hast thou heard the saying of the wise man,
Arguing concerning wealth?
What the fool acquires will not prosper.

121

Hast thou heard the saying of Matholwch,
Who loved all tranquility?
Peace is a feast to every pious man.

122

Hast thou heard the saying of one Mwynwas,
Who was a king of great dignity?
Carnage is a feast to the raven.

123

Hast thou heard the saying of the hoary-headed man,
To the associates of his hearth?
The food of every pious man is corn.

124

Hast thou heard the saying of Mevennydd,
A Bard of book-loving disposition?
Except God there is no chief ruler.

125

Hast thou heard the saying of Nonn?
—The mother of St. David was she—
There is no madness like contention.

126

Hast thou heard the saying of Pryderi,
The wisest person in counseling?
There is no wisdom like silence.

127

Hast thou heard the saying of Maelog,
The knight of far-extending sight?
The good will not make friendship with the wicked!

128

Hast thou heard the saying of Peredur,
Sovereign of the Island of Britain?
Harder is the brave than a blade of steel.

129

Hast thou heard the saying of Lleuddad,
For the instruction of a peevish man?
Unloved is every unamiable person.

130

Hast thou heard the saying of Dysgyvundawd,
Who was chief of his host?
The best possession is the present.

131

Hast thou heard the saying of Cadell,
The prince whose better never was found?
Good will not come of much deceit.

132

Hast thou heard the saying of Anarawd,
The king of Gwynedd, an abundant land?
The unwise will not watch his swath of corn.

133

Hast thou heard the saying of Merlyn?
—King of Powys was he—
Without beginning we cannot finish.

134

Hast thou heard the saying of Gwrgan,
The renowned king of Morganwg?
God is on the side of every merciful person.

135

Has thou heard the saying of Elystan
Glodrydd, the wisest in design?
Better too stern than too helpless.

136

Hast thou heard the saying of Elvyw,
A man wise without a fellow?
Let every sort go to wherever it belongs.

137

Hast thou heard the saying of the poor old man,
When he could not get alms?
Whoso has meal shall have meal.

138

Hast thou heard the saying of St. Cybi,
Of Anglesey, to the son of Gwrgi?
There is no misfortune like wickedness.

139

Hast thou heard the saying of the just old man,
A chief teacher of knowledge?
Urgent is the truth for the light.

140

Hast thou heard the saying of the truth-telling man,
The possessor of accurate knowledge?
The wise will not associate with the wicked.

141

Hast thou heard the saying of old Uriad
The Bishop, the wisest man in his country?
It is easy to reconcile where there is love.

142

Hast thou heard the saying of the Son of Mervyn.
In discoursing with his sister in Coed y Glyn?
Confide not in thine enemy.

143

Hast thou heard the saying of the poor hoary hermit,
Where there was no hand stretched out?
Every ditch is a shelter to the beggar.

144

Hast thou heard the saying of the experienced man,
Who had seen many events?
Better a handicraft than the favor of a lord.

145

Hast thou heard the saying of Divwg,
The aged bard of Morgan Morganwg?
Whoso will not seek good, let him await evil.

146

Hast thou heard the saying of Einion Sais,
Greatly desirous of wisdom?
He's a fool who quarrels with his own garment.

147

Hast thou heard the saying of the wise man,
To one who lost his property?
Wealth will not prosper with the fool.

148

Hast thou heard the saying of Davydd
Brophwyd, to the irreligious man?
Seek after God whilst thou hast a day.

149

Hast thou heard the saying of Gwiawn
Bach, teaching a just law?
Every claim is right where there is justice.

150

Hast thou heard the saying of the old Poet,
Who in his day was a teacher?
The produce of falsehood is shame.

151

Hast thou heard the saying of Gwaithvoed,
When he loved not long delay?
Let the longest tarrier go furthest into the wood.

152

Hast thou heard the saying of the discreet man,
To one who would not act with discretion?
What is acquired through fraud will not long prosper.

153

Hast thou heard the saying of the Druid,
Who had seen the state of nations?
Scarcely is there, in a thousand, one happy.

154

Hast thou heard the saying of the eloquent man,
Who knew the befalling of destiny?
Every one longs for the object of his fancy.

155

Hast thou heard the saying of Cadair,
Who in every answer was of brief words?
The light load brings the hay.

156

Hast thou heard the saying beneath the foliage,
Of the wise old man, whose equal was not found?
God guards every pious one.

157

Hast thou heard the saying of the captive,
After subduing every longing?
The good God will not undo his work.

158

Hast thou heard the saying of Ceredig,
A wise and select king?
Every one has his foot on the fallen.

159

Has thou heard the saying of the enlightened man,
Revolving his meditations?
Above all remember death.

160

Hast thou heard the saying of John
The Apostle, of clear declaration?
Have God's grace, and have all things.

And thus terminate eight score of the Sayings of the Wise; and wise is the man who understands them, and acts accordingly.

Other Sayings of the Wise–
To the Wise who may Understand Them

1

Hast thou heard the saying of the white crow,
Predicting fate?
A clean hand, safe its owner.

2

Hast thou heard the saying of the nightingale,
In the woods in the summer night?
Often over the head of the godly is seen a shelter.

3

Hast thou heard the saying of the torn tit,
Playing with the birds?
Death comes in every shape.

4

Hast thou heard the little saying of the wren,
In the nest where she lived?
Let every sort go where it belongs.

5

Hast thou heard the saying of the hawk,
Conversing with the kite?
The friend of the wolf is the slothful shepherd.

6

Hast thou heard the saying of the owl,
In the wood by herself?
Happy is he who obtains his object.

7

Hast thou heard the saying of the bird,
From the midst of the holly bush?
Good will not come of long intending.

8

Hast thou heard the saying of the ant,
In the winter, out of its mound?
Summer sleep, winter famine.

9

Hast thou heard the saying of the wood-pigeon,
In the woods, instead of complaining?
God portions out man's provision.

10

Hast thou heard the saying of the blackbird,
Hiding from the hawk?
There is but a season for the proud.

11

Hast thou heard the saying of the magpie,
Where there was a nest to shelter her?
Labor is better than idleness.

12

Hast thou heard the saying of the grouse,
To the kite in the top of the oak?
The wise and the vicious will not associate.

13

Hast thou heard the saying of the toad,
Whilst caressing its baby?
Every sort loves its own likeness.

14

Hast thou heard the saying of the cat,
Whilst searching for the mice?
Every kind seeks its fellow.

15

Hast thou heard the saying of the lion,
Whilst casting his coat?
There are some brave in every country.

16

Hast thou heard the saying of the chaffinch,
In the thicket avoiding pursuit?
Bad is sin of long following.

17

Hast thou heard the saying of the puppy,
When the time of accusation came?
There is no deceit like the flattery of a maid.

18

Hast thou heard the saying of the fish,
Whilst moving amongst the reeds?
Stronger is nature than learning.

19

Hast thou heard the saying of the goose,
After seeing every occurrence?
The idle will not seek his duty.

20

Hast thou heard the saying of the crow,
On the highest tree in the orchard?
Better too stern than too helpless.

21

Hast thou heard the saying of the jay,
Screaming about the divulging of secrets?
Make not thy wife thy confidante.

22

Hast thou heard the saying of the kite,
To the insolent rapacious man?
Quick comes the doom of the rash.

23

Hast thou heard the saying of the thrush,
To him who walked the wilderness?
Make not thy enemy thy fellow-traveler.

24

Hast thou heard the saying of the sow,
Wallowing in the mud and mire?
The monstrous love monstrosity.

25

Hast thou heard the saying of the dog,
In the ditch, having become lame?
Let judgment be understood, before hanging.

26

Hast thou heard the saying of the eagle,
After traversing every land?
Consideration will not hinder any work.

27

Hast thou heard the saying of the linnet,
Feeding on the bogberries?
Wait for evil, it will come.

28

Hast thou heard the saying of the lark,
In the sky at the dawn of day?
Evil will not harm the pious.

29

Hast thou heard the saying of the sea-mew,
Conversing with her sister?
He who complains too much complains not very much.

30

Hast thou heard the saying of the golden- crested wren,
Who sang amidst the woods of the valley?
He dishonors God who injures man.

31

Hast thou heard the saying of the cuckoo,
Which she uttered on a dewy morning?
Willful is every ill-bred person.

32

Hast thou heard the saying of the red-breast,
Where he had been from his infancy?
Seek not the dishonest man at home.

33

Hast thou heard the saying of the pig,
Recoiling from dirty actions?
There is none so hateful as the drunkard.

34

Hast thou heard my own saying,
After all sayings have been rehearsed?
There is no wisdom like choosing the best.

And thus ends this portion of the Sayings of the Wise; and happy is the man who is as wise as the Pig.

Chapter VII Elements of Druid Ritual - Rites & Magic of the Cymry

Illuminated by Myrddin Cerrig,

Bard of the Twelfth Chair

Adapted from "Druid Compleat"

Druid Magic

Rituals are predetermined formulas for channeling energetic currents toward a specific goal. In most practical applications, ritual magic is elemental-oriented. The ritual structure itself has elemental alignments. In addition to these, the elemental forces are called by the presence of the elementally-aligned ritual tools.

1. Earth Phase: Physical preparations, outer environment, grounding, meditation and preparation of the circle (ritual space - *nemeton*).

2. Water Phase: Inner preparations, internal set and focus, the focus of intentions and altering personal energy vibrations to match the energy being attracted.

3. Air Phase: Internal intention communicated via vocalization (the spell), sound and smell (incense), all of which represents the first step toward manifestation.

4. Fire Phase: Visualization, reconnection to the original intention, using will-power to raise personal energy, incorporating external forces and finally releasing the energy toward the goal.

Earth Phase

Personal Preparations: Before conducting any physical ritual, be completely prepared, internally (whether that be your spiritual and mental set or emotional state) and externally (including everything from the physical body to the tools being used).

Firstly, cleanse the body and wear clean clothing (or robes) for the ritual. Being clean and wearing freshly laundered linens will help deter any static or disruptive energy that might otherwise be attached. Secondly, a Druid must be mentally prepared prior to the ritual working. Review all relevant magical lore and related knowledge concerning *Druidry*, the elements, ritual magic, and any of the other facets that might be incorporated. If there are incantations to be spoken, it is best (though not necessary) to have them memorized to be spoken fluent and sincerely during the operation. Finally, all physical items that need to be present during the ceremony must be gathered and placed within the work space (ritual *nemeton)*.

Physical Preparation of the Circle: Once the work area has been determined, all physical aspects of the circle (*nemeton*) must be considered. Cleanse the existing (static) energy of the location. This can be done by 'sweeping' with a broom which has both physical and spiritual connotations to it. Unnecessary ruble (if outside) or distractions (such as wall-hangings, if inside) should be cleared from the space. If desired, the physical boundaries of the circle (work area) can be defined by some object (or objects). When conducted outside, the ritual circle, especially in accordance with the Druidic tradition, can be supplemented with the erection of a stone circle (*henge*) or else the selection of a proper clearing within a circle of trees (*grove*).

Neutralization of Existing Energies: The Druid must meditate to bring unifying harmony to the energies of all the implements present - tuning them all into a similar vibration or frequency (essentially activating them by recognition of their magical qualities). To Clear, Ground and Concentrate or Focus on the ritual, the space being used must be made Sacred or Consecrated. This can be accomplished with a prayer or incantation to the Spirit of the Place just as easily as it can be visualized, feeling and seeing the boundary of the *nemeton* and charging the interior work space with the appropriate intention.

The Druid may raise their awareness or enter what is known as the *Body of Light.* This is accomplished by consciously recognizing the astral body or light body and projecting personal consciousness into it while simultaneously working from the physical body. This awareness is maintained for the duration o the ritual. When the Druid has raised their own personal awareness and they have extended that awareness out to the boundaries of their microcosmic *nemeton,* then they are ready to consecrate the energetic space of the sphere with some conscious form of circle casting.

Water Phase

Awakening the Elemental Currents: The Druid then proceeds to open the channels to the elemental currents, as if opening an energetic flood-gate. Doing so creates a communicative link for the exchange of energy between the *nemeton* and the Elemental Kingdoms - between the seen and unseen. Since each of the cardinal directions is seen as a representation of the four elements, the currents of energy are considered as 'coming in' by way of each of these directions.

To aid in attracting these forces to the circle, the tool that is best aligned to each element is placed at that quarter of the circle along with a candle of an appropriate color, a lamp or a bonfire.

Summoning Elemental Currents from the Quarters: Each of the four elements is perceived as possessing a unique current of energy that flows from one of the four directions. Within the spectrum of visualization, the currents can be seen as bands of colored light. The Druid could, for example, fill the *nemeton sphere* with a watery-blue tranquil and peaceful energy to charge a healing ritual, and so forth

At this stage of the ritual, the Druid openly invites in the energetic presence from the Elemental Kingdoms using invocation, active visualization and intention. Using the appropriate elemental tool, a sign or glyph can be traced in the air at each corresponding direction, visualized in an appropriate color.

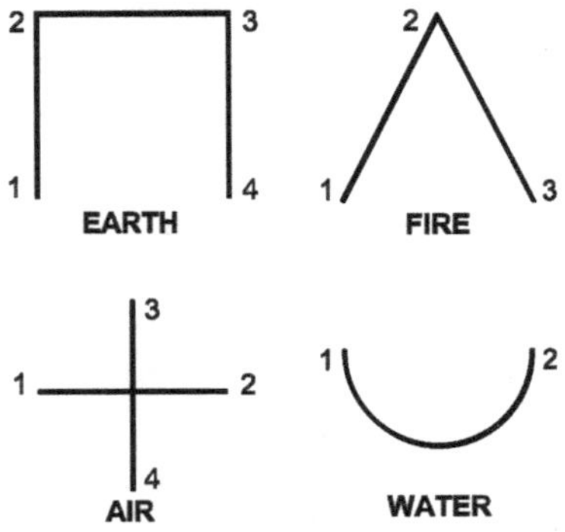

Statement of Purpose: After having called forth external or elemental energy, the Druid makes a firm statement of intention (purpose) to inform the external energy of the intention, but most importantly to refocus the consciousness of the operator back onto the ritual goal after having performed the ceremonial preliminaries. Some lore suggests that the intention of the ritual was stated by the Druid three times during the duration of the ceremony before energy was finally released to it.

Air Phase

Expression of Intention via Catalysts: The Druid will use various tools and implements to carry out an operation energetically linked to the goal. The Druid may light a candle of an appropriate color representing the intention; fumigate the circle with an incense that is sensually aligned to the goal; even empower or charge a talisman or amulet to project the effects of the ritual long after the working has ended.

The First Phase of Manifestation: For energy to manifest it must have a precise direction. The air may have the freedom of movement to blow in many directions but it is generally focused on only one direction of travel at a time. Just as the wind must choose a specific direction to blow in, so too much the air-aligned mind maintain the singular clarity of the intention. The intention must be entirely clear before you direct any energy in order to prevent 'wild magic'.

Precision Awareness of the Goal: The need is examined to be sure it is for the highest good. Then, being certain that the intent is clear, he gathers his own attention in combination with the forces culled into the pool and prepares to fix the whole of the ritually raised energy on the goal.

Fire Phase

Visualization of the Desired Change: The Druid fixes the goal in their mind, seeing the outcome as if it has already happened - the complete and final picture. This is to alert the subconscious mind that this change has *already* taken place. By assimilating that knowledge, the energy of this new reality is interacted with first internally, and then projected outward to engage into the greater sea of the Universe.

Belief imparts reality. In ritual magic, the visualizations are used as a catalyst to actually implement action, even if by only energetic and psychological expressions in ceremony. Direct action comes from right thinking and so the problem solving experience in ritual can be brought to the world in daily life.

The Second Phase of Manifestation: Energetic alchemy ensues. The idea is to combine or merge the internal personal stores of energy with the external energies summoned and then to direct them as a single current and ultimately uploading them into the Universal consciousness (releasing the energy toward the goal in the universal mind).

Resolution: When the ritual is completed, it is customary to formally thank and dismiss the energies called into the *nemeton,* particularly the representatives of the Elemental Kingdom and any other spirits or entities that had been called forth by name. For psychological reasons, this procedure is sometimes done in reverse order, beginning with the last name called in to the ritual at the start. Likewise, the elemental forces are dismissed counterclockwise, opposite of how they are called.

In order to keep the energy that has been sent out by the Druid toward the goal form lingering or remaining attached to themselves, it is best if the ritual is not thought about or contemplated after its completion. Worrying about the results and charging the work with *that* energy will do nothing positive for you. Since the use of magic and concentration does consume energy, it is often advised to follow a ceremonial working with a meal and perhaps rest and sleep.

The Grove Festivals

The ceremonial formula is divided among the eight "Grove Festivals" observed each year.

a) Winter Solstice: Rebirth of the Sun King (Dec. 21-22)

b) Imbolc: festival of Light (Feb. 1)

c) Spring Equinox: Festival of Life (Sept. 21-22)

d) Beltane: festival of Flowers and Fire (May 1)

e) Summer Solstice: Festival of Oaks and Stones (June 21-22)

f) Lughnassadh: Marriage of Lugh (Aug. 1)

g) Autumn Equinox: Harvest Festival (Sep. 21-22)

h) Samhain: festival of Ancestors and Spirits (Oct. 31-Nov. 1)

The remembrance of the *pagan* Wheel of the Year is one of the more authentic revival efforts conducted by modern neodruids. Druids of the *Gorsedd* or Initiates of the Third Circle are responsible for leading and executing the primary solar festival ceremonies. The liturgy may be used by working groups or adapted for solitary practitioners.

The Sacraments of Earth - A Druidic Liturgy

1. Formation of the 'Circle of Stones' or nemeton.

2. Lighting the ceremonial incense: 1 part mistletoe, and 1 part oak.

3. Light a white candle in the centre of your workspace and say:

Here I stand on the threshold between worlds, at a time that is not a time, in a place that is not a place, on a day that is not a day. Yet I am here to occupy this sacred *nemeton*, to be at one with the many gods, who are but faces of the One and True God. I claim for the moment outside of time and space, to attain the right of Godhood for myself.

4. Consecration of the Circle and ritual implements. Hold you hands over a cup/bowl of water and a plate of salt, and say:

I ask the water spirits to come and bless this water. I ask the earth spirits to come and bless this salt. Water and earth are manifest here, blessed, and contained before me.

Dip the magical items into the salt, then the water (you might sprinkle water on something as opposed to dunking it) and say:

Blessed are these elements and all that makes contact with them. Almighty are the Elder Gods, the ancient, eternal, and ever-shinning Masters.

Drop the salt from the plate into the container of water, and say:

Blessed is the alchemical change. Elements unite. Energies swirl. Fusion and transformation creates.

Walk clockwise around the inside perimeter of the *nemeton* (beginning in the east, or perhaps north) and sprinkle the alchemical mixture. When you have returned to the east (or place of beginning), say:

This sacred *nemeton,* the Holy Mandala, is sealed, protected, and blessed by the forces of earth and water.

Return to your workspace and hold your hands over the incense and burner. This is not the same as the incense from Step 2, and may be selected as the occasion demands, say:

I ask the air spirits come and bless this incense. I ask the fire spirits to come and bless this burner.

Light the incense in the burner (charcoal, stick, cone, resin incense, etc.) and pass the ritual implements (objects) to be blessed through the sacred smoke, and say:

Blessed are the elements of air and fire, and all that makes contact with them. Almighty are the Elder Gods, the ancient, eternal, and ever-shinning Masters.

Walk clockwise around the boundary of the circle as before, this time with the burning incense, which consecrates and purifies the energies of the sacred space. Say:

This sacred *nemeton*, the Holy Mandala, is sealed, purified, and blessed by the forces of air and fire.

5. Calling the Inspiration of Awen. See three rays of light descending down upon you from above. One is silver, one is crystalline white, and the last is gold. Hold this image for thirty heartbeats (seconds), then speak:

Today (tonight) I call upon the strength of the heavens: light of sun, radiance of moon, splendor of fire, speed of lightning, swiftness of wind, depth of sea, stability of earth, firmness of stone. I call upon the clear and omnipresent light.

6. The Call to the Elementals. Say:

I do now invite all helpful and friendly energies of other realms to witness and defend this circle, and to aid in the magic performed here. I stand between the gates of realization and manifestation. The perceptual doors to the elemental kingdoms open wide by the sound of my voice. May the Great Universal Spirit be within the hearts of all.

7. The Eastern Ward. Go to the east and see an equal-armed yellow cross hanging in the air before you (or you can visualize yourself tracing these archetypal symbols) representing the four winds. As you speak the following, you see a faerie sylph come up to the edge of your circle:

Let there be peace in the east. Let the winds of the east blow in perfect harmony with all of Creation. By these words of the east: Gorias, Esras, Paraldas, Powers of Air, Kingdom of Wind, I do summon your infinite powers. Come forth from the east that you will be known. You are welcomed.

8. The Southern Ward. Go to the south and see a triangle of flame burning before you, suspended in the air. As you speak the following, you see a dragon emerge and come forth to the *nemeton*:

Let there be peace in the south. Let the flames of the south burn in perfect harmony with all of Creation. By these words of the south: Finias, Uscias, Djinas, Powers of Fire, Kingdom of Flame, I do summon your infinite powers. Open now to me and reveal thy mysteries. Come anger of fire. Come fire of oak. Come oak of knowledge. Come now forth from the south. Come flaming sword of song. Come song of razor edge. You are here welcomed.

9. The Western Ward. Go to the west and see your perception of the Holy Grail suspended before you. Take and drink from the cup of life, feeling the soothing energy wash over you. Speak the following and see a beautiful sea-nymph come to the *nemeton*.

Let peace rule in the west. Let the tides of the western seas flow in perfect harmony with all of creation. By these word of the west: Murias, Semias, Niksas, Powers of Water, Kingdom of Sea, I do summon your infinite powers. Sea full of fish. fish swarming up. Fertile land. Under-wave bird. Wise salmon. Come forth from the west that you can be known. You are welcomed.

10. The Northern Ward. Go to the north and see a megalithic trilithon portal before you (two standing stones with a lintel topping them both). As you speak the following, you see an elf emerge from between the two stones and move toward the *nemeton*:

Let there be peace in the north. May the trees and stones, grow and rest in perfect harmony with all of Creation. By these words of the Northern Portal: Falias, Morfessas, Ghobas, Spirit of the Land, I invoke you and call you in. Powers of Earth, Kingdom of Stone, be here now. Spirit of the trees, vibrations of the stone, from the north you are called to this magick circle. You are welcomed.

11. Benediction. Return to the centre of your workspace, lower your palms (faced down), and say:

Nid Dim on Duw. Nid Duw ond Dim.
Y Gwir yn Erbyn Byd.
The Truth Against the World.

12. Light intention candles as you verbalize the purpose of the ceremony (e.g. "I am here..."). The following are suggested colour combinations for the 'Grove Festivals'.

a) Winter Solstice: 1 green, 1 red, 1 white.

b) Imbolc: 2 white, 1 green

c) Spring Equinox: 2 green, 1 white

d) Beltane: 2 white, 1 red

e) Summer Solstice: 1 red, 1 white, 1 yellow

f) Lughnassadh: 1 red, 1 yellow, 1 green

g) Autumn Equinox: 1 red, 1 white, 1 black

h) Samhain: 2 black, 1 white

13. Calling the Higher Divine Powers of Creation and the Archetypes. You may wish to, but need not, further familiarize with the Celtic Mythos so that you can better envision deity forms at your festivals.

If you feel the need, you could even substitute a different pantheon. Say:

Awen, Menw, Akasha, IAO (*ee-ah-oh*), Pharon. Powers of the Earth, rising up from the stone, wind, flame and sea, encircle and empower me. Strengthen my aura. Archetypes of the festival, you are here honored, as you have been for thousands of years. You do I call forth on this day (night) to join this sacred ceremony.

a) Winter Solstice: Kernunnnos, Mabon

b) Imbolc: D'anu, Brighid

c) Spring Equinox: Taliesen, Epona

d) Beltane: Bel, Blodduwedd

e) Summer Solstice: Araianrhod, Oghma

f) Lughnassadh: Lugh, D'Anu

g) Autumn Equinox: Bran, Branwen

h) Samhain: Gwyn ap Nudd, Samham

14. The Summoning/Conjuring. Say:

Moon, stars, mist, and sun: By the powers above, my will be done. Earth, air, water, and fire: I summon forth what I desire. Oak, ash, thorn, and vine, conjured here are powers Divine. Dragons deep and faeries bold: As above, so below.

15. Blessing of the Grove. Say:

I come forth to bare witness to the strength and unity of the Grove, where rests this sacred *nemeton,* the Holy Mandala. Between the roots and branches of the sacred trees, I standfast. I possess the strength of Oak with deep roots and reaching branches. Blessed is the earth. Blessed is the Grove. Blessed be the All.

16. The Festival Incantation. If these formulae were being used for another purpose, that ritual working would be performed here.

a.) Winter Solstice: Farewell to the Dark Lord. All gather and witness the rebirth of the Sun King. Hail to the Sun King who is reborn. Spirits of the Yule-log and the candles thereon, bring to us all good health and cheer. Divine child of light, rejoice in thy existence.

b.) Imbolc: Rekindle the flame. Clear out the old in the house and heart. Enter the new. Shedding skin. Purification. Infinite possibilities uniting to manifest. Earth's slumber soon comes to the end. Great Earth dreaming, remember me.

c.) Spring Equinox: Now I do plant the seed of new beginnings. I ask the Forces of Nature to allow it to grow in the time of new growth. Good tidings and welcome, awakening Earth. Equality. The balance of power. Renewal. Warmth and love are strengthening the heart of Creation. The Darkness has been dispelled.

d.) Beltane: The Earth has now come alive to breed and multiply. Fertility and growth bring maturity. Ah, the Fires of Bel. Oh, the May Queen of Flowers. Look, the Rainbow Children. See, the May Poll. The Cauldron of Inspiration and fertility is overturned, pouring forth blessings upon all of Creation.

e.) Summer Solstice: We gather at the nemeton to celebrate life and the maturity of life. This day marks the annual peak of the Sun King's potency. Yours is the life-giving force, burning within the heart and soul of every being in Creation. Burn deeply within my spirit. Might Sun King, yours is the power that burns and blesses. I stand to give vigil to thy power. Make me a vessel of sacred fire.

f.) Lughnassadh: Lord of the wheat and the corn, bless me now as I come upon the harvest season. Help me to use the fruits of the seed that was planted and has matured. Change comes. The darkness is drawing ever near. I reap the sown seed as I prepare for a time of great hibernation. Now comes a time of looking inward. Bless the first harvest, that it may sustain me through the dark months.

g.) Autumn Equinox: From life to death, I am renewed. The face of the Earth is ready for renewal. Now comes the second harvest. My lord and lady of the shadows gain reign. Maintain and protect me, my home, and my family. May the harvest of my efforts be plentiful for the coming winter. I watch and wait in silence as the darkness draws near.

h.) Samhain: Death comes upon us in full circle. The veil is lowered between this world and the next. Now, I do reap the third and final harvest. The shadow of the dark goddess falls upon the land, spreading out frozen waters of ending and new life. Here do I call my ancestral spirits and the shades of the ancient Druids and Masters, to join me in this sacred festival. We feast to good health and happiness. May both health and happiness be in abundance, now and forever more

17. Ceremonial Feast and retelling of Celtic/Bardic Tales.

18. Dismissal and Thanks to the Archeypes and Deities called.

19. Dismissal and Thanks to the Faeries, Nature Spirits, Elemental, and Directional Wards called.

20. Extinguishing the Energies of the Active Nemeton.

Bardic Druidism - The Eisteddfodd

This rite can be used by any number of participants and can be amended for any type of group work or circle magic. The ceremonial observation is most effective in a circle of trees and/or stones. Once the participants are prepared, procession to the northeast corner of the Nemeton bringing all tools and items with you and begin.

I. Opening Benediction

Druid King/Arch Druid: May the Source of All Being and Creation grant us favor and protection; and in protection, strength; and in strength, peace; and in peace, understanding; and in understanding comes the True Knowledge of the 'Right Way'; and in the grace of this knowledge may we be granted the will to use it; and in that will, the wisdom to temper the use of knowledge; and in temperance comes mercy; and thru mercy, love; and in love we find the Source of All Being and Creation.

Druid Queen/High Priestess: The recursive spiral path passes through Annwn ('ah-noon') and returns to the love and favor of the Source. Blessed be the All.

All: Blessed be the Universe.

II. Grand Invocation

Druid King/Arch Druid: To bathe in the aethyr of new light and life that swirls about the galaxy. To cleanse away iniquity and mortality so we may join in the harmony of all living beings. Here we stand, beneath the Oaks, beneath the Stones, coming to the place we watched our ancestors go to commune with the Spirit of the Universe.

Druid Queen/High Priestess: The stars shine brightly upon this meeting of our people. The Divine Star shines brightly on us now at the hour of our meeting.

III. Elemental Benediction

Druid Queen/High Priestess: Let peace ring out through the four quadrants of the Universe. Within our being may we find peace at the center. In the Secret Grove we meet to share peace. Then, as we go about the lives we lead on the 'Surface World,' we radiate the currents of love and peace and attract the same.

Druid King/Arch Druid: Here we stand strong, coming together in answer to the call of our inner vow as Guardians and Keepers of the Earth. Here we stand, side-by-side, heart-to-heart and [the circle joins hands] hand-in-hand. [Release hands.]

Northern Druid Guard: Guardian of the North, realm and spirits of the Earth Element, 'nature spirits,' Gnomes, Kobold and Drwyds of Falias, hail and welcome to this Nemeton. Extend the currents of peace and stability.

Eastern Druid Guard: Guardian of the East, realm and spirits of the Air Element, Ancient and Shinning Ones, Elves and Drwyds of Gorias, hail and welcome to this Nemeton. Extend the currents that enable enlightenment.

Southern Druid Guard: Guardian of the South, realm and spirits of the Fire Element, Dragon Priests, fiery sprytes, pict-sidhe and Drwyds of Finias, hail and welcome to this Nemeton. Extend the necessary energy for strengthening the will.

Western Druid Guard: Guardian of the West, realm and spirits of the Water Element, ancestral spirits, merfolk, Drwyds of the past and the Otherworld city of Murias, hail and welcome to this Nemeton. Extend the currents of personal well-being and those that enable the insight of wisdom.

IV. Bardic Verse & Story

Traditionally, a gathering of Bardic Druids will recite lore and legend at ceremonial gatherings and festival celebrations for the purposes of the preservation of those stories. This is called an 'Eisteddfodd' in the Gaelic-Welsh language, an ancient ceremonial tradition of processions, candle-lighting, stories and "sermons" that were shared.

V. Festival Observations

Perform ceremonial celebration or operations the group has come together to accomplish.

VI. Thanking & Dismissing Elemental Spirits

Druid King/Arch Druid: May the Source of All Being and Creation grant us favor and protection; and in protection, strength; and in strength, peace; and in peace, understanding; and in understanding comes the True Knowledge of the 'Right Way'; and in the grace of this knowledge may we be granted the will to use it; and in that will, the wisdom to temper the use of knowledge; and in temperance comes mercy; and thru mercy, love; and in love we find the Source of All Being and Creation.

Druid Queen/High Priestess: Let peace ring out through the four quadrants of the Universe. Within our being may we find peace at the center. In the Secret Grove we meet to share peace. Then, as we go about the lives we lead on the 'Surface World,' we radiate the currents of love and peace and attract the same.

Western Druid Guard: Guardian of the West, spirit of the Wave and realm of Sea, we thank thee for thy attendance this day/eve as you witness and remember the ceremony we practice in memory of the rites of our ancestors. May you return again when hence we call. Hail and Farewell. Go in peace.

Southern Druid Guard: Guardian of the South, spirit of the Flame and realm of Fire, we thank thee for thy attendance this day/eve as you witness and remember the ceremony we practice in memory of the rites of our ancestors. May you return again when hence we call. Hail and Farewell. Go in peace.

Eastern Druid Guard: Guardian of the East, spirit of the Wind and realm of Air, we thank thee for thy attendance this day/eve as you witness and remember the ceremony we practice in memory of the rites of our ancestors. May you return again when hence we call. Hail and Farewell. Go in peace.

Northern Druid Guard: Guardian of the North, spirits of Stone and Wood and realm of Earth, we thank thee for thy attendance this day/eve as you witness and remember the ceremony we practice in memory of the rites of our ancestors. May you return again when hence we call. Hail and Farewell. Go in peace.

VII. Closing Benediction

Druid King/Arch Druid: Before departing from this place, we release the field surrounding the Nemeton, grounding the energy of Earth, releasing to the Sky the energies of Air, pushing down the currents of Fire deep into the 'Core of Gaea' and pouring the Water back into the Sea.

Druid Queen/High Priestess: As we have come in peace, so do we leave in peace. We are the 'Children of the Stars,' beings of light, life and love. In departing, we project and radiate peaceful energy and positive power throughout the Universe, dispersing the energies gathered here.

All: Blessed Be.

Druid King/Arch Druid: Y Gwir Yn Erbyn Byd.

All: The Truth Against The World.

Druid Queen/High Priestess: May our circle now stand open, though it is still a circle and never broken. The 'Magick Sphere' of the 'Grove of [group name]' ever rests here.

All: Awen [*ah-oo-een*]

Chapter VIII
The Book of Taliesin:

Hanes Taliesin - Part One

Transliterated by Edward Davies

Bard of Glamorgan

From Rites of the British Druids

Ceridwen's Cauldron & The Books of Pheryllt

1: In former times, there was a man of noble descent in Penllyn, the end of the lake. His name was Tegid Voel, bald serenity, and his paternal estate was in the middle of the lake of Tegid, or Pemble meer. His espoused wife was named Ceridwen. By this wife he had a son, named Morvran ap Tegid, raven of the sea, the sow of serenity, and a daughter called Creirvywrf the sacred token of life. She was the most beautiful damsel in the world.

But these children had a brother, named Avagddu, utter darkness, or black accumulation, the most hideous of beings. Ceridwen, the mother of this deformed son, concluded in her mind, that he would have but little chance of being admitted into respectable company, unless he were endowed with some honourable accompiishments, or sciences; for this was in the first period of Arthur, and the round table.

2: Then Ceridwen determined, agreeably to the mystery of the Books of Pheryllt, to prepare for her son a cauldron of *Awen a Gwybodeu,* water of inspiration and sciences, that he might be more readily admitted into honorable society, upon account of his knowledge, and his skill in regard to futurity.

The cauldron began to boil, and it was requisite that the boiling should be continued, without interruption, for the period of a year and a day; and till three blessed drops of the endowment of the spirit could be obtained.

She had stationed Greion the Little, the son of Gwreang the Herald, of Llanvair, the fane of the lady, in Caer Einiawn, the city of the just, in Powys, the land of rest to superintend the preparation of the cauldron: and she had appointed a blind man, named Morda, ruler of the sea, to kindle the fire under the cauldron, with a strict injunction that he should not suffer the boiling to be interrupted, before the completion of the year and the day.

In the mean time Ceridwen, with due attention to the books of astronomy, and to the hours of the planets, employed herself daily in botanizing, and in collecting plants of every species, which possessed any rare virtues.

On a certain day, about the completion of the year, whilst she was thus botanizing and muttering to herself, three drops of the efficacious water happened to fly out of the caul-dron, and alight upon the finger of Gwion the Little. The heat of the water occasioned his putting his finger into his mouth.

As soon as these precious drops had touched his lips, every event of futurity was opened to his view: and he clearly perceived, that his great-est concern was to beware of the stratagems of Ceridwen, whose knowledge was very great. With extreme terror he fled towards his native country.

As for the cauldron, it divided into two halves; for the tl whole of the water which it contained, excepting the three efficacious drops, was poisonous ; so that it poisoned the horses of Gwyddno Garanhir, which drank out of the channel into which the cauldron had emptied itself. Hence that channel was afterward called, The poison of Gwyddno's hones.

3: Ceridwen entering just at this moment, and perceiving that her whole year's labor was entirely lost, seized an oar, and struck the blind Morda upon his head, so that one of his eyes dropped upon his cheek.

Thou hast disfigured me wrongfully, exclaimed Morda, seeing I am innocent: thy loss has not been occasioned by any fault of mine.

True, replied Ceridwen, it was Gwion the Little who robbed me. Having pronounced these words, she began to run in pursuit of him.

Gwion perceiving her at a distance, transformed himself into a hare, and doubled his speed: but Ceridwen instantly becoming a greyhound bitch, turned him, and chased him towards a river.

Leaping into the stream, he assumed the form of a fish: but his resentful enemy, who was now become an otter bitch, traced him through the stream; so that he was obliged to take the form of a bird, and mount into the air.

That element afforded him no refuge; for the lady, the form of a sparrow hawk was gaining upon him she was just in the act of pouncing him. Shuddering with the dread of death, he perceived a heap of clean wheat upon a floor, dropped into the midst of it, and assumed the form of a single grain.

Ceridwen took the form of a black, high-crested hen, descended into the wheat, scratched him out, distinguished and swallowed him. And, as the history relates, she was pregnant of him nine months, and when delivered of him, she found him so lovely a babe, that she had not resolution to put him to death.

She placed him, however, in a coracle, covered with a skin, and, by the instigation of her husband, cast him into the sea on the twenty-ninth of April.

4: In those times, Gwyddno's wear stood out in the beach, between Dyvi and Aberystwyth, near his own castle. And in that wear, it was usual to take fish, to the value of a hundred pounds, every year, upon the eve of the first of May.

Gwyddno had an only son, named Elphin, who had been a most unfortunate and necessitous young man. This was a great affliction to his father, who began to think that he had been born in an evil hour. His counselors, however, persuaded the father to let this son have the drawing of the wear on that year, by way of experiment; in order to prove whether any good fortune would ever attend him, and that he might have something to begin the world.

The next day, being May-eve, Elphin examined the wear, and found nothing: but as he was going away, he perceived the coracle, covered with a skin, resting upon the pole of the dam.

Then one of the wear-men said to him, Thou hast never been completely unfortunate before this night ; for now thou hast destroyed the virtue of the wear, in which the value of a hundred pounds was always taken upon the eve of May-day.

How so? replied Elphin that coracle may possibly contain the value of a hundred pounds.

The skin was opened, and the opener perceiving the forehead of an infant, said to Elphin, Behold Taliesin, *Radiant Front*!

Radiant Front be his name, replied the prince, who now lifted the infant in his arms, commiserating his own misfortune, and placed him behind him upon his own .horse, as if it had been in the most easy chair.

Immediately after this, the babe composed for Elphin a song of consolation and praise; at the same time, he prophesied of his future renown. The consolation was the first hymn which Taliesin sung, in order to comfort Elphin, who was grieved for his disappointment in the draught of the wear; and still more so, at the thought that the world would impute the fault and misfortune wholly to himself.

Further Notes on the Pheryllt

Ceridwen, like Ceres and Isis, appears to have been a great botanist, and well skilled in the virtues of plants. The Pheryllt, according to whose ritual she proceeds in her selection, are often mentioned by the Bards, as well as by the prose writers of Wales.

The Pheryllt also had an establishment at Oxford, prior to the founding of the university by Alfred. These Pheryllt are deemed to have been the first teachers of all curious arts and sciences; and, more particularly, are thought to have been skilled in every thing that required the operation of fire. Hence some have supposed, that the term implies chemists or metallurgists. But chemistry and metallurgy seem rather to have taken their British name from these ancient priests, being called *Celvyddydau Pheryllt*, the arts of the Pheryllt, or some of those mysteries in which they were eminently conversant.

As primary instructors in the rites of Ceridwen, or Ceres, I regard the Pheryllt as priests of the Pharaon, or higher powers, who had a city or temple amongst the mountains of Snowdon, called also *Dinas Emrys*, or the ambrosial city.

Whatever route these ancient priests may have pursued; and whether they belonged to the original establishment of the nations here mentioned, or were imported from other people; their rites, as described by the learned author, are clearly to be distinguished amongst the Celts of Britain; and with those Pheryllt or Druids, who directed the mysteries of Ceridwen.

Chapter IX
Pheryllt High Magic:
Channeling & Summoning Dragon Energy

Illuminated by Myrddin Cerrig,

Bard of the Twelfth Chair

Adapted from "Draconomicon"

The Dragon Force

Dragons directly represent actual power feeding any system of the ancient mystery school. Electromagnetic currents on the planet and energy systems that move throughout the human organism all came to viewed as the "power" of the dragon. We can consider outer "e-magnetic" and *ley lines* as "dragon lines" and internal currents of what eastern schools know as *Kundalini* and *Chakras* as "dragon currents" in the Pheryllt Tradition.

Dowsing for Dragons

Dowsing is one of the oldest practical forms known for channeling the dragon lines of the earth planet. The method has been used for locating underground water, locating missing objects, and of course, dowsing or divining the locations of *Ley Lines*. Dowsing is a form of "radiethesia," operating by the same principles as pendulum divination. Practicing this form of magic requires the use of special rods or wands, called dowsing rods or dragon rods. Traditionally, they are made from either a hazel or willow branch and appears reminiscent of a "Y." It is preferable if the tree it is taken from grows near a natural source of water. Y-types are the original forked-form of the rod, gripped by the ends of two "legs" with the central stem extended outward.

Recently an L-type became popular, which actually requires a set of two L-shaped rods held apart in each hand. Modern L-rods are constructed from bent or fabricated metal, usually copper (modern innovators have used coat-hangers), with a long arm and a shorter base (at a 90-degree angle to the arm). The base-handle should be wrapped in cardboard or a drilled out length of dowel, allowing the arms to extend freely when held. When the energy frequency (or object) visualized and projected from the mind has been reached, the Y-stem drops downward and the L's swing inward towards each other or crossing over each other (depending on how they are held).

The mind emits a particular vibration when focusing on a specific visualization, a frequency maintained until it becomes noticeably stronger by constructively interfering with a similar current of energy. This can be felt through muscular tensing, the involuntary reactions to energy, caused by internal impulses. This means that you can also use dowsing rods to "test" or "measure" the boundaries and strength of energy fields like auras and ley lines. With auras, L-rods have a tendency to swing outward, not in, when encountering the energy. With movement in two directions on this axis, "yes/no" answers can also be determined. Experienced wizards and magicians have a natural sensitivity to energy and can even use their own muscular inclinations (without tools) to "test" energies.

Calen - Inner Starfire & The Dragon Within

Chakra and Kundalini work of the East are mirrored in Druid Doctrine of Calen, the prana or light-centers of lifeforce, a personal energetic distribution system within all living creatures. The word *chakra* is derived from Sanskrit, meaning "wheel." They are described as such because they act like fan-blades or turbines, continually gathering and projecting a particular *dragon current* or Ray of Light (as it is perceived in the realm of forms). This projected energy creates an energetic field, called a *light shield,* around the body - and such an electro-magnetic field is generally called the *aura.*

Calen (chakras) are an energetic link between the metaphysical mind-spirit and the physical body. Together with the aura this personal energy system contributes to who you are (personality), how you feel (emotion) and whatever others feel or perceive from you (persona). Each individual light-center operates with a specific *dragon current.* The projected vibrations you come into contact with from you external environment, via transference and resonance, also get perceived and processed through the appropriate Calen filter.

The Starfire System comprises the very wiring by which the human experience is composed. With the auric field, this personal energy system contributes to (and constitutes) who you are (personality), how you feel (emotionally) and your projected persona, including every thing from your behaviors to what others feel or perceive from you.

Each type of energy is concentrated on a specific relative position within the body. Your lower faculties, connected to your lower animal survival-driven self, exists relatively low on the body (below the heart). By comparison, the higher faculties (most often attributed to a higher self) are all processed closer to (and including) your head. Auric emanations are typically stronger in the higher regions of spiritually-minded seekers, which can also lead them to be more susceptible to the distractions of the lower if these other centers go unchecked.

Calen - Inner Starfire & The Seven Light Centers

Maintaining and balancing the entire *chakra* system does not require advanced and obscure rituals or ceremonial observations. Awareness and consciousness, the use of *will* and *intention,* is sufficient in manifesting these personal energetic changes. Since the *chakras* are color (light ray) based, it has been suggested that colored stones, crystals or fabric squares can be used as focal aids to this type of energy work. A basic description of the *dragon currents* are as follows:

1: Base or Root: located at the base of the spine (or feet), and controls basic survival instincts, the wild/animal nature and physical ability required to exist and function. Colors: Ascension = white, Elven = green; red (if underactive) or green (if overactive). Stones: [green] Amazonite, aventurine, emerald and moss agate.

2: Sacral or spleen: located just above the penis or between the ovaries, and controls sexual reproduction and carnal pleasure. Colors: Ascension = violet, Elven = blue; orange (if underactive) or blue (if overactive). Stones: [blue] Hematite, lapis lazuli, pearl and topaz.

3: Solar plexus: located near the stomach, and controls digestive, emotional and ritualistic faculties. Colors: Ascension = purple (and gold), Elven = red; yellow (if underactive) or purple (if overactive). Stones: [red] Agate (red), jasper (red), and ruby.

4: Heart or Merkaba: located near the heart, and controls the circulatory system, balance of the other rays and personal healing faculties. Colors: Ascension = pink, Elven = purple (and pink); green (if underactive) or pink (if overactive). Stones: [purple spectrum] Rose quartz, quartz, sapphire and turquoise.

5: Throat: located at the throat near the thyroid, and controls communication, speech, some telepathy and voice. Colors: Ascension = blue, Elven = orange; blue (if underactive) or orange (if overactive). Stones: [orange] Amber, carnelian, jacinth and opal.

6: Third Eye or brow: located near the pineal gland, and controls the endocrine system, immunity, personal magnetism, imagination and visualization. Colors: Ascension = green, Elven = yellow; indigo (if underactive) or soft orange/ yellow (if overactive). Stones: [yellow] Diamond, gold, tiger's eye and topaz.

7: Crown or Flower of Life: located just above the head, and controls our spiritual/metaphysical inter- connectedness, the subconscious mind and the use of intention. Colors: Ascension = yellow, Elven = violet; violet (if underactive) or yellow (if overactive). Stones: [violet] Particularly amethyst.

Light Shields - Light Rays & The Radiance of Awen

The color – and thereby, nature – of the auric "Light Shield" may be altered to meet an energy desired to be attracted. Call the energy down as a beam of light from the stars allowing yourself to absorb and radiate its essence. Three Divine Rays of Awen – "silver," "crystalline" and "gold" – are divided (fragmented or condensed) into a spectrum seven bands of light, matching the *dragon currents* that form the basis of reality.

The Silver (Left) Ray

- Sound/Letter: I ("ee")
- Polarity: Female, dark, passive, lunar.
- Quartile Element: Water (some Earth)
- Elvish Element: The Sea
- Physical Manifestation: The Mineral Kingdom
- Threshold Time Period: Dusk, sunset, autumn.
- Elessar (Elf-Stone): Silver (hematite)
- Light Bands (Rays): Indigo, violet and blue.

The Silver Properties of the Light Rays:

- Violet (Saturn): Astral vision, darkness, Otherworld work, wisdom, wards.
- Manifestation: Element of Vapor/Cloud
- Indigo (Jupiter): Beauty, enchantment, emotions, love, music, play.
- Manifestation: Element of Rain
- Blue (Luna): Compassion, dreams, healing, peace and understanding.
- Manifestation: Element of Sea

The Gold (Right) Ray

- Sound/Letter: O ("oh")
- Polarity: Masculine, light, active, solar.
- Quartile Element: Fire and Air
- Elvish Element: The Sky
- Phys. Manifestation: Animal & Human Kingdoms
- Threshold Time Period: Dawn, sunrise, spring and summer.
- Elessar (Elf-Stone): Gold (tiger's eye)

- Light Bands (Rays): Yellow, orange and red.

The Golden Properties of the Light Rays:

- Yellow (the Sun): Knowledge, intellect, confidence, and inspiration.
- Manifestation: Element of Skyfire
- Orange (Mercury): Communication, courage, being aware, wishes.
- Manifestation: Element of Star
- Red (Mars): Transformation, healing, strength, willpower, and leadership.
- Manifestation: Element of Flame

The Crystaline (Middle) Ray

- Sound/Letter: A ("ah")
- Polarity: Neutral, crystalline, reflective
- Quartile Element: Earth ('Quintessence.')
- Elvish Element: The Land
- Physical Manifestation: Plant & Tree Kingdom
- Threshold Time Period: Twilight, midnight, winter.
- Elessar (Elf-Stone): Black or Green (obsidian)
- Light Band (Ray): Green

The Crystalline Properties of the Light Ray:

- Green (Venus): Life-force, balance, healing, growth, true love.
- Manifestation: Element of Earth

Calling the Dragon

Dragons are called, summoned and even alchemically formed by Druids and *mages* on the Astral Plane. Occasionally, the Druid may seek to call *dragon energy* to concentrate in a physical locale or internal invoke its nature. The *nemeton* must be made receptive to vibrate a *dragon current* of energy. Raise energy of the ray of light corresponding to the fire element and any other elemental (specific to the alchemical "type" of *dragon energy* you are calling).

To attract any *draconic energy,* you must first attune your internal and external environment to *dragon-friendly* vibrations. This can be easily achieved with the use of an exercise called the "Dragon's Breath." You should use this as a preliminary to all forms of dragon magick that require this ritual style of operation. First, go to your nemeton (sacred space) and speak the *Charm of Making* three times:

Anail nathrock (anail NaDrack)
Uthvass Bethudd (Orth'bhais is Beatha)
Dochiel Dienve (Docheal Denmha)

Begin "Quad Breathing" or "Fire Breathing" (breathing in for four counts and exhaling for four). Feel, visualize and sense the fiery energy all around you. When you breathe in, take this fiery energy into yourself through every pore of your body. Continue to build up the pressure of the "Dragon's Breath" within, feeling it stream throughout your entire body, emanating into and out of your aura and charging the space occupying the *nemeton.* Dragon calling may effectively raise the temperature of the ambient space in the *nemeton.* Buildup of fire energy in the body for the "Dragon's Breath" may also raise the body's personal temperature, a sensation that may be uncomfortable for some.

Although iron is recorded in lore as anathema to the *faerie folk* in some traditions, alchemical lore correlates it with the fire element and Mars, making it a suitable attractant for specifically *draconic* energy. The triangular *Dragon's Eye* is an ancient sigil that can be traced on the ground with the sword, the elemental weapon sacred to the dragon. You can use *Dragon's Blood essence* as either a stone or incense. Stand in the center of the *Dragon's Eye* and hold the sword upright with blade pointed down and speak:

Draig Draig Draig
Draconis Draconis Draconis
Vovim Vovim Vovim
Oi Ia Salman ca Vovim

Hear the words of the master

Pheryllt High Magic:

Cum Saxum Saxorum,
In aduersum montum oparum da,
In aeitibulum, in quinatum, draconis.

Using a single quick motion thrust the sword into the ground. This gesture is archetypal to "piercing the dragon" and the "sword in the stone." To dismiss the energy, remove the sword from the Earth Planet, the "Body of the Dragon" and ground the "Dragon's Breath" by returning it to its source.

Blood and Breath are critical components of 'true' dragon magick. The Dragon's Breath equates back to Mesopotamia and the "Breath of Life" given to human beings by the creators. The *Dragon's Blood* is a genetic component of Dragon Kings and the Pheryllt (*Dragon Priests*). Elsewhere it came to be substituted in herbal form by the resin (incense) carrying the same name.

Chapter X
The Quatrains of Bran

Translated by Llywelyn Sion

Bard of the Glamorgan Chair

Transliterated in Lost Books

I:

In 462 new stars will burn over Albion
Draco will enter the world
A great city will arise and fall
The fathers brought low by the Queens hand

II:

The eagle shall have his day
Twenty plus One escape the tyranny
In the dawn a sun-pact of blood
A voice of iron to call them forth

III:

A boy to magic will be born
Island son and abbots bane
Seven years the cave-mans heir
Final hope against the siege

IV:

The Celtic fathers, time honored
Brought to their lowest level
Called to return by a dying world
An army hidden for future dreams

V:

Giants in the earth will settle
Sea-side tomb will teach its wisdom
Sunken ship will ferry some over
A new land will blossom

VI:

From the sky a new wave breaks
Fresh order among the trees
One brought back to teach the words
His name written across Three Books

VII:

A simple box of wood will be heard
In green field the song of Solomon
Two great spirits under one tree
Their destiny divided

VIII:

The white oak plundered by the black cross
Captives move from lowest dungeon to highest tower
Middle years the worst
2005 rising out of the mire. 21 victors close the Age

IX:

A new state yields a new forest
Lone giant leads an army of elves
Shackled within a keep of steel
After, the blood of three covers all

X:

Of wind sea fire and stone
Fire shall reign supreme
The thrice three lost will re-appear
Son of sun to heal the Dragon

XI:

The moon will vanish three days without a trace
The Son-God will falter
Then will a Great Dragon rise up
From the city bearing the horseshoe falls

XII:

Yet the sea shall not have them
Those who will lead a great people
The scourge passes
Uncertain victory awaits the younger

XIII:

The greatest of new prophets
Shall make deepest forest his realm
Will wander hidden in his final days
Only the Apple Isle a solace

XIV:

An army of academics condemn
The dweller from the River Roe
99 passes into 2000
Twenty-one into the twenty-first shall be re-armed

XV:

The Haunted Mountain will live again
A new law in a new land
Not far from the Millennium
The once-burned shall rise from their own ashes

XVI:

Dark moon summons old friends together
One faltering sun rekindled a while
Armies of fanatics lost in the mist
Beneath the Apple Hill
An Ancient Book in ancient hands

XVII:

Upon this hallowed ground
A once-great spirit will be awakened
Newhill begets a great spokesman
The world again his stage

XVIII:

When rules a Son of the Dragon
Bones of the Future King are found

A tomb beneath a stone
Ends the reign of a dreaded Queen

XIX:

The garden unhappy and abandoned
Cries out as the sun rises
The earth trembles
All await the Equinox of Autumn

XX:

Following long years of hope
He will never come in Albion
Born again in the lands of Colomb
The old province yields the new forest

XXI:

Sacred night again overcomes the wooden cross
An age of ritual sacrifice ends
New clergy don the white of old
Law no longer dictated by the Black Book

XXII:

To save Gaia, a mighty challenge issued
The voice of a rare song will be heard
Seized and sung among green
The world forced to drink sacred waters

XXIII:

All that glitters is not gold
Twenty plus one freed from the hunger
David and Solomon rule once again
Legends born of three guilded flames

XXIV:

Past and present join weeping
A circle of stones top Dragon Hill
Plundered into foundations of Mary
Isle lost to the summer sea

XXV:

Great lodges of stone and timber
Old names restored to Twenty
Forgotten oracles will whisper among the trees
Words of Bran shall live again

XXVI:

A time of confused identity will come
Women wishing to partake of manhood
Men attuned to the lunar sea
One born to walk between

XXVII:

From an ancient list. Three counted as one
By Dragon sought in the land of sweet death
Tree words buried within one soul
Mined by a foreign worker of wood

XXVIII:

Then shall a Roman come forth
Beloved protector of the Bear
Falling star from the frozen north
His light will uphold a great darkness

XXIX:

Seven, six and eleven
The numbers of the letters of the name
Three red ones will stain three parchments
After adjoining, a great wonder is seen

XXX:

Beyond word and deed
A book of Twenty-One will forge the path
Three lost scrolls are made as one
then four new hands elected to cross

XXXI:

Late into the blackest night
Silver tree knocks silver boy
Forgotten words call forth a sudden flood
Voices dead from Gobannium

XXXII:

Songspells resound from a forgotten lake
Echoes so beautiful one will awaken
At midwinter an unearthly thaw
The old bard plays his harp making twenty

XXXIII:

Slowly the great blue temple falls
Sky stones yield up their power
Those who seek to wear the stones
Find refuge in the new forest

XXXIV:

Deadliest of her species
A Queen resplendent wounds without weapons
stirring in sleep, the clergy smile
Vows no longer honored by the King

XXXV:

The anointed trapped between two worlds
A perfect child chosen as successor
As the century approaches rebirth
Wondrous scandal in the form of Christos

XXXVI:

Echoes of ancient stone cry forth
A vast gigantum slowly crumbles
Church and state plundered by ghosts
Fresh forest winds cause the siege to be lifted

XXXVII:

Dragon Isle will regain its honor
From the needles three found by one
Bound by serpents blood burned in iron
After 91 a strange era among the Twenty

XXXVIII:

All the Gods will become as one God
A comet stands, burns alone in the Autumn Sky
Wood and stone forge a tower
A new temple not acceptable to the clergy

XXXIX:

Born during Hunters moon
The battle of Marcus rekindled
Third homestead will prove the one
An ancient priest from the frigid north descends

XL:

The power of a word turns back the eagle
Rightful heiress regains the Apple Cottage
Two hearts with one soul
Sword and chalice again united under the oaks

XLI:

Rites of Passage from the Wizards hand
Two will be born forth, awaiting a final
Dialogue between countries
North and south meet in the third

XLII:

The world lingers between worlds
Great masses lament the ancient teachings
Fire again kindled in the Kings head
Twenty old trees planted anew

XLIII:

The north rose is bluer than ever
Slowly the chosen awaken from their dreams
As sons run and swing amidst green forest boughs
From tower'd high, a giant descends in white

XLIV:

Beyond word and deed
Beyond past and present
Written verse sets forth forgotten lessons
Dead men reborn of three tales

XLV:

The Mouth of Pharon speaks once more
Twenty plus One called to the promised land
Old lodges of timber and stone erected
Like a shadow, the tower rises from slumber

XLVI:

Wildfire will burst over the forests
Elder trees singing out their marks
Ogma returns with an army of poets
Voices long lost echo throughout the world

XLVII:

The song of the forest trees
Summons forth the forests greatest Prophet
Many condemn his mind as troubled
Yet a great clan is liberated

XLVIII:

And the trees walk where he walked
The priests sang a new song
For an age, The wolf howled all night
Stone hanging from a tree his voice returns

XLIX:

Refuge of fire and blood cases
Death cries to be heard within the Twenty
A terrible tumult stirs the Isles
Gold hidden within the mystic deed

L:

Nemeton remembered
Quest set forth in dreams
A great fire is seen amid green
Roses fill the night air with poison

LI:

The head falls forever silent
Until the moon truly falters
Then eagle and sun will both be victorious
True flame consumes a lady of water

LII:

Draglais the flying fire
Tongues of flame, the Prophets song
Carven faces outshine the dark
Ancient circle, messages hidden within a stone

LIII:

The Silver Branch will be the Key
The golden bough upholds
White for black, old for new
The newly anointed bring a long peace

LIV:

A Warrior Angel
Will be chosen saying nothing
Devil above ground, Angel beneath
His wings bear ruin upon the greatest

LV:

At long last the summons!
His family nearly torn asunder
Ancient thunder from the tallest
Love for a chosen one upholds the new state

LVI:

Behold all fresh will be reborn
Roman and Celt work side by side
The duke of Camel rebuilds his throne
Shunamitism the key to all

LVII:

The mists of Calen draw down
Time becomes one through one
Unity, peace and change: The new triad
Four Albans upheld among the Twenty

LVIII:

From nothing nothings comes
Beginning and end must echo the wheel
He who races against the Millennium
Need only heed the cypher of Bran.

Chapter XI
The Gorchan of Maeldrew

Adapted by Myrddin Cerrig,

Bard of the Twelfth Chair

From the Gododin Verses

of the Book of Aneurin

and Myvyrian Archaeology

The Gorchan of Maeldrew

The noise of two Abers around the Caer!
Arouse thyself to arms and splendor!
Cold is the passing and re-passing of the breach of battle.
Lover of fame, you seek to sleep?
The variegated texture, the covering of heroism,
For the shelterless assault shall be woven.
The breach that has been attempted will not be effected.
Bear the patient exertion of heroism.
Sharply in arms he used to frown,
But mildly allured he the intellectual world.
A man that will run when you pursue,
Will have the rounded house of the sepulcher for his bed.
Call together, but do not reproach the over-anxious;And meddle not with the fierce and violent.
Let him who has a just claim break the boundary.
He does not calculate upon praise
Who defends his shelter.
Praise is the meed of those who have made impressions.
The victor gazed towards the fair one.

Of bright and prominent uplifted front,
On the ruddy dragon, the palladium of Pharaon,Which will in the air accompany the people
Dead is every one that fell on his mouth
In the repulsion of the march of Teth and Teddyd.
Courteous was the great retinue of the wall, of ashen spears.
To the sea thou mayst not come;
But neither thy retreat nor thy counsel will fail.
Thou magnanimous soul in the defense of his boundaries.
No more can they extricate themselves,
Extricate themselves before the barrier of Eiddyn.
Cenan, the fair wall of excellence,
Placed a sword on the entrenchment of warriors.
Victorious was the chief
In dispossessing the sovereign,
The inconstant
Gray-headed chief of ministers,
Whose counsels were deep.
The mutually sweet will not produce the mutually bitter.
I have mutually wished,
I do mutually wish for the repose of Enlli
The fair aspect of which is filled with deep interest,
On the course on a serene morning.
It allures me, it plays upon my strong desire.
I will ask the men for a dwelling,
In order to lessen the loss.
Happiness was lost and recovered.
The northern Eun, chieftain, thou hast caused to withdraw;
The fat one in returning thou wilt cause to return to me.
They call more for large trees than for honeysuckles.
{ Three lines untranslated }
Let the sovereign stand firm between the looks of Dremrudd,
The ruddy glancer, whose purpose cannot be viewed for a sufficient time.
Whose purpose cannot be viewed for a sufficient time,
By those who with impunity plough the noisy sea.

First to be satisfied is the pale one.
The eccentric, whose throne is of complete form.
Before he was covered, Gownddelw
Was a tall man of great worth like Maeldrew.
I will extol him who wields the spear.
Whose course is like that of the ruler of the mount.
The pervader of the land, by whose influence I am moved.
With active tumult did he descend to the ravine between the hills.
Nor was his presence a running shadow.
Whatever may befall the high land,
Disgrace shall never happen to the assembled train.

The Gorchan of Maeldrew (Histories of Aneurin)

I.

In the dales where the courses surround the Caer, arouses, who is partly covered and partly bright soon shall the breach of slaughter be repaired.

Let the renowned, the enterprising, be lulled in sleep; and with speed let the variegated web of heroism, with unbroken threads, be woven the breach which has been made shall not furnish a passage.

Train up his valor to endure the toil of conflict: let him frown in arms, expert and active; but let Hu mildly warm him with his divine presence!

2.

The man who rushes forth, when the foe lie in ambush, is the bedfellow of him who rests in the narrow house, under the tumulus. Let him have the habit, but not the disposition of the over-cautious.

Mix not thou the cruel with the brave! If the brave be broken, fair is his unblemished character his fame is not carried away.

I have devised a huge standard the mysterious glory of the great field of battle, and its excessive toils. There the victor directs his view over Manon, the luminary, the Arkite with the lofty front, and the red dragon, the Sudd (victory) of the Pharaon (higher powers) it shall accompany the people, flying in the breeze,

3.

He should have perished! Even he who brought down ruin with his mouth, by causing the army to halt on the march, when the ranks were drawn out, and his effective train was as a huge wall, mounted with ashen spears.

In the fluctuating sea,f thou canst mark neither cooperation, design, nor counsel the front of the circling mound protects their lives; but no more can they extricate themselves, nor be delivered, before the barrier of Eidin. Kenan, the fair bulwark of excellence, set his sword upon the rampart of the celebrators of May.

4.

Beneficent was the exertion of the supreme the sovereign inclosed, for the unadvised, grey-headed chief ministers, who devised deep counsels.

The mixture of sweet will not produce the mutually bitter I have joined in the common wish, the general wish of those who saw Enlli, filled with the fair aspect of returning prosperity, in the sacred course, on a serene morning, when Hu sent forth his dancing beams, making this demand "I require men to be born again, in consideration of those liberal ones who will be lost!" Those blessed ones - they have been intoxicated and lost!

5.

Is it the Northern Rhun, O thee supreme, that thou drawest forth! The gross chief, who has returned to me, shall be forced to retrace his steps For steeds they call, more than for the circling mead.

In the network which surrounds the sovereign, dispose thou the threads of wrath. Dispose wrath in the flowing streamer. Irksome in front he the glance of the radiant presence! Let the sovereign stand firm, amongst the rays of the ruddy glancer - the ruddy glancer, whose purpose cannot be viewed in perfect freedom whose purpose cannot be viewed, in a state of security, by those who plow the sea.

By a shout which cannot be disparaged, the chief of pale and livid aspect even he whose throne is involved in utter confusion, will be first convinced, before Gounddelw ("the white image") is covered, that Maeldrew ("proficient of the oaks") is a mighty operator.

6.

I will immortalize the form of him who brandishes the spear, imitating, in his career, the ruler* of the mount, the pervader of the land, by whose influence I am eminently moved. With active tumult did he descend to the ravine between the hills; nor did his presence form a running shadow.

Whatever fate may befall the lofty land, disgrace shall never be the portion of this assembled train!

Lludd and Llefelys -or- Cyfranc Lludd Y Llefelys

(from the Mabinogion)

1.

To Beli the Great, son of Manogan, were three sons: Lludd and Caswallawn and Nyniaw; and according to the story a fourth son of his was Llefelys. And when Beli died and the kingdom of the Island of Britain fell into the hands of Lludd his eldest son, and Lludd ruled it prosperously, he rebuilt the walls of London and girt it about with innumerable towers; and after that he bade the citizens build houses within it. So that there might not be in the kingdoms houses of such splendor as would be therein. Moreover, he was a good warrior and generous and liberal in giving meat and drink to all who sought them. And though he had many castles and cities he loved this one more than any; and he dwelt in it the greatest part of the year, and on that account it was called Caer Ludd, and at last Caer Lundein. And it was after the coming of the foreign folk thereto that it was called Lundein, or otherwise Lwndrys.

Best of all his brothers Lludd loved Llefelys, for a wise and prudent man was he. And when he heard that the king of France had died, leaving no offspring save an only daughter, and had left the dominions in her hands, he came to Lludd his brother to seek of him counsel and aid, and that not more for his own advantage, but to seek increase in honor and dignity and status for their kindred, if he might go to the kingdom of France to seek that maiden as wife. And straightway his brother agreed with him, and he was pleased with his counsel in that matter.

And straightway ships were made ready and filled with armed knights and they set out for France. And straightway after their coming to land they sent messengers to declare to the nobles of France the reason for the quest he was come to seek. And by common counsel of the nobles of France and its princes the maiden was given to Llefelys, and the crown of the kingdom along with her; and thereafter he ruled the land prudently and wisely and happily, so long as his life lasted.

2.

And after a space of time had passed, three plagues befell in the Island of Britain, whose like none in the Islands had seen before. The first of these was a certain folk that came and was called the Coranieid. And so great was their knowledge that there was no discourse over the face of the Island, however low it might be spoken, that they did not know about if the wind met it. And because of this no hurt might be done them.

The second plague was a scream which was raised every May-eve over every hearth in the Island of Britain. And that would pierce folks' hearts, and strike them with such terror that men would lose their hue and their strength and women the fruit of their wombs, and the young men and maidens would lose their senses, and all animals and trees and the earth and the waters be left barren.

The third plague was that however much might be the provision and food prepared in the king's courts, even though it were a year's provision of meat and drink, never a thing of it would be enjoyed save what was consumed the very first night.

Yet the first plague was open and manifest, but of the two other plagues there was none who knew what their meaning might be, and for this reason there was greater hope of winning deliverance from the first than there was from the second or from the third. And thereat king Lludd felt great trouble and care since he knew not how he might win deliverance from those plagues. And he summoned to him all the nobles of his kingdom, and asked counsel of them what they should do against those plagues; and by the common counsel of his nobles, Lludd son of Beli went to Llefelys his brother, king of France (for a man great in counsel and wise was he), to seek advice from him. and then they made ready a fleet, and that in secret and in silence, lest that folk should know the reason for their mission, or any besides the king and his counselors. And once they were ready, they went into their ships, Lludd and those he chose along with him; and they began to cleave the seas towards France.

And when those tidings came to Llefelys, since he knew not the reason for his brother's fleet, he came from the other side to meet him, and with him a fleet of vast size. And when Lludd saw that, he left all his ships out on the deep save one ship, and in that one he came to meet his brother. And he came in one other ship to meet his brother, and when they were met together each embraced the other, and each welcomed the other with brotherly affection.

3.

And after Lludd had made known to his brother the reason for his mission, Llefelys declared that he himself knew the reason for his coming into those parts. And then they took counsel together to discuss their business in some way other than that, so that the wind might not catch their discourse, lest the Coranieid should know what they were saying. And then Llefelys had made a long horn of bronze, and through that horn they conversed; and whatever words they said one to the other through the horn, it came to each of them as nothing but hateful contrariety.

And when Llefelys perceived that, and how there was a demon thwarting them and making mischief through the horn, he had wine poured into the horn, and had it washed, and by the virtue of the wine had the demon driven out of the horn. And when their talk was unhindered, Llefelys told his brother that he would give him certain insects and that he should keep some of these alive to breed, for fear lest a plague such as that should perchance come a second time, and other of the insects he should take and mash them with water; and he affirmed that was good for destroying the Coranieid folk. That is to say, when he returned home to his kingdom he should summon together all the people, his own folk and the Coranieid folk, to one assembly, under pretense of making peace between them; and when they were all assembled he should take that magic water and sprinkle it over all alike. And he affirmed that that water would poison the Coranieid folk, but would neither slay nor injure any of his own folk.

"The second plague", said he, "which is in thy dominion, that is a dragon, and a dragon of another foreign folk is fighting with it and striving to overcome it. And therefore," said he, "this dragon of yours raises a dire scream. And this is how thou canst prove it. After thou hast returned home, have the Island measured in its length and its breadth, and in the place where thou shalt find the exact point of centre, have a pit dug in that place, and then have set in that pit a tub full of the best mead that can be made, and a covering of silk over the face of the tub. And then keep watch in thine own person, and then thou shalt see the dragons fighting in the shape of monster animals. But at last they shall go in dragon-shape aloft in air; and last of all, when they shall have grown weary of their dire and frightful combat, they will fall in the shape of two little pigs upon the covering, and will make the covering sink down with them, and will drag it to the bottom of the tub, and they will drink up all the mead, and after that they will fall asleep. And then do thou straightway wrap the covering about them, and in the strongest place thou canst find in thy dominions bury them in a stone coffer, and hide them in the earth. And so long as they are in that strong place no plague shall come to the Island of Britain from elsewhere.

"The cause of the third plague,' said he, 'is a mighty man of magic who carries off thy meat and thy drink and thy provisions. And he through his magic and enchantment causes every one to fall asleep. And on that account thou must needs in thine own person keep watch over thy feasts and thy provisioning. And lest that sleep of his should overcome thee, let there be on hand a tub of cold water, and when sleep bears hard upon thee, get into the tub."

4.

And then Lludd returned to his country. And straightway he summoned to him each and every one of his own folk and of the Coranieid. And as Llefelys instructed him, he mashed the insects with water and sprinkled it over all alike, and there and then destroyed so the whole folk of the Coranieid, without hurt to any of the Britons.

And a while thereafter Lludd had the Island measured in its length and in its breadth, and in Oxford he found the point of centre. And in that place he had a pit dug in the ground, and in that pit he set a tub full of the best mead that might be made, and a covering of silk over the face of it, and he himself keeping watch that night. And as he was thus, he saw the dragons fighting; and when they were worn and weary they descended on top of the covering, and dragged it with them to the bottom of the tub. And when they had made an end of drinking the mead they fell asleep.

And in their sleep Lludd wrapped the covering about them, and in the safest place he found in Eryri he hid them in a stone coffer. The form by which that place was known thereafter was Dinas Emreis, and before that Dinas Ffaraon Dandde (Dinas Pharaon). He was one of Three Noble Youths who broke their hearts with consternation. So ended the tempestuous scream that was in his dominion.

And when that was over, king Lludd had prepared an exceeding great feast. And when it was ready he had a tub of cold water set near at hand, and he himself in his own person kept watch over it. And while he was thus, clad in arms, about the third watch of the night, lo, he heard much rare pastime and variety of song, and drowsiness compelling him to sleep. And thereupon, lest his design be hindered, and his drowsiness overcome him, he went often into the water. And at last, lo, a man of huge stature, clad in strong heavy armour coming in with a hamper, and as he had been wont, putting all the provisions and store of meat and drink into the hamper, and making off with it. And nothing was more wonderful to Lludd than that so much should be contained in that hamper.

And thereupon king Lludd made after him, and spoke to him thus: "Stop, stop!" said he, "though thou hast wrought many wrongs and losses ere this, thou shalt do so no further, unless thy skill at arms show thou art stronger and braver than I." And straightway he placed the hamper on the ground and waited for him to come up. And a terrible encounter was there between them, until sparks of fire flew from their weapons. But at length Lludd came to grips with him, and fate willed that victory should fall to Lludd, by casting down the oppressor between him and the ground. And when he had been overcome by might and by main, he asked for quarter. "How could I give thee quarter," asked the king, "after the many losses and wrongs thou hast wrought me?"

"All the losses that I have ever wrought thee," he answered, "I will make good even to the extent I have inflicted them. And I will never do the like henceforth, and a liege man will I be to thee for evermore." And the king accepted that of him.

And in this wise Lludd rid the Island of Britain of the three plagues. And from that time till his life's end Lludd son of Beli ruled the Island of Britain in prosperous peace.

Chapter XII
The Dragon Legacy
Divine Right & Dragon Blood

Illuminated by Myrddin Cerrig,

Bard of the Twelfth Chair

Adapted from "Draconomicon"

The Royal Dragon

Strong tides of emotional and political impact swept through human consciousness from the inception of civilization and its foundation in the Babylonian "Epic of Creation" called the *Enuma Elis.* Raising Marduk (*Jupiter*) to power in Babylon required the fragmentation of the "Universal Dragon" into the Currents or Gates that Marduk - and his chosen priests and kings - could govern as acting intermediaries between the human population and the "Divine," thereby controlling the reality affecting human experience of *Heaven and Earth* under the banner of the Royal Dragon. Later appearances of the *dragon* motif outside the domain of Mesopotamia came swiftly and sure.

To the Pheryllt Druids, the *dragon* represents not only the "greater universe" and cosmic order existing seemingly apart from the immediately affecting physical world of earth-life, but also political and religious mastery of the same as represented on earth. This is best realized with the "charge" that the "Holy Church" was given at its inception that "on earth as it is in heaven," implying that what "chosen dragon rulers" decreed on "earth," would also be in "heaven" -- suggesting its being "blessed by God" and enacted on "earth" by *Divine Right.* In essence, this is what has been meant by *dragon power* since the time of Babylon, including the proto-Druid founders - the *Pheryllt Priesthood.*

Whether represented by a cosmic spiritual entity, a biological form, or a reptilian humanoid, there are some very key "currents" or moves of energy that are connected to the Dragon. In and of itself, this should be suggestive to an inquisitive mind that there is *some kind* of unification behind it all. The Dragon represents:

Order, Science, Intellect, Sovereignty, Ancientness, Primeval, Primordial, Esoteric, Secret, Animal, Material, Reptile, Energy, Power, Stars, Strength, Will, Action, Information, Creation.

The Dragon is depicted in the most ancient lore as representative of everything as one! It is both the primeval and undistinguished ocean of consciousness and chaos as well as the fragmented and pointedly manifest physical existence. It is the epitome of the most spiritual and intangible of abstract ideals in the cosmos as much as it is the definitive representation of the solid physics we most closely identify as "real."

Between the Earth and Sky (or Universe), both of which are in themselves referred to as the *dragon,* we find the "ambassadors" *between the worlds* - aliens, sky gods, kings, Druids, etc. - also referred to as *dragons,* or carrying *dragonblood* thereby linking them to the "legacy" genetically. By some abstract semantics, the "sacred knowledge" of the Great Work Mystery Tradition of the Ages is called "star-knowledge" or "dragon-knowledge" not only because of its source, but as a result of its relay to the population: using "Divinely Ordained" *Dragon Kings* and *Priest-Scribe Dragons* (bards and magicians).

The mythologies surrounding the "Sky Gods" and *dragons* (regardless of the cultural pantheon or semantics adopted) have yet another *key* element involved that not only links them to each other, but also to the practices and beliefs that erupted as well: *mountains.* It is the "mountaintops" and "high places" that seem to be of significant interest to the *dragon-like* "deities" themselves as well as those half-mortals and demi-gods who came to serve as their ambassadors. In the case of non-mountainous terrain without such geology, "artificial peaks" in the form of pyramidal structures were raised in their stead - and we should not be surprised that they are also sacred to these *dragon gods.* Using the historical and verifiable (and visible) sources of tradition, we can attribute a *dragon-energy* to the socio-poltical and religio-spiritual use of the mountains in relation to the later emerging "Sky God" traditions, including: pyramids, ziggurats, temple (and burial) mounds and other artificial hillsides.

By some interpretations of the migration of the Dragon Tradition from Sumeria to Europe, the focus becomes "blood" (often referred to as *dragonblood* or *dragon's blood*). The preservation of these mysteries in the forms they survived as in Europe appeared to be a threat to the structure of the new spiritual-political organization in power by that time, the Roman Empire - and eventually the Roman Church. In order for them to secure their own hold on "worldly power," all of the other claims to such, including those of specific lineages of *dragonblood*, were thwarted or destroyed altogether. Rather than risk the rise of potential enemies, all of those who were suspect were killed.

This emphasis of the *Dragon Blood* living in the ancient lineages of Europe, its priest-kings and dynasties, proved significant in the preservation of the Sumerian, Babylonian, Egyptian and otherwise "Hermetic" mysteries of the ancients into the "secret societies" and otherwise underground occult schools surviving to this day. The *demonization of the dragon* by the Church forced those who did pursue these mysteries underground under the penalty of death! For thousands of years, a monopolized dictatorship on the freedom of *true knowledge* (gnosis) has prevented the masses from having direct experience with the *truth.* What's more: there is sufficient programming existent within the human psyche to prevent the accumulated and unified understanding of these things *fully*, as was intended by *man's creators*.

The Pheryllt Priesthood

For thousands of years, since the height of their power in *Keltia,* the entire subject of the *Druids* has been enshrouded in mystique and misinformation - much like the *dragon* as a whole. Among these aspects is the *Pheryllt Priesthood* of Welsh organization known as none other than the *Dragon Alchemists*. The Pheryllt were based in the mountaintops of Snowdonia in ancient Wales - a place where communion with the Sky Gods was most accessible, particularly by way of their ambassadors: the dragons!

The *Pheryllt* represent an element of "Celtic" history that is not altogether the same as the contemporary "Celtic Druidism" that seekers might be better acquainted with. While there are some aspects that do appear one-to-one with the often-biased perspectives offered in the Roman literary renderings, the vision of the *Pheryllt* is reminiscent more of the archetypal *wizard* and *priestly-magician* image than that of the later *Druids,* which appear to have become a governmental organization to guide and unify the Celtic nations as a whole. Such was not the original intention or functional purpose of the *Pheryllt* alone.

There is sufficient reason to plant *Mesopotamia* as the source for the Pheryllt Dragon Tradition. Given the time of the recorded Druidic histories, the Greek and post-dynastic Egyptian Hermetic traditions had already begun to affect the way in which the Great Mysteries were being interpreted. The simplicity of the *primum mobus* move to fragment and relay the totality of the tradition in Babylon had become further and further fractured into socio-political and otherwise religious interpretations of emerging and human populations in civilizations of differing languages all over the world. The *Pheryllt* are presented in current Bardic literature as the "first systematizers of the ancient *Cymry*" (Cymry meaning theWelsh Celts) and their knowledge or wisdom-based tradition. Given such a description the seeker is reminded of the "first systematizers" of global knowledge as an archetype, which can be found in *Mesopotamia.*

In addition to being represented by the image of the *dragon* (which can be easily seen in *blood red* gracing the national flag of Wales), the *Pheryllt Druids* were known as "dragons" themselves, a title later adopted by the Druids as a whole. In the times of St. Patrick when the legacy of the Druids had been excluded to Ireland by the efforts of the Milesians and later Romans, he considered the final *annihilation of the Druids* as an act of ridding the isle of "snakes" or dragons - an image of archetypal dragonslaying that has never seemed to escape the consciousness of men.

The Pheryllt and Stonehenge

One of the first subjects of controversy connecting the *Druids, Pheryllt* and *Dragons* is "Stonehenge." Located on a hillside in the Salisbury Plains (England), this circle or henge of stones remains one of the most infamous ancient mysteries. Debate over whether or not Druids literally built Stonehenge concerned historians for a long time. Regardless of the time-line issues between the construction of Stonehenge and the existence of the organized Celtic Druids that we are most familiar with by classical writings, it seems matter-of-fact that the local Druids at the very least *used* Stonehenge, regardless of its original design and purpose.

Local legends of England often attribute the construction of Stonehenge to "Merlyn" (also Myrddin or Merlin), specifically one from the Arthurian period (as this title was carried by several persons), but this too would support a significant time-line issue, with the era in question being c. 5th century AD and the construction of Stonehenge thousands of years prior to this, marking the turn or shift of the observed celestial (zodiac) ages in c. 2160 BC, the *Age of Aries*.

Dragon Alchemy

Pheryllt Druidism, as it is originally recorded, is likened to *alchemy* - an "Egyptian" originating term used to describe the "black arts" of science that were imported from Mesopotamia to the Mediterranean. It is most often expressed in Druidism - and perhaps the whole of "New Age" ritualism and magic - in the form of "Elementalism," which is to say the "elements" of Nature, or else the 'natural' forces of the 'universe'.

At some juncture or another in ancient lore, the energy currents themselves as well as the natural forms and background reality of the universe that the Druid is working to manipulate, are all referred to as the dragon. The idea that the Great Mystery can be coiled and veiled in countless layers of mystery - and levels of understanding - is by definition the very nature of the dragon and the dragonmind. This means that the existence of the dragon as the first-form, and the programming of the cosmos with the dragonmind, which is infinite knowledge, in essences makes the occult and esoteric possible.

Not only such, it makes for the manifold geometric and mathematical forms possible in our Realm of Light where ordered-patterns of chaotic shapes and forms occupy the whole of our experience of reality.

Volume Two

Chapter XIII Cad Goddeu - The Battle of Godeu

Adapted by Myrddin Cerrig,

Bard of the Twelfth Chair

From the Book of Taliesin

and Myvyrian Archaeology

The Battle of Goddeu - Cad Goddeu

("Battle of the Trees")

I have been in a multitude of shapes,
Before I assumed a consistent form.
I have been a sword, narrow, variegated,
I will believe when it is apparent.
A hundred souls through sin
I have been a tear in the air,
I have been the dullest of stars.
I have been a word among letters,
I have been a book in the origin.
I have been the light of lanterns,

A year and a half
I have been a continuing bridge,
Over three score Abers.
I have been a course, I have been an eagle.
I have been a coracle in the seas :
I have been compliant in the banquet.
I have been a drop in a shower;
I have been a sword in the grasp of the hand :
I have been a shield in battle.
I have been a string in a harp,

Disguised for nine years.
In water, in foam.
I have been sponge in the lire,
I have been wood in the covert.
I am not he who will not sing of
A combat though small,
The conflict in the battle of Godeu of sprigs.
Against the Guledig of Prydain,
There passed central horses,
Fleets full of riches.

There passed an animal with wide jaws,
On it there were a hundred heads.
And a battle was contested
Under the root of his tongue ;
And another battle there is
In his occiput.
A black sprawling toad.
With a hundred claws on it.
A snake speckled, crested.

Shall be tormented in its flesh.
I have been in Caer Vevenir,
Thither hastened grass and trees,
Minstrels were singing,
Warrior-bands were wondering,
At the exaltation of the Brython,
That Gwydyon effected.
There was a calling on the Creator,
Upon Christ for causes,
Until when the Eternal

Should deliver those whom he had made.
The Lord answered them,
Through language and elements :
Take the forms of the principal trees.

Arranging yourselves in battle array,
And restraining the public.
Inexperienced in battle hand to hand.
"When the trees were enchanted,
In the expectation of not being trees,
The trees uttered their voices"

From strings of harmony.
The disputes ceased.
Let us cut short heavy days,
A female restrained the din.
She came forth altogether lovely.
The head of the line, the head was a female.
The advantage of a sleepless cow
Would not make us give way.
The blood of men up to our thighs.
The greatest of importunate mental exertions

Sported in the world.
And one has ended
From considering the deluge,
And Christ crucified,
And the day of judgment near at hand.
The alder-trees, the head of the line,
Formed the van.
The willows and quicken-trees
Came late to the army.
Plum-trees, that are scarce,

Unlonged for of men.
The elaborate medlar-trees,
The objects of contention.
The prickly rose-bushes,
Against a host of giants,
The raspberry brake did
What is better failed
For the security of life.
Privet and woodbine
And ivy on its front,

Like furze to the combat
The cherry-tree was provoked.
The birch, notwithstanding his high mind,
Was late before he was arrayed.
Not because of his cowardice.
But on account of his greatness.
The laburnum held in mind.
That your wild nature was foreign.
Pine-trees in the porch,
The chair of disputation,

By me greatly exalted.
In the presence of kings.
The elm with his retinue,
Did not go aside a foot;
He would fight with the centre.
And the flanks, and the rear.
Hazel-trees, it was judged
That ample was thy mental exertion.
The privet, happy his lot.
The bull of battle, the lord of the world.

Morawg and Morydd
Were made prosperous in pines.
Holly, it was tinted with green,
He was the hero.
The hawthorn, surrounded by prickles,
With pain at his hand.
The aspen-wood has been topped,
It was topped in battle.
The fern that was plundered.
The broom, in the van of the army,

In the trenches he was hurt.
The gorse did not do well,
Notwithstanding let it overspread.

The heath was victorious, keeping off on all sides.
The common people were charmed.
During the proceeding of the men.
The oak, quickly moving.
Before him, tremble heaven and earth.
A valiant door-keeper against an enemy,
His name is considered.

The blue-bells combined.
And caused a consternation.
In rejecting, were rejected.
Others, that were perforated.
Pear-trees, the best intruders
In the conflict of the plain.
A very wrathful wood.
The chestnut is bashful,
The opponent of happiness.
The jet has become black,

The mountain has become crooked.
The woods have become a kiln,
Existing formerly in the great seas,
Since was heard the shout :

–

The tops of the birch covered us with leaves,
Transformed us, and changed our faded state.
The branches of the oak have ensnared us
From the Gwarchan of Maelderw.
Laughing on the side of the rock,
The lord is not of an ardent nature

Not of mother and father,
When I was made.
Did my Creator create me.
Of nine-formed faculties.
Of the fruit of fruits,
Of the fruit of the primordial God,

Of primroses and blossoms of the hill,
Of the flowers of trees and shrubs.
Of earth, of an earthly course,
When I was formed.

Of the flower of nettles.
Of the water of the ninth wave.
I was enchanted by Math,
Before I became immortal,
I was enchanted by Gwydyon
The great purifier of the Brython,
Of Eurwys, of Euron,
Of Euron, of Modron.
Of five battalions of scientific ones,
Teachers, children of Math.

When the removal occurred,
I was enchanted by the Guledig.
When he was half-burnt,
I was enchanted by the sage
Of sages, in the primitive world.
When I had a being ;
When the host of the world was in dignity,
The bard was accustomed to benefits.
To the song of praise I am inclined, which the tongue recites.
I played in the twilight,

I slept in purple;
I was truly in the enchantment
With Dylan, the son of the wave.
In the circumference, in the middle,
Between the knees of kings,
Scattering spears not keen,
From heaven when came,
To the great deep, floods,
In the battle there will be
Four score hundreds,

That will divide according to their will.
They are neither older nor younger,
Than myself in their divisions.
A wonder, Canhwr are born, every one of 900.
He was with me also.
With my sword spotted with blood.
Honor was allotted to me
y By the Lord, and protection (was) where he was.
If I come to where the boar was killed,
He will compose, he will decompose,

He will form languages.
The strong-handed gleamer, his name.
With a gleam he rules his numbers.
They would spread out in a flame.
When I shall go on high.
I have been a speckled snake on the hill,
I have been a viper in the Ilyn.
I have been a bill-hook crooked that cuts,
I have been a ferocious spear
With my chasuble and bowl

I will prophesy not badly,
Four score smokes
On every one what will bring.
Five battalions of arms
Will be caught by my knife.
Six steeds of yellow hue
A hundred times better is
My cream-colored steed.
Swift as the sea-mew
Which will not pass

Between the sea and the shore.
Am I not preeminent in the field of blood ?
Over it are a hundred chieftains.

Crimson (is) the gem of my belt,
Gold my shield border.
There has not been born, in the gap.
That has been visiting me,
Except Goronwy,
From the dales of Edrywy.
Long white my fingers,

It is long since I have been a herdsman.
I traveled in the earth.
Before I was a proficient in learning.
I traveled, I made a circuit,
I slept in a hundred islands.
A hundred Caers I have dwelt ia
Ye intelligent Druids,
Declare to Arthur,
What is there more early
Than I that they sing of.

And one is come
From considering the deluge,
And Christ crucified,
And the day of future doom.
With a golden charm set in a gold
I am the feat of splendor
and am offered royalty
Born from the Craft of the Fferylt.

The Cad Goddeu - The Battle of Godeu

"Battle of the Trees" – Archaic Version

[1] I have been in many forms

[2] before I reached my current existence.

[3] I have been the sleek blade of a sword.

[4] I believe in what appears.

[5] I have been a tear in the air.

[6] I have been a distant star.

[7] I have been the letters written in a book.
[8] I have been the book.
[9] I have been the illumination of a lantern.
[10] For a year and a half
[11] I have been a bridge crossing
[12] sixty rivers.
[13] I have been an eagle in the sky.
[14] I have been a boat on the sea.
[15] I have been a general at war.
[16] I have been a stand of thread in a child's blanket.
[17] I have been a sword in a warrior's hand.
[18] I have been a shield protecting in battle.
[19] I have been the sting of harp.
[20] Enchanted for a year
[21] I have been the foam of the sea.
[22] I have been a poker stirring the fire.
[23] I have been a tree in a secret grove.
[24] There is no existence I have not been.
[25] Though slight, I have fought
[26] on the battlefield of Goddeu Brig,
[27] before the rule of Britain,
[28] marching in brigade formation.
[29] Indifferent Bards conjure
[30] they conjure a fierce beast
[31] with one hundred heads
[32] and death battles
[33] at the root of the tongue.
[34] Another fight exists

[35] at the back of the head.
[36] A toad possessing on his legs
[37] one hundred claws
[38] and a spotted crested serpent
[39] for punishing the bodies
[40] of one hundred sinners.
[41] I was in Caer Feffynedd
[42] and beheld the hastening grasses and trees.
[43] Wanderers beheld this
[44] warriors are amazed
[45] at a renewal of conflict
[46] such as Gwydion made.
[52] Through charms and magick
[53] discover the nature of the trees,
[54] with you in line
[55] temper the folk
[56] who are inexperienced in warfare.
[57] When the trees were enchanted (awoken)
[58] there was hope for the trees
[59] that they should hinder the progression
[60] of the surrounding fires.
[61] Better are the three-in-one
[62] united in a circle.
[67] The alder trees in the front line
[68] commenced the attack.
[69] Willow and rowan
[70] were slow in their arrival.
[71] The plum tree

[72] is not beloved by men.
[73] The medlar is the same,
[74] overcoming laborious toil.
[77] The raspberry
[78] does not make the best food.
[79] In shelter resides
[80] privet and woodbine.
[81] The ivy was in its season;
[82] the gorse great in battle.
[83] The Cherry tree is compromised.
[84] The birch is encompassing
[85] but was late in joining the fight
[86] not because of cowardice or sloth
[87] but because of immense size.
[90] The pine in court
[91] strong in battle
[92] greatly exalted
[93] in the presence of kings.
[94] The elms are his subjects;
[98] the hazel, his judge
[99] and his berries are your dowry.
[100] The privet is blest.
[. . .]
[103] Prosperous is the beech tree.
[104] The dark green holly,
[105] he was very valiant:
[106] he defended on all sides, with spikes,
[107] wounding hands.

[108] The long enduring poplars
[109] broke easily in battle.
[110] The embezzled fern
[111] and the broom with her children
[112] and the unruly furze
[113] were eventually tamed.
[114] The heath consoled,
[115] it comforted the people.
[116] Black cherry pursued.
[117] The oak moved quickly
[118] shaking the heavens and the Earth
[119] a strong door against evil
[120] his name in all languages.
[128] The cruel and gloomy ash
[129] and the bashful chestnut tree
[130] were seen retreating from happiness.
[131] There shall be a black darkness.
[132] The mountains shall shake.
[133] There shall be purification by fire
[134] and a great wave of sea.
[135] When the shout is heard,
[136] the beech sprouts new leaves
[137] transforming, renewed from a withered state.
[138] The oak canopies entangle.
[139] (From the Gorchan of Maeldrew)
[142] Neither of mortal mother or father
[143] was I made,
[144] except for my blood and body.

[145] Of nine faculties,
[146] nine fruits
[147] God birthed me.
[148] From the blossom of the primrose
[149] from trees and shrubs
[150] from Earth and earthly elements
[151] I was made.
[152] From nettle flowers
[153] and waters from the ninth wave
[154] I was enchanted by Math
[155] before I ascended to immortality.
[156] I was enchanted by Gwydion
[157] the British conjurer
[158] of Eurys, of Eurwn,
[159] of Euron, of Medron
[160] in a pool of secrets
[161] I have become as learned as Math.
[164] I know the star knowledge
[165] and of the existence of stars before the Earth was made.
[166] From where I came from
[167] many dimensions exist.
[168] It is the function of the Bards
[169] to create verse in praise of their nation.
[189] I know of the slaying of the boar,
[190] its illusionary aspects,
[191] its language of languages.
[192] I know the light whose name is Splendor
[193] and the secret number of the lights

[194] that scatters rays of fire.
[195] High above the deep
[196] I have been a spotted serpent on a hill.
[197] I have been a sea serpent in the lake.
[198] I have once been an evil star.
[199] In a mill I have been an anvil.
[200] I wear a red cassock.
[201] I foresee no evil.
[202] Eighty puffs of smoke
[203] carry all the willing away:
[204] and one million angels
[205] on the point of a dagger.
[206] Handsome is the yellow horse
[207] but one hundred times better
[208] is my cream-colored one,
[209] quick as the sea mew,
[210] which cannot overtake me
[211] between the sea and the shore.
[214] My wreath is embellished with red jewels,
[215] a gold border graces my shield.
[216] There has not been born one so good as I,
[217] or is to be known,
[218] except Goronwy
[219] from the valley of the Edrywy.
[220] My fingers are long and white.
[221] Much time has passed since I worked the field.
[222] I traveled across the Earth
[223] before finding wisdom.

[225] I have slept in one hundred islands

[226] and dwelled in one hundred cities.

[227] Learned Druids,

[228] prophecy of Arthur?

[229] Or, do they honor me,

[230] and the crucifixion of the messiah

[231] and the Day of Judgment upon us,

[232] and one uniting

[233] history of the flood?

[234] With a jewel set in gold

[235] I am enriched:

[236] indulgent in pleasure

[237] at the labor of the Pheryllt.

The Cad Goddeu - Battle of the Trees

Robert Graves' abridged version

1.

The tops of the beech tree had sprouted of late, are changed and renewed from their withered state (lines 136-137). When the beech prospers through spells and litanies, the oak-tops entangle, there is hope for the trees (lines 102, 52, 138 & 58).

2.

I have plundered the fern, through all secrets I spy, Old Math ap Mathonwy, knew no more than I (lines 110, 160 & 161). From nine sorts of faculty, God has gifted me: I am the fruit of fruits gathered from nine sorts of tree (lines 145-147).

3.

Plum, quince, whortle, mulberry, raspberry, pear, black cherry and white, with a sorb in me share (lines 71, 73, 77, 83, 102, 116 & 141). From my seat at Fefynedd, a city that is strong, I watched the trees and green things hastening along (lines 41-42).

4.

Retreating from happiness, they would fain be set in the forms of the chief letters of the Ogham alphabet (lines 130 & 53). Wayfarers wondered, warriors were dismayed at the renewal of conflicts such as Gwydion made (lines 43-46). Under the tongue root a fight most dread, and another raging behind in the head (lines 32-35).

5.

The alders in the front line began the affray, willow and rowan tree were tardy in array (lines 67-70). The holly, dark and green, made a resolute stand; he is armed with many spear-points wounding the hand (lines 104-107). With foot-beat of the swift oak the heavens and earth rung; stout guardian of the door, his name in every tongue (lines 117-120).

6.

Great were the gorse in battle, and the ivy in his prime; the hazel was arbiter at this enchanted time (lines 82, 81, 98 & 57). Uncouth and savage was the fir, cruel the ash tree, turns not aside a foot-breadth, straight as the heart runs he (lines 88, 89, 128, 95 & 96).

7.

The birch, though very noble, armed himself of late: A sign not of cowardice but of high estate (lines 84-87). The heath gave consolation to the toil-spent folk; the long-enduring poplars in battle much broke (lines 114, 115, 108 & 109).

8.

Some of them were cast away on the field of fight, because of holes torn in them by the enemy's might (lines 123-126). Very wrathful was the vine whose henchmen are the elms; I exalt him mightily, the ruler of realms (lines 127, 94, 92 & 93).

9.

Strong chieftains were the blackthorn with his ill fruit, the un-beloved hawthorn that bares the same suit (lines 101, 71-73, 77 & 78). The swift pursuing reed, the broom with his brood, and the furze but ill-behaved until he is subdued (lines 116 & 111-113).

10.

The dower-scattering yew stood glum at the fight's fringe, with the elder slow to burn among the fires that singe (lines 97, 99, 128, 141 & 60). And the blessed wild apple laughing for pride, from the incantations of Maeldrew by the rock side (lines 100, 139 & 140).

11.

In the shelter linger privet and woodbine, inexperienced in warfare, and the courtly pine (lines 79, 80, 56 & 90). But I, although slighted, because I was not big, fought, trees, in your array, on the fields of Goddeu Brig (lines 83, 54, 25 & 26).

Chapter XIV The Coelbren of the Bards:

A Tradition of the Ogham

Translated by Llywelyn Sion

Bard of the Glamorgan Chair.

From the Iolo Morganwg MS.

Introduced by Myrddin Cerrig

The Ogham and Coelbren

Ancient Bards & Druids used secret alphabets in Council and to preserve secret knowledge. Burning or carving Ogham characters onto the wood is known as "coelbren." This tradition is twinned by "coelvain," which is carving of same characters onto stone. A ritual or magic act of coelbren is performed during the construction of Ogham Sticks and Ogham Wands, which includes a form of runic magic.

Books of the Ancient Cymry

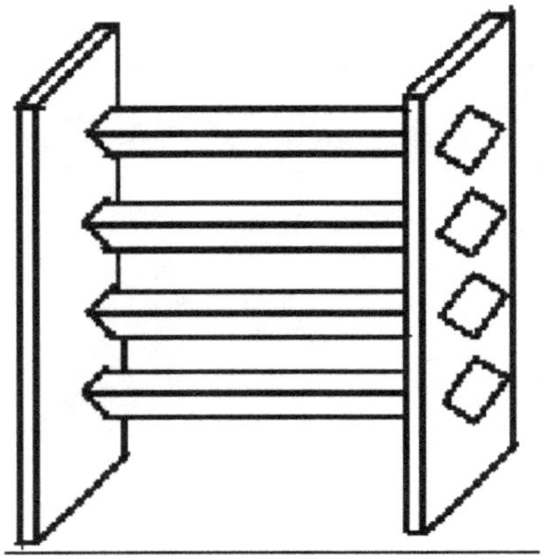

The Coelbren of the Bards:

Student - What were the first books that were first known to the nation of the Cymry, and what were their materials?

Teacher - Wood, that is, trees, and that mode was called Coelbren, from which comes the Coelbren of the Bards, as it is still on record by the nation of the Cymry.

Student - Pray, my teacher, is it meet that thou should show me instruction of how to make the Coelbren of the Bards, and the art that ought to belong to it?

Teacher - The Coelbren of the Bards is made with the genial wood of oak plants, split into four parts, that is, of greenwood as thick as a boy's wrist. These are hewn square, that is, into four sides, a cubit in length, their breadth and thickness being equal one to the other, namely the length of a barley corn, which is the third of an inch.

The Most Ancient Marks

Coelbren Alphabet of the Bards Ieuan Llawdden

Arrangement

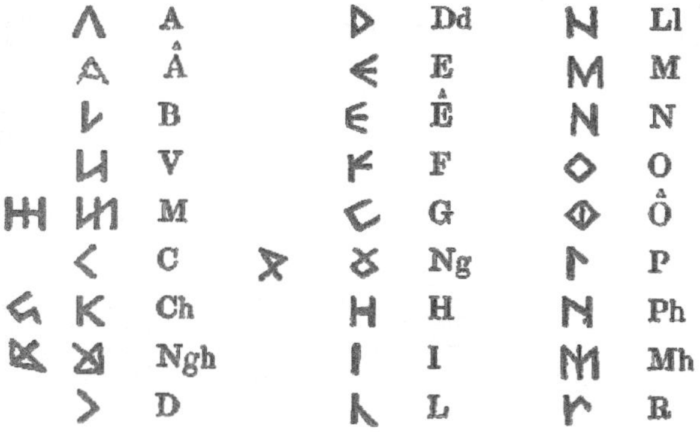

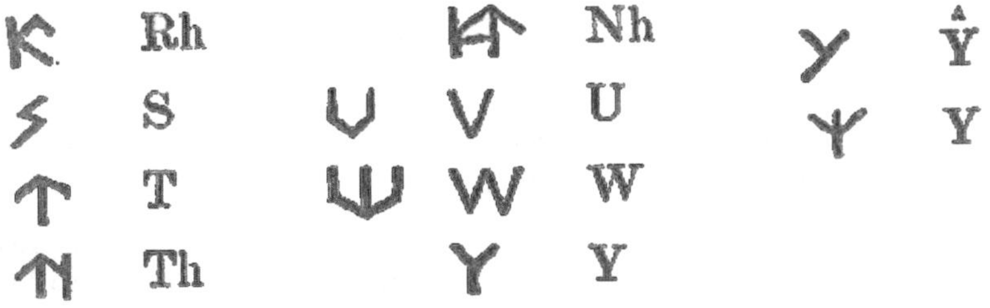

The Coelbren of the Bards According to Llywelyn Sion

The primitive Cymry, and their poets, and book-wise men, were accustomed to cut letters on wood, because in their time from the beginning there was no knowledge either of paper or *plagawd,* and here is exhibited the manner in which they constructed their books and the figure of the mode and manner.

The first thing made was the *pillwydd*, or the side posts, each post

being in two halves, thus:

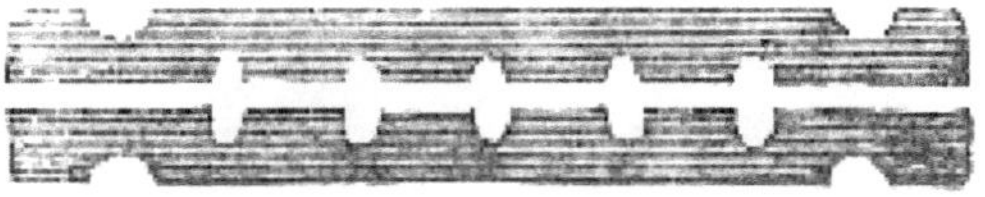

That is, there is a number of holes in the post, the halves of the holes being in either half, and the other halves in the other, so that when the two halves are put together, there will be a row of perfect holes in a line from one end to the other, in the middle of the post, or *pill*. There will be also another post of the same kind and size. After that, other staves, called *ebillwydd*, each of them thus:

At one end and the other let a neck be formed, as is delineated here, and let a closed and tied pill be placed round the necks of as many *ebillwydd* as may be required, at both ends. And thus let them be joined together, *pillwydd* and *ebillion*, in the form of a hurdle; the *ebillion*, each one of them, turning all round by their necks in the *pillwydd*, or posts.

On the *ebillion* the letters are cut with an efficient knife, that is, on each of the four sides of every *ebill;* and when one side has been read, the second side is turned upwards, after that the third side, and after that the fourth side, each side being read as it is turned upwards. The corners, along each of the *ebillion* as far as the necks, must be trimmed down, that the cutting of a letter on one face may not become one with, or break into the letters of the other face, and so with every one of the four faces. A sharp knife is required to cut the grooves fairly and clearly, with a skilful, dexterous hand. Take care that every letter, in respect of its groove, be of uniform thickness, otherwise it will be unseemly to the sight.

Coelbren Alphabet of the Bards

from "Barddas"

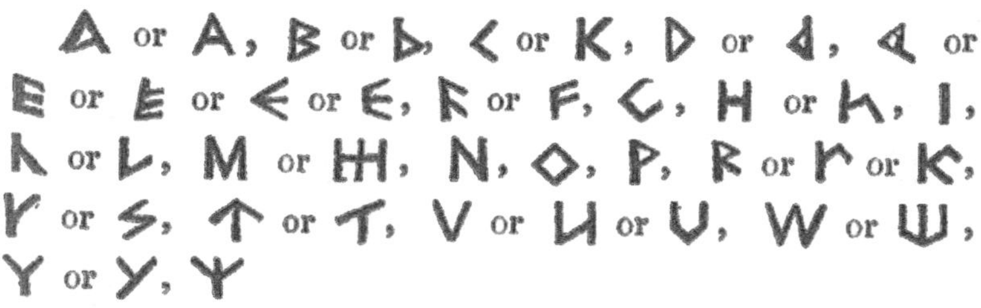

Chapter XV Enchantment of the Greenwoods:

Communing with Nature - Pheryllt High Magic

Illuminated by Myrddin Cerrig,

Bard of the Twelfth Chair

Adapted from "Book of Elven-Faerie"

The Triad Rite of Awen: Three Rays of Radiance

Managing personal Calen (Light Centers and Light Shields) primarily involves the more mundane spectrum of seven rays of manifestation. The high magic of the Pheryllt and Druids concentrates on light-work aligned to the Three Rays of Awen, using the Triad Rite to activate an awareness of the personal Light Body.

The Triad Rite of Awen

Face the northern direction. Call down the Radiance in the form of the Silver Ray, feeling and seeing it descend upon you and to the left as you intone the sound "I" (or "ee"). Raise your arms as you inhale the tone and bring them down to your sides as you exhale or intone the sound, using your arms to draw or pull down the air (Ray). Do this with the Middle Ray descending through you with the sound "A" ("ah"), and the Gold Ray upon you and down to the right with the utterance "O" ("oh"). In some Bardic interpretations, the three letter forms are O, I and W (or O, I and U) from *Coelbren* lore.

The Auric Light Shield

The Light Shield is the auric covering of a being that filters the energy that is projected and received. The color of the energy will determine which Calen center of the body is projecting the most into the shield. Each color possesses "positive" and "negative" qualities based its over- or under-activity and on whether the effects appear "constructive" or "destructive" to our spiritual evolution, emotional well-being, psychological state and physical health. Nothing is usually what it seems on the surface alone.

At the very core of your being there is a violet egg or oval-like sphere that represents the essence of our spirit. The rest is part of an elaborate biochemical vehicle. First, the violet egg (the fragmented shard of the "dark crystal") is encased in a pink shell for protection, composed of true love and purity. This violet-pink spirit is the true part of us that came from and can return to *Ceugent*. It is our connection to the Source, the Middle Ray, and is responsible for the activation of our entire internal Calen (energy propulsion) system that projects our Light Shield.

The Etheric Light Body System

The Light Body is your link to *Gwynedd*, the Astral, Otherworld or Realm of Light. When the white energy of the Light Body has stabilized (or equalized) it is then able to manifest the colors of the spectrum. These Rays use the body's Calen system as a "step-down transformer" to conduct energy from the Divine Radiance. The fourth level of your spiritual existence consists of both a silver and a gold encasement that seals the auric energy in. The fifth level is the Light Body itself, the outer aura and Light Shield. It is the part of us that people see when they say they can see auras.

Your energy and emotional state will influence the nature and strength of your auric Light Shield, which affects your environment. It is possible to neutralize negative or destructive aspects of an emotion (color) by changing the Light Shield to an opposing color. For example, you might counter "red" anger with "blue" peace. However, an hyperactivity of blue can cause depression. Meditate on the nature of the multiplicity and oneness of the perceived levels of the "spiritual self," and see your auric energy strong.

The Enchanted Forest

Tree Magic is a unique and personal practice descended from Pheryllt and Elvish Druids and used to awaken individual consciousness of trees one by one. These awakened trees form groups or chains, completing a complex network of communication with other awakened trees of the "Enchanted" forest. Through the ability known as "Communion with Nature," the Druid is capable of learning spiritual lessons, gaining access to the "Earth Memory."

Advanced use of these abilities include activating a ring of awakened trees to guard an area. Linking with Forces of Nature, sensitive adepts can feel when surrounding charged area has a "visitor" or is being disturbed. To 'Commune with Nature,' your mastery over the initial visualization and willpower will be tested. The following prerequisites must be met before any further work is performed.

Communion with the Forest

1.

Go to the sacred woods where you practice your art of energy-play and light-weaving. This will most likely by the *nemeton* or place where you have developed your aptitude in the Druid Way. Spend some time meditating on the Pheryllt materials.

2.

Project awareness into your Light Body.

3.

Adjust your Light Shield to match the green energy (crystalline ray) of the woodlands.

4.

Use muscular inclination ('dowsing with your feet') to guide you to a tree. At first you will want to work with only a few tree types. Eventually you will be able to awaken the entire forest.

5.

When working with individual trees, approach slowly and from the north (when possible.) Be sure to have meditated and quieted your mind before doing so. Do not bring a mind cluttered with worldly matters to your energy-work.

6.

Sit close, within arm's reach, focus on both your Light Shield and the auric radiation of the tree. Match the frequency and color vibration and then merge the two energy fields as you spread your palms wide on the surface of the trunk.

7.

Retain contact with your left hand, completing the circuit with your right by using some catalyst for the energy like sticks, stones or the ground.

Tree Energy Systems & Tree Communication

What follows after your preliminary communion depends on what type of Green Magic you have intended. Not all communions are intended for actual communication, which can be a lengthy process. For communion you must clearly visualize the circuit of energy you are conducting.

The pillar of the tree represents the "Tower of the Green Ray," the pure Middle Ray of crystalline reflection and refraction. Take this into your circulatory and nervous system via your left (or receptive) hand spread on the trunk. Make it a part of you, and then send it forth to the ground after passing through your catalyst, forming a circuit. The life-force energies actually get filtered (increase in their strength and purity) from this process, beneficial to both (like removing corrosion from a wire connection or contact.) Energy projected from the Druid is returned, permanently changed and empowered by the "signature" of the partner, in this case the tree. Mortals have a habit of not using the Pillars and Rays (often unknowingly) in their sexual activity and thus cause damage to their Calen system and Light Bodies.

Once you have communed, you can communicate. Close your eyes; see a whitish etheric cloud between you and the tree, slightly above your head. Both of you share this field and have the ability to project into it. Understand, the tree will not verbally "talk" to you. It prefers to communicate in the timeless language of symbols and imagery; hence the picture is worth a thousand words.

Sometimes there is an etheric spirit inhabiting or attached to the tree that is more likely to communicate in words, otherwise, when in communion with the forest, any verbal use of communication (with a few exceptions) is for mainly your own psyche and your ability to attune to the proper dragon current. Trees are more likely to hear and feel the emotion and tone of your words than the words themselves, and it is to this they will respond to. Use the cloud as a thought-bubble to project your desire to communicate. Then wait and see what happens.

Forest Magic - Oghamancy: Tree Ogham Tools

There are different sets of Ogham tools that are often haphazardly all referred to as "Ogham Sticks." Each set is kept in their own "Crane Bag" or magical pouch.

Ogham Sticks are sticks/twigs of the same type, cut to the same size and polished. An alternate version uses wood-chips as "runic wood-stones." Each of the sticks or chips will have one of the Ogham glyphs burned (preferably) or painted thereon. "Ogham Sticks" are used for high-divination and "cryptomancy."

Ogham Wands range from eight to sixteen inches in length and should be constructed from the correlating tree for each Ogham rune, or a tree of similar energy for the ones you can't find. The "handle" of the wand should be shaved flat on one side so that you have a surface to put the runic glyph. The other end should be shaved to a stake-like or spear-like point so that it can be pushed several inches into the ground. The Wizard maintains hold of the handle to complete the circuit. Ogham Wands are used mainly for communication and spiritual communion with Nature.

Ogham Rods are used specifically for divination. They are pieces of dowel or thin wood that are cut to equal lengths, twenty-one in all. Some scholars suggest this ancient tool set is responsible for the children's game "pick-up-sticks," which is what an objective observer might see when they are cast, interpreted and retrieved. They are held in one hand about a foot away from the ground, and then dropped. Using the rune and Ogham symbols as reference, the Wizard interprets any omens found or "read." When used in conjunction with tree communication, simple acts of divination can become powerful workings of high magic of the forest.

Forest Magic - Arbormancy: The Elf Stones Triscale

Elf Stones are sacred of tools used in Sylvan forest magic. They may be used for tree communication, energy/light-work and as an energy testing divinatory tool in lieu of pendulums, etc. Each of the stones taps the heart of one of the Three Rays of Awen and with the Seven Rays of Divine Radiance.

Traditional sets of Elf Stones are usually Tiger's Eye (Gold Ray,) Hematite (Silver Ray) and an Obsidian (black) for an indicator. Some traditions use Aventurine-type (green) to represent the crystalline "Middle Ray."

Elf Stones indicate a positive or negative response depending on where the gold and silver stone lay in relation to the black (or green) indicator.

Forest Magic - Arbormancy: Tree Awakenings with Elf Stones

Link your Calen to a tree from your Light Body and ask it if it is in need of a Guardian and Caretaker or if it wishes to begin a mystical and spiritual relationship with you. Drop the stones at the base of the tree and see how they fall. If the gold one is closest to the indicator, the answer is "yes," and the answer is "no" if the silver stone is closer.

Elf Stones operate on the same principle that "foot dowsing" and "muscle testing" (intuitive inclination) work. These methods are all great for forest magic, but are dependent on the sensitivity and awareness of the practitioner and are not as blatant interpretable as other forms of divination. The lore of the "Tree Awakening" comes down to us from the original

"Greenwood Forest Grimoire." It is a powerful rite when performed by Pheryllt Sylvan Adepts (yet anyone can follow these steps.)

Call down the Three Rays and enter your Light Body. Make physical contact with the tree. Speak the Celtic name for the tree three times, followed by the English name, and finally the names "Aldaron," "Daghda" and the Guardian of the particular tree you are working with. Knock three times. As you break contact know that the tree is awakened.

Chapter XVI
Auraicept Na N'eces - The Scholar's Primer

Written by Three Bards of Ballymote

Translated from the Ogham Tracts,

Book of Lecan and Book of Leinster

Primer of the Poets

I*ncipit Auraicept na n'Eces,* Primer of the Poets, that is, Eraicept, beginning of lessons, for every beginning is ER. To what is this a beginning? Not hard. To the selection that was selected in Gaelic since this is the beginning which was invented by Fenius after the coming of the school with the languages from abroad, every obscure sound that existed in every speech and in every language was put into Gaelic so that for this reason it is more comprehensive than any language.

ER then is every beginning, for this was the beginning with the poets, that every obscure sound should come in the beginning, to wit, the *Beithe-Luis* of the Ogham on account of obscurity.

Query, what is the reason why select language should be said of Gaelic? Not hard. Because it was selected from every language; and for every obscure sound of every language a place was found in Gaelic owing to its comprehensiveness beyond every speech.

Query, then, did not Gaelic exist before it was selected? It did indeed, for the 72 languages are not found otherwise.

Query, in what land was Gaedel born? Not hard. In Egypt. And what particular place? Not hard. In the plain of Ucca in the South-Western division of Egypt. Who of the school went to it thither? Not hard. Gaedel son of Ether, son of Toe, son of Baracham, a Scythian Greek. Query, how much did he bring of it? Not hard. The whole of it except what poets added by way of obscuration after it had reached Fenius.

Query, what language of the 72 was published by Fenius first? Not hard. The Irísh Language, for it is he whom he preferred of his school, and whom he had reared from his youth, and it is he that was the youngest of the school, and on account of its comprehensiveness beyond every speech, and it was the first language that was brought from the Tower of Babel. Fenius had Hebrew, Greek, and Latin before he came from Scythia, and he had no need to establish them at the Tower, wherefore on that account it was published first.

Query, was there not among the many languages something nobler to take precedence of Gaelic? Not hard. No indeed, on account of its aptness, lightness, smoothness, and comprehensiveness.

Wherefore is it more comprehensive than any speech? Not hard. Because it was the first speech that was brought from the Tower, it was of such extent that it was more comprehensive than any speech so that it was the one to be published at first.

What are the place, time, person, and cause of Gaelic? Not hard. Its place, the Tower of Babel, of Nimrod, for there it was invented at first. It's time the time of building the Tower by Adam's children. Its person Sachab son of Rochemhurcos and Gaedel son of Ether, son of Toe, son of Baracham, a Scythian Greek. What is its cause? Not hard. The building of Nimrod's Tower. Others say the cause was that Gaedel went into the land in which he was born so that he was the first that wrote it on tablets and stones in the particular place which is named Calcanensis. There Gaedel wrote Gaelic.

That this is the reason for the Irish Language (that is Fenius' speech); a deed wonderful, unlawful, that is, an unusual deed, unusual for its infrequency, unlawful for its pride, an attempt on heaven in their fleshly bodies without permission of God. Which happened there, i.e., the building of the Tower of Babylon.

Nimrod and the Tower of Babel

Now that Nimrod was champion of all Adam's seed in his time, Nimrod, son of Cush, son of Ham, son of Noah. There was not then any king over the world till the time of Nin, son of Bel, but only counselors and chiefs were in existence up till that time. Seventy-two counselors accordingly were in the world at the time ín which the Tower was made.

Now one of the 72 was Nimrod. A mighty man was he and a man famous in hunting, to wit, for stags; and in coursing, to wit, for hares; and in trappings, to wit, wild pigs; and in snarings, to wit, for birds. So that thus multitudes of men were following him so that he was more numerous, to wit, in armies and so that he was thus more powerful than a counselor, So that it was he who united those 72 counselors to one counsel to make the Tower with the grandson of his father's brother, to wit, with the great grandson of his grandfather's brother, to wit, with Peleg son of Ragau, son of Arphaxad, son of Shem, son of Noah. And he was one of the 72 counselors, too, up to that time. And they say therefore that Peleg was the one counselor and the same parent of them all.

A question here is, the names of the 72 counselors by whom the Tower was made, only that writings do not enumerate but the names of the 17 men who were most illustrious among them, to wit, Peleg, Nimrod, Eber, Latinus, Rabiath Scot, Nabgodon, Assur, Ibath, Longbardus, Bodbus, Brittus, Germanus, Garath, Scithius, Gotius, Bardanius, and Sardain.

After the flood the first king according to nature was Nimrod. That was the first king according to art, the Peleg aforesaid. According to authority, however, it was Nin son of Bel, son of Plosc, son of Pluliris, son of Agomolis, son of Fronosis, son of Gitlis, son of Tiras, son of Assur, son of Shem, son of Noah, He obtains, then, that thing. Nimrod said that it was his name that should be on that work for ever. Adrodamas, i.e., that thing also was granted him.

Three things, then, on account of which the building of that Tower was accomplished by Adam's children, to wit, for dread of the flood again, and that they should go to heaven in their bodies from the earth, and to render their names illustrious after them, so that on that account said the King of heaven to the people of heaven - *Venite tit videamus et confundanius linguas eormn* - that is, come that we may see and confound those men's speech.

Now great was the power of Adam's seed and their strength at that time in making the Tower, that they might know thus whether the power of heaven's King was over them, He confounded them, that is, He confused them. When one of them would say to another "fetch me a stone" it was a stick he would bring, to wit, the slabs on which the mortar was mixed and the mallets by which it was mixed, these are the sticks and stones which they were talking about.

Now poets came from Scythia a little time after these doings to seek to learn the many languages at the Tower since they thought i.e. they supposed, i.e. they expected, of a place from which were dispersed and in which had been invented the many languages by Adam's children that they would remain there in perfection.

They went therefore to the plain of Sumer unto the Tower, that is, the plain of Ucna or the plain of Doraimh in the North West of the plain of Shinar, a special name of the point on which is the Tower. The poets numbered seventy-five, that is, one for each language, and the three sages, to wit, a sage for each of the three principal languages, Hebrew, Greek, and Latin. Seventy-four languages, which is every one of these languages, that was what was dispersed there.

Fenius Farsaidh was the name of their chief, and he was a sage in the principal languages even before he came from the North out of Scythia. The reason why superiority is claimed on behalf of these three languages is owing to the amount of compositions that were made out of them, and owing to the mingling wherewith they mingled with every language, or again it was owing to the superscription that was written out of the three of them upon the board of the Cross.

Since Fenius did not get a perfection of the languages at the Tower, he dispersed his school and his disciples abroad throughout the cities and territories of the earth on every side to learn the languages, and Fenius supported them with both food and clothing whilst they were so learning, to wit, seven languages [years], and Fenius stayed at the Tower and dwelt till his school came unto him from every direction, and he kept instructing the many races of the world at the Tower during that space of time. Hence he said ĺn the body of the book that Fenius himself remained there at the Tower and there he dwelt.

The Hebrew (Semitic) language is the tongue that was in the world before any building of the Tower, and it is it too that will be after doomsday, and some say that it was ít which the people of heaven had. Now after the disciples came to Fenius from learning, and after showing their journeys, to wit, their wanderings, and their works, to wit, their studies, then they asked the sage, to wit, Fenius to select for them out of the many languages, a language that no one else should have but which might belong to them alone. Wherefore on that account for them was invented the Select Language with its super-additions, the Language of the Irish, and the Additional Language, and the Language Parted among the principal letters as he has related in the Great Book of Trees, and the Language of the Poets whereby each one of them converses with another, and the Common Language which serves for every one from many races.

At the end of ten years after their dispersion from the Tower in every direction this language was selected for them Now there were 25 persons that were the noblest of them. These are the names of them after whom are named the Ogham vowels and consonants.

Here are their names: Babel, Lot, Pharaon, Saliath, Nebuchadnezzar, Herod, David, Talamon, Cae, Kaliap, Muiriath, Gotli, Gomers, Stru, Ruben, Achab, Oise, Urith, Essu, lachim, Ethrocius, Uimelicus, ludonius, Affrim, Ordines.

These are the names of the 25 persons, the noblest that were in Fenius' school. Others again say that that is the alphabet which was invented in Achaidh, and at the Causeway of the Great Estuary that Amergen, son of Mil, invented, the Beithe Luis of the Ogham.

What letter, what character, what sound is that with which no word is ended? dinin disail, or F. And what sharp sound is found with which no strong word is begun? NG.

The five principal vowels of the Ogham however, it was from the five persons who were noblest of them that they were named, A, O, U, E, I. Others again say that seven principal vowels are there, and that it is from the seven persons that were noblest there that they are named, and the two vowels that were added to those five vowels are EA, OI.

Query, what are the definite numbers of Nimrod's Tower? Not hard. Eight of them, to wit, 72 counselors, 72 pupils, 72 races of men, 72 languages, the languages in his school, 72 peoples whose were those languages, and the races, 72 artificers to work at it, 72 building materials including lime, bitumen, earth, and cement in equal layers, 72 paces in width, as he said:

The number of the chosen Tower
Of Nimrod, it was a shelter to men,
Four and seventy paces,
Five paces, and five thousand.
Two and seventy counselors,
They took companies on an expedition,
Two and seventy languages
God gave to confound them.
Two and seventy free races
Of the men, it was hard;
Two and seventy pupils,
Fenius sends them to learn.
Two and seventy free peoples
He subdivided, men of the earth;
Two and seventy chief artificers
For the skilful working of the materials.
Two and seventy building materials,
In equal quantity, he used,
Including lime and pitch
And earth and cement.
Seventeen cubits certified,
Near heaven upwards with a roaring wind,
And two and seventy paces
In breadth to reckon it.

Others say, however, that only nine materials were in the Tower, to wit, clay and water, wool and blood, wood and lime, acacias, flax thread, and bitumen, *de quibus dicitur*:

Clay, water, wool, and blood,
Wood, lime, and flax thread of a full twist,
Acacias, bitumen with virtue,
The nine materials of Nimrod's Tower.

Division of the Ogham

There are, then, two divisions in the *Beithe-Luis-Nin* of the Ogham, i,e., vowels and consonants, *Dano -i- da n-ui,* two of them, that is, *da n-ui,* two questions are there. *N-ae* is question, that is, the question on the *Beithe-Luis-Nin* of the Ogham, that is, *ind oguamma* of the perfect alliteration, or on the undying literary knowledge of the Ogham.

As to Fedha, wood vowels, moreover, two kinds are reckoned of them, to wit, artificial tree and natural tree. Artificial tree, i.e., the tree of the Ogham; and natural tree, the tree of the forest. As regards artificial wood, moreover, they are regarded as having two sorts of origin.

Fidh, wood, then, is from the word *funo,* sound, or from the word *fundamentum,* i.e., foundation, and that derivation, to wit, *fundamentum,* is common to artificial and natural wood.

Now, as to Fid, wood, good law is its meaning, both artificial and natural. Foundation, however, is its use, both artificial and natural. It is strange what makes the artificial wood have the two derivations and the natural wood one, to funo, and fundamentum?

Not hard. Funo in respect of sound, and fundamentum in respect of foundation; and common to artificial and to natural wood is foundation.

Fid, wood, that *Fedh Ae,* extent of them, since five forms of AE - AE in existence, AE that nourishes, AE that sings, AE that sues, AE that judges, and AE that sits. Now AE that nourishes, i.e., while it is on the mind, and AE that sings at giving it, and AE that sues while asking the reward for it, and AE that considers about its greatness or its smallness, and ae that sits after being paid his reward.

Taebomnai, consonants, that is, *taebuaim n-ai,* side seam of them; or to the sides of the oaks they are, that is, to the sides of the chieftain wood they are; or *taebomna*i, i.e., cutting of material, from the fact that material for the words is cut out of them. Why did he say taeb uaim n-ui, that is, side harmony of poetry, for there is no poetry without the consonants? Why is it said of the sides of the oaks, i.e., the vowels, for it is not at the sides they are, but before or behind them in the words that the consonants are? Cutting of material, however, that is the peculiar meaning of that expression. There is a correspondence to a word which he gave Ín the Latin alphabet when he said: There are two divisions in the Latin alphabet. It was a correspondence to nature, however, which he gave when he said: There are two divisions in the *Beithe-Luis* of the Ogham.

Chapter XVII
The Ogam Alphabet of Ogma Sun-Face

From the In Lebor Ogaim manuscript

being Ogham Tracts (Book of Ogham)

of Autaicept na n'Eces (Scholar's Primer)

The Ogam of Ogma Sun-face

What are the place, tíme, person, and cause of the invention of the Ogham? Not hard. Its place: *Hibernia insula quavi nos Scoti habitamus*. In the time of Bres son of Elatha king of Ireland it was invented. Its person Ogma son of Elatha son of Delbaeth brother to Bres, for Bres, Ogma and Delbaeth are the three sons of Elatha son of Delbaeth there.

Now Ogma, a man well skilled in speech and in poetry, invented the Ogham. The cause of its invention, as a proof of his ingenuity, and that this speech should belong to the learned apart, to the exclusion of rustics and herdsmen.

Whence the Ogham got its name according to sound and matter, who are the father and the mother of the Ogham, what is the first name that was written by Ogham, in what letter it was written, the reason why it was written, by whom it was written, and why B precedes every letter, *hic uoluuntur omnia*.

Ogham from Ogma *suo inventore privio* in respect to its sound, *quidem*; according to matter, however, *ogum* is *og-uaim* perfect alliteration, which the poets applied to poetry by means of it, for by letters Gaelic is measured by the poets; the father of Ogham is Ogma, the mother of Ogham is the hand or knife of Ogma.

This moreover is the first thing that was written by Ogham, (the birch) B was written, and to convey a warning to Lug son of

Ethliu it was written respecting his wife lest she should be carried away from him into faeryland, to wit, seven B's in one switch of birch: Thy wife will be seven times carried away from thee into faeryland or into another country, unless birch guard her. On that account, moreover, B, birch, takes precedence, for it is in birch that Ogham was first written.

How many divisions of Ogham are there, and what are they? Not hard. Four: B five, H five, M five, A five, besides diphthongs.

How many groups of Ogham? Not hard. Three, viz., eight chieftain trees, eight peasant trees, and eight shrub trees. Eight chieftain trees first:—alder, oak, hazel, vine, ivy, sloe, furze, heath. Eight peasant trees, viz., birch, quicken tree, willow, ash, whitethorn, whin, apple tree. As to their letters all other shrubs are peasant trees.

Secundum alios it is from the trees of the forest that names were given to the Ogham letters metaphorically.

Moreover *beithe*, B, is from the birch of the forest for the first letter on the path of the Ogham alphabet. To continue:

Luis - L, that is, elm in the forests.

Fern - F, that is, alder in the forest.

Sail - S, of the Ogham, that is, willow, again, in the forest.

Nin - N, of the Ogham, to wit, maw of spear, or nettles in the woods.

Uath - H, of the Ogham, that is, test tree or whitethorn, on account of its thorniness.

Dur - D, of the Ogham is oak, again, in the forest.

Tinne - T, of the Ogham, to wit, holly or elderberry in the forest.

Coll - C, of the Ogham, to wit, hazel.

Quert - Q, of the Ogham is the quickening tree, or aspen.

Muin - vine, M, to wit, mead.

Gort - cornfield, G, to wit, fir.

Getal - NG, to wit, broom.

Straif - STR, willowbrake in the forest.

Onn - O, to wit, furze or ash.

Ur - U, to wit, thorn.

Edad - E, to wit, yew.

Ida - I, to wit, service tree.

Ebad - EA, to wit, elecampane.

Oir - OI, to wit, spindle tree.

Uilleann - UI, to wit, ivy.

Pin - IO, of the Ogham, pine, again, in the forest. Hence are named *caera pinne,* gooseberries; ifin, again *secunduni alios* is the name of that letter.

Eniancoll - witch hazel, AE, to wit, C doubled according to fact or according to form, to wit, C across C in its form.

The Word Ogham of Morann Mac Main

Feocus foltchain - faded trunk and fair hair, that is for birch, B, in the Word Ogham, because names which Morann gave of himself to the Ogham letters, these are they which take the effect of letters in the Word Ogham. *Feocus foltchiain* for B, for these are two aspects of the birch, and it was hence put for the Ogham letter which has taken a name from it.

Li súla - delight of eye, that is *luis,* quicken tree, L, to wit, the flame.

Airinach Fian - i.e., shield of warrior-bands, i.e., shield for *fern,* F, with him owing to their redness in the same respect: or because the alder, the material of the shield was from fernce, given to the Ogham letter which has taken a name from it. *Airenach Fian,* i.e., shield, that is fern, F, with him.

Li n-aimbi - hue of the lifeless, i.e., hue of one dead, to wit, *am* for denial, so that he is not living but is dead. *Li n-aimbi* again, to wit, that is sail, willow, S with him, and hence it was put for the Ogham letter.

Cosdad sida - checking of peace, that is *nin,* ash, N: it is the maw of a weaver's beam as applied to wood: a sign of peace is that. A checking of peace with him is that from the ash of the weaver's beam.

Conal cuan - pack of wolves, to wit, that is *uath*, thorn H, for a terror to any one is a pack of wolves. *Conal cuan* said of the Ogham H, owing to the affinity of the name, for they are a thorn, in the same way.

Ardavi dossaibh - highest of bushes, that is *dur*, oak, D, with respect to its wood in the forest.

Trian - T, another thing the meaning of that to-day.

Cainiu fedaib - fairest of trees, that is hazel, C, owing to its beauty in woods.

Clithar mbaiscaill - shelter of a hind, i.e., a fold: to wit, *boscell*, lunatic, that is *bas-ceall*, death sense, it is then his sense comes to him when he goes to his death. *Clithar boiscell*, again, that is an apple tree: or *boscell*, that is, hinds, to wit, they are light. *Clithar boiscell*, again, i.e., lunatics or hinds: *quert*, an apple tree, Q, with reference to its letter.

Tresim fedma - strongest of effort, that is *muin*, vine, M, with him, i.e., owing to identity of name with *muin*, back of a man or ox, for it is they that are the strongest in existence as regards effort.

Milísiu feraib - sweeter than grasses, that is *gort*, ivy, G, with him owing to the identity of the name with the cornfield. When it is in the blade, sweeter than any grass is that grass, to wit, the cornfield. Hence for that letter in OGHAM owing to the complete identity of the name between them.

Luth legha - a physician's strength, that is broom, NG, to wit, because it is strength with the physicians, and there is an affinity between *cath*, panacea, and *getal*, broom.

Tresiiu ruamna - strongest of red, to wit, that is STR with him in Ogham. *Straif*, sloe, according to fact; for in the sloe red for dyeing the things is stronger, for it is it that makes the pale silver become azure, making it genuine silver. It is it which is boiled through the urine into the white gold so as to make it red. *Tresiiu ruamna* is the sloe according to fact. Hence it was put in the letter named STR, owing to identity of name between them, i.e., straif is the name of each of them.

Timieui rucce - intensest of blushes, that is *ruis*, elderberry, R, to wit, from the reddening or shame according to fact, for by R it is written, and it is a reddening that grows in a man's face through the juice of the herb being rubbed under it. *Tiudi rucce,* an ingot of blush, again, said of the *ruis*, elderberry, from *shamc* or reddeníng, for it is by R that it is itself written.

Ardam iachtadh - loudest of groanings, that is wondering, to wit, that is *ailm,* fir, A, with him; for it is *ailm* or A, a man says while groaning in disease, or wondering, that is, marveling at whatever circumstance.

Conguauiaid echraidc - helper of horses, to wit, the *ennaid* of the chariot, i.e, the wheels, to wit, that is *onn*, furze, with him, for it is by *onn*, O, that the wheels of the chariot are written, Aliter, *comguinidech*, equally wounding, i.e. *whin*. Hence it was put for that letter which is named *onn*, O, owing to identity between them, for *onn* is a name for each of them; and it is from *whin* that the name *onn* was put for the Ogham letter *secundum alios*.

Etiud midach - robe of physicians, to wit, *cath*, panacea. Hence it was put *íor getal*, broom, NG.

Uaraib adbaib - in cold dwellings, to wit, that is *ur*, fresh, with him, for from *uir,* the mould of the earth is the name *uaraib adbaib*. Hence it was put for the letter named *ur*, heath, in Ogham, owing to identity of name between them, to wit, each of them is *ur*, and it is written by U.

Ergnaid fid - distinguished wood, to wit, that is aspen with him, for *ergnaid fid* is a name for the trembling tree. Hence it was put for the Ogham letter named *edad,* aspen, for hence was *edad,* E, put for it.

Siniu fedaib - oldest of woods, to wit, that is *idad,* yew, with him; for *siniu fedaib* is a name for service-tree. Hence it was given to that letter in Ogham named *idad,* yew, I, for hence the name *idad* was put for it; for *idad,* yew, is a name for *ibur,* service-tree.

Snamchain feda - most buoyant of wood, to wit, that is *ebad,* aspen, with him, for fair swimming is wood: to wit, that is a name for the great raven. Hence it was put for the letter named the Ogham *ebad,* for E is a name for salmon, and it is written by EA like the alphabet of the fauna: i.e., by stag (deer), EO by *eonasc (ousel).*

Sruitem aicdi - most venerable of structures, i.e., *oir,* OI, spindle tree, according to fact. Hence it was put for the letter owing to the identity of the name that is between them, to wit, oir is the name of each of them.

Tutmur fid uilleann - juicy wood is woodbine, that is woodbine with him, for it is a name for honeysuckle. Hence it was put for the Ogham named woodbine, UI; for hence was woodbine put for it, for it is a name for honeysuckle.

Millsem feda - sweetest of wood, that is gooseberry with him, for a name for the tree called *pin* is *milsem feda.* Gooseberries are hence named. Hence it was put for the letter named pin, for hence pin, or ifin, IO, was put for it.

Luad scethaig - expression of a weary one, i.e., *ach,* ah! *uch,* alas! that is *emancoll,* AE, with him, for *omancoll* is taken for *ach,* though it may be taken for something else.

The Word Ogham of Mac Ind Oic

Glaisiuni cnis - most silvery of skin, to wit, that is the birch of the Ogham from birch of the forest, for hence birch, B, was put for it; *sic in reliquis sequentibus.*

Cara ceathra - friend of cattle, to wit, elm. *Cara,* to wit, dear to the cattle is the elm for its bloom and for down. Hence it was put for the Ogham *luis,* quicken tree, L, for hence was quicken tree, L, put for it.

Comet lachta - guarding of milk, to wit, that is the Ogham alder, F, from alder of forests, for it is it that guards the milk, for of it are made the vessels containing the milk.

Luth bech - activity of bees, to wit, that is willow, S, for its bloom and for its catkin. Hence it is put for the cognate Ogham letter.

Bag ban - fight of women, to wit, ash, N, of weaver's beam, i.e., maw of weaver's beam. Hence for its cognate letter.

Banadh gnuisi - blanching of face, to wít, fear, *huath,* H, for blanched is a man's face when he is encompassed with fear or terror. Hence for the Ogham letter owing to identity of name between the same two, to wit, *uath* stands for each of them.

Gres sair - carpenter's work, to wit, oak, D. Hence it was put for its cognate Ogham letter.

Smir guaili - fires of coal, to wit, that is holly. Hence for its cognate Ogham letter, i.e., *tinne,* T, *secundum alios;* for *tindi* is a name for holly, *ut alii dicunt.*

Cara bloisc - friend of cracking, to wit, *coll,* hazel, C. Hence for its cognate Ogham letter.

Brigh an duine - force of the man, to wit, *queirt,* Q, apple tree. Hence for its cognate letter.

Arusc n-airlig - condition of slaughter, to wit, a man's back, M. Hence for its synonymous letter.

Med nercc - to wit, ivy, G. Hence for its synonymous letter.

Morad run - increasing of secrets, to wit, sloe, STR. Hence it was put for its synonymous letter.

Ruanma dreach - redness of faces, to wit, sap of the rose which causes the redness of the faces, so that blushing is in them. *Ruamna dreach,* again, said of the Ogham *ruis,* elder, R, from the blush or from the reddening, for it is by elder, R, it is itself written.

Tosach fregra - beginning of an answer, to wit, that is *ailm,* A; for the first expression of every human being after his birth is A.

Fethim saire - smoothest of work, or *fedem,* to wit, *onn* stone, O.

Silad clann - growing of plants, that is *ur,* heath, U with him, for it is *uir,* the soil of the earth, that causes the growing of the plants that are put into it. Growing of plants, again, said of the soil of the earth, is said of the Ogham letter which has taken the same name with it, to wit, each of them is *ur.*

Comainm carat - synonym for a friend, to wit, aspen, E, in the forest. Hence for its synonymous Ogham letter.

Crinem feda – most withered of wood, or sword, to wit service tree, I. Hence for the Ogham letter, which has taken a name other than it, to wit, *idad*, yew.

Cosc lobair – corrective of a sick man, to wit, woodbine for the Ogham letter, which has taken a name other than it, to wit, *ebad*, aspen, EA.

Li crotha - beauty of form, to wit, heath. Hence for íts synonymous letter, to wit, the Ogham Oi.

Cubat n-oll - great equal-length, to wit, woodbine, i.e., honeysuckle. Hence for the Ogham letter which it has taken from it, to wit, woodbine, UI.

Amram blais - most wonderful of taste, to wit, *pin* or *ifin*, gooseberry. Hence for the letter that has taken its name from it, to wit, *pin* or *iphin*, IO.

The Bird Ogham

Group B. *besan*, pheasant; *lachu*, duck; *faelinn*, gull; *seg*, hawk; *nescu*, snipe.

Group H. *hadaig*, night raven; *droeíi*, wren; *truith*, starling; (?); *querc*, hen.

Group M. *inintan*, titmouse; *ge'is*, swan; *ngeigh*, goose; *stniólach*, thrush; *rócnat*, small rook.

Group A. *aidhircleóg*, lapwing; *odoroscrach*, scrat; *uiseóg*, lark; *ela*, swan; *illait*, eáglet.

The Color Ogham

Group B. *bán*, white; *liath*, grey; *flann*, red; *sodath*, fine-coloured; *necht*, clear.

Group H. *huath*, terrible; *dub*, black; *tenien*, dark grey; *cron*, brown; **quiar,** mouse-coloured.

Group M. *mbracht*, variegated; *gorm*, blue; *nglas*, green; *sorcha*, bright; *ruadh*, red.

Group A. *alad*, piebald; *odhar*, dun; *usgdha*, resinous; *erc*, red; *irfind*, very white.

Chapter XVIII The Ballymote Ogham Scales

From the Book of Ballymote

for Autaicept na n'Eces as

Illuminated by Myrddin Cerrig

The Book of Ballymote

Written in 1390-91 near the town for which it is named, the Book of Ballymote constitutes the knowledge basis of modern "New Age" Ogham lore. It contains the most vast collection of "Ogham Scales" ever uncovered, as preserved by three scribes - Solamh O' Droma, Robertus mac Sithigh and Maghnus O Duibheannain - from a secret order of Celtic Culdee Bardic monks working on commission from Tonnaitagh McDonagh (whose clan kept possession of the manuscript until 1522).

The following - Ladder of Fionn - is perhaps the best known of the scales, demonstrating the standard by which we understand the Ogham today.

The scales given in the Book of Ballymote are indicative of the

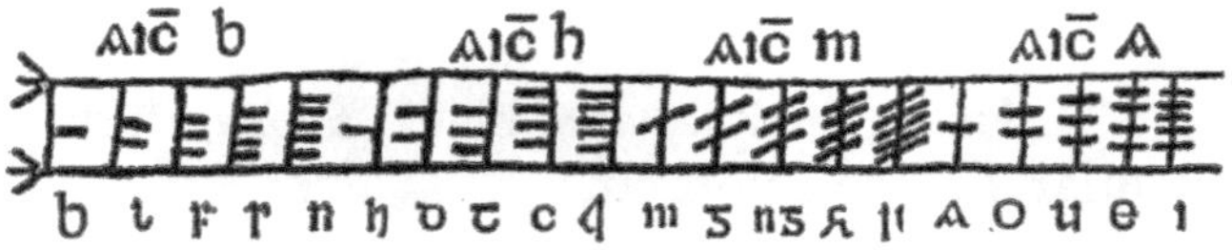

B-L-F alphabet, which differs from the B-L-N alphabet only for the letter given as third. All else being equal, the two alphabets assign different Oghams to the third position of the first (B) aicme (group). Systems in use today generally follow a B-L-N

format, assigning the N - Ash (*Nin*) - to the third position rather than F - Alder (*Fearn*).

The shift in alphabets occurs synchronously with the Cad Goddeu or Battle of the Trees, when a cultural shift in methodology occurred among the Druids between the older Pheryllt one and a newer Celtic one.

Fionn's Ladder represents the Druid Path, a cabala of progressive lessons that symbolize the ascension of the SOUL from its birth in the Cauldron of Annwn - where it is separated as an identity from the Source of All-Being and Creation - and its ascent through three circles of existence whereby it returns to the Source, for it is writ:

We stand upon the earth at the center of All - the first circle; Caer Sidi, the sacred stone circle, exists as the Otherworld boundary all around us, the second circle; and beyond these lies the Eternal Ocean of the Unknown, the third circle of Infinities.

Ogham Scales all follow the same standard progression of notches to represent letters. The only difference is the ornate elaborateness of the characters. For example, a single straight notch crossing the stemline means "A" (*ailm*) whether left by itself or as part of a more ornately depicted scale:

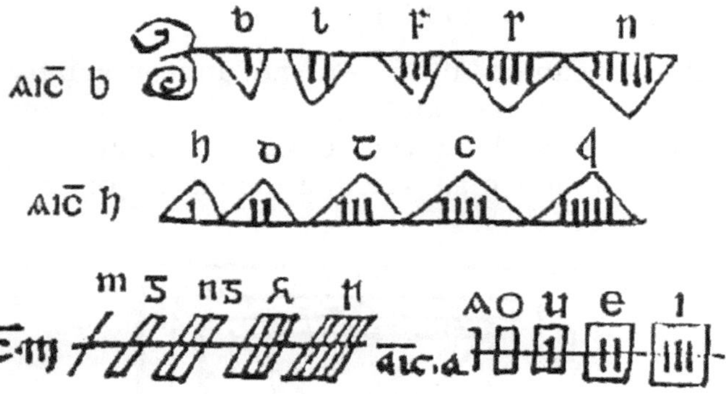

Much like the first writing system - cuneiform in Mesopotamia - the figures themselves are not indicative of language. This means that they can be used to represent communications in the chosen language of the scribe.

Ogham Scales are all phonetically arranged in the same groups (*aicme*) of five letters: a "B" group (labials), a "H" group (dentals/aspirants), a "M" group (gutturals) and the vowels appear in the final "A" group. This system of 20 Ogham is usually called the Fedha. An additional 5 characters were added, called Forfedha.

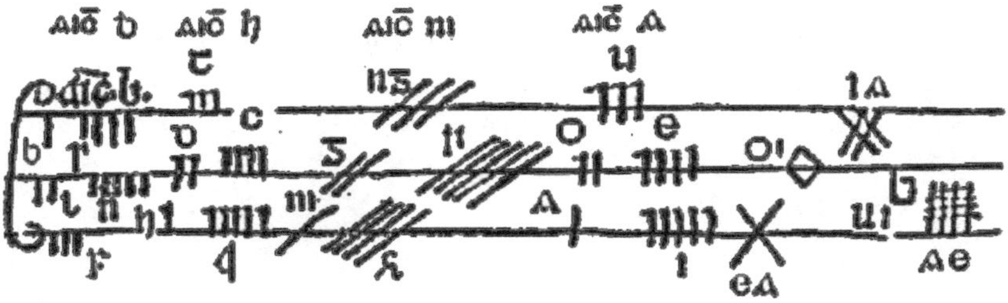

The Forfedha are traditionally given as:

Koad – grove – "EA" (and "CH")

Oir – spindle – "OI" (and "TH")

Uileand – honeysuckle – UI (and "PE")

Phagos – beech – "IO" (and "PH")

Mor – the sea – "AE" (and "XI")

The Forfedha – meaning "fifths" – do not appear on most Ogam Tracts of the Forest Trees, but they are particularly useful as an interpretation "spread" when casting Ogham sticks for divination – also known as "Casting the Fifths" or Crannchur, "Casting the Woods."

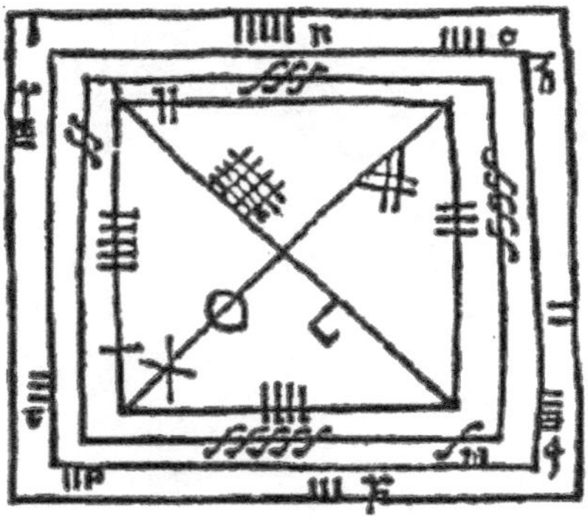

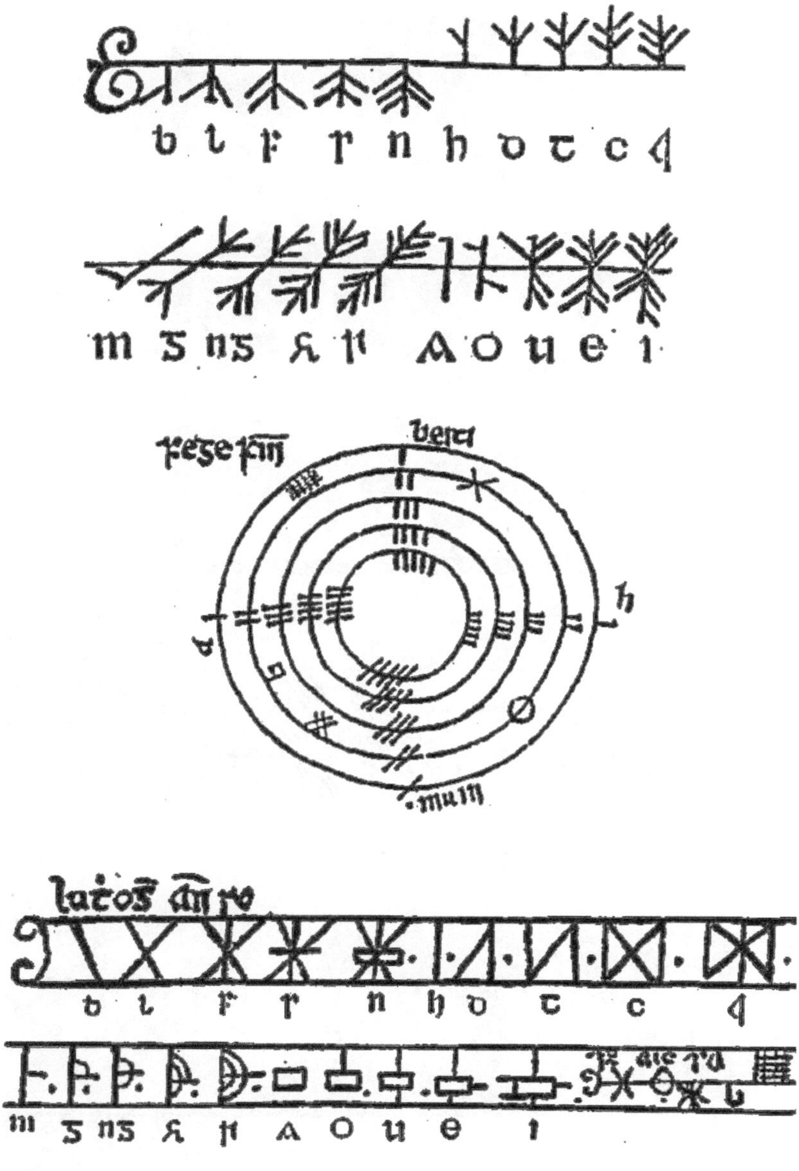
b l f s n h d t c q
m g ng z r a o u e i
b l f s n h d t c q
m g ng z r a o u e i

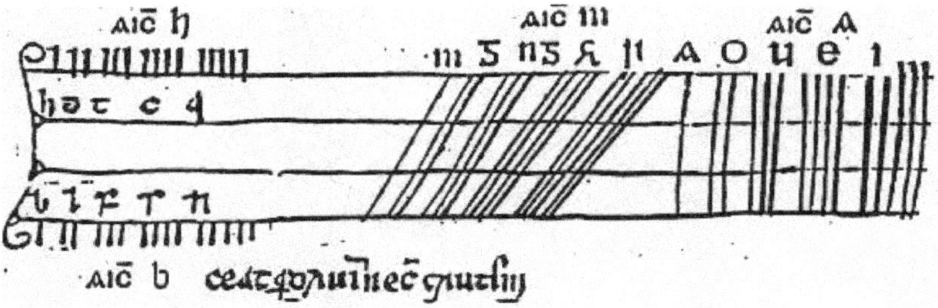

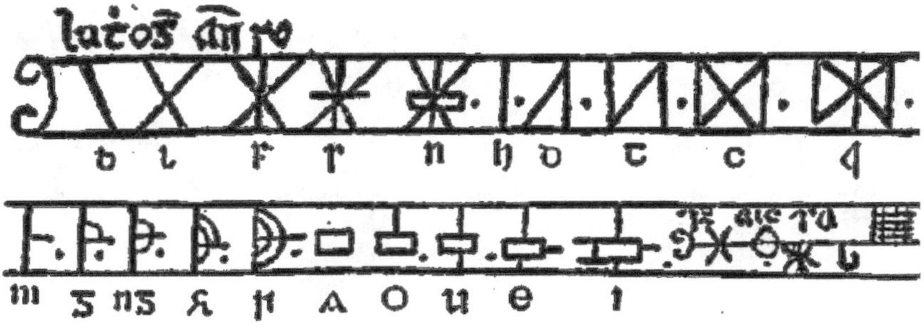

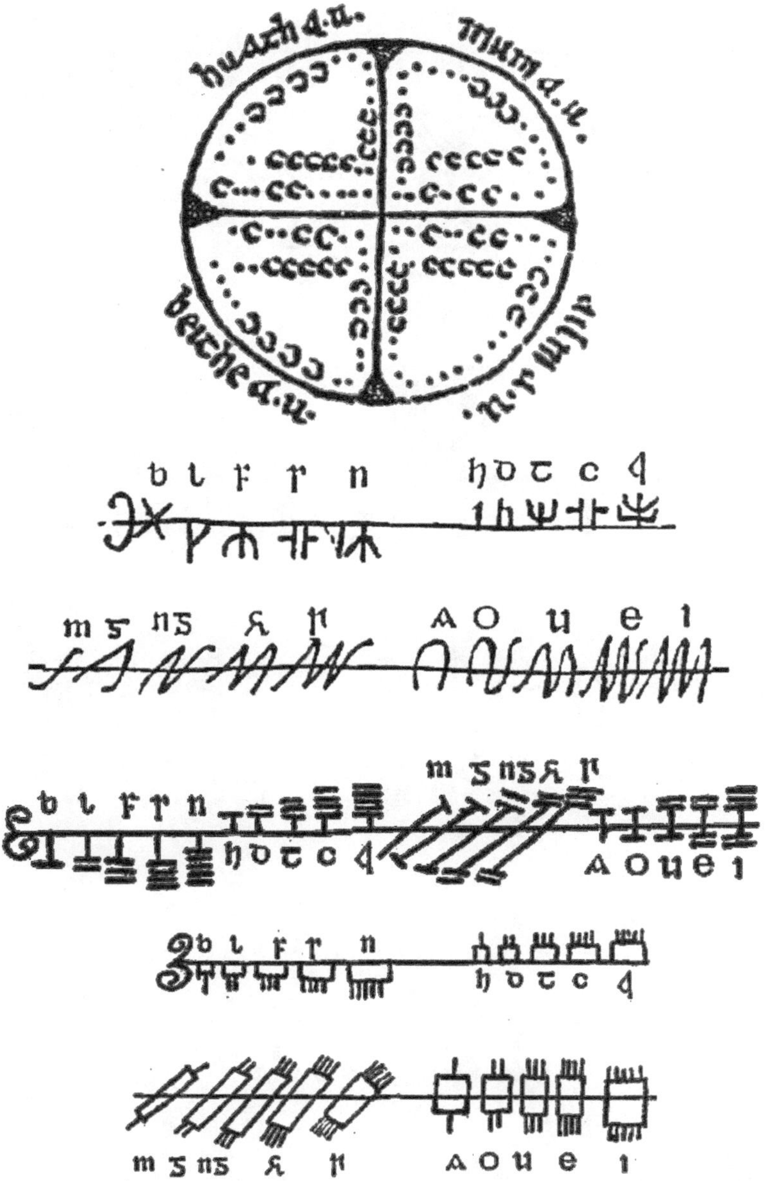
huath a.u.
muin a.u.
beithe a.u.
ailm a.u.
b l f s n
h d t c q
m g ng str r
A O U E I

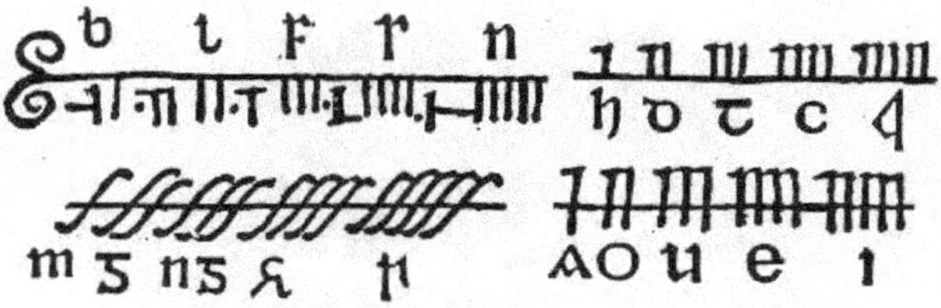
b l f r n
h d t c q
m g ng z r
a o u e i

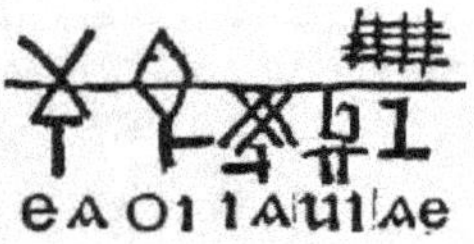
ea oi ia ui ae

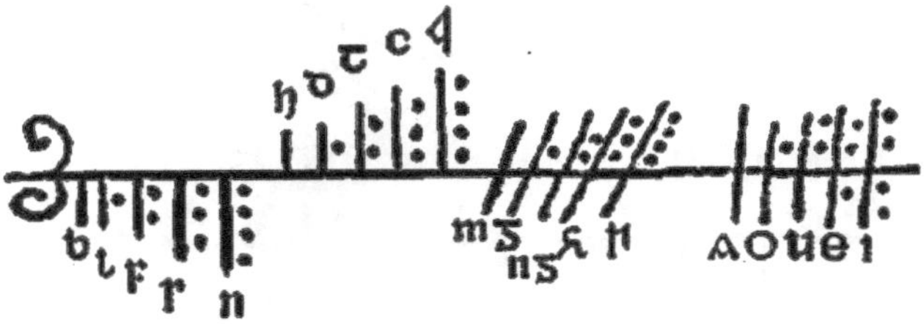
h d t c q
b l f r n
m g ng z r
a o u e i

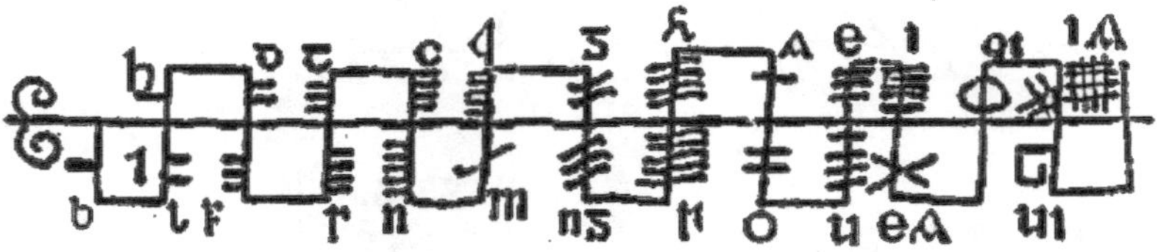

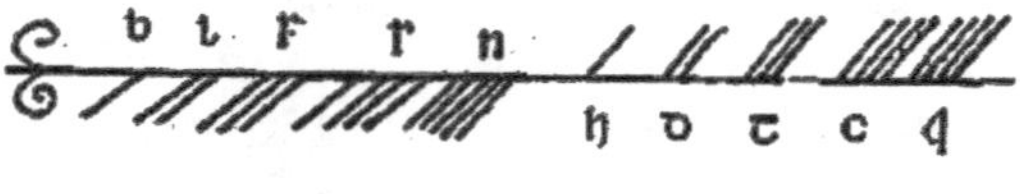
b l f r n
h d t c q

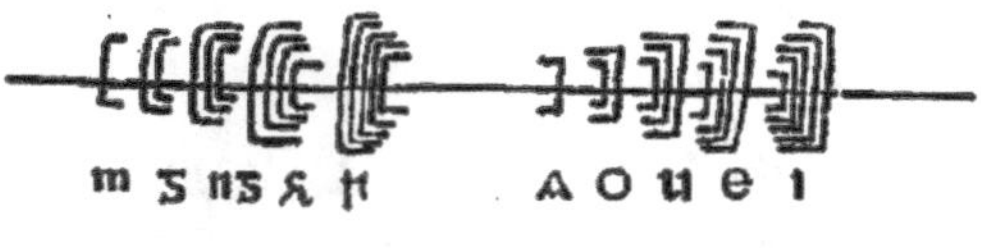
m g ng z r
a o u e i

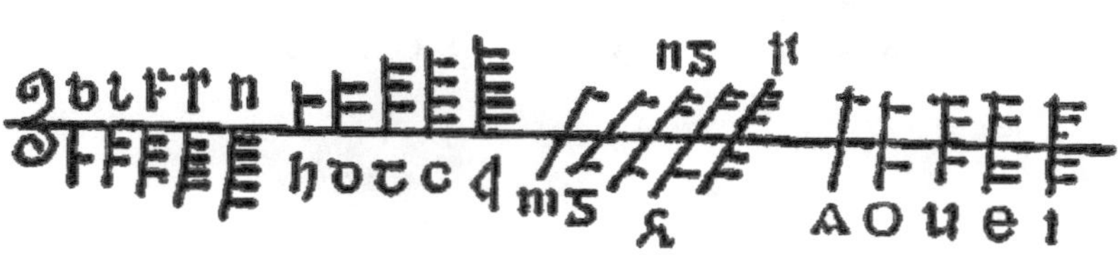
b l f r n
h d t c q
m g
ng z
a o u e i

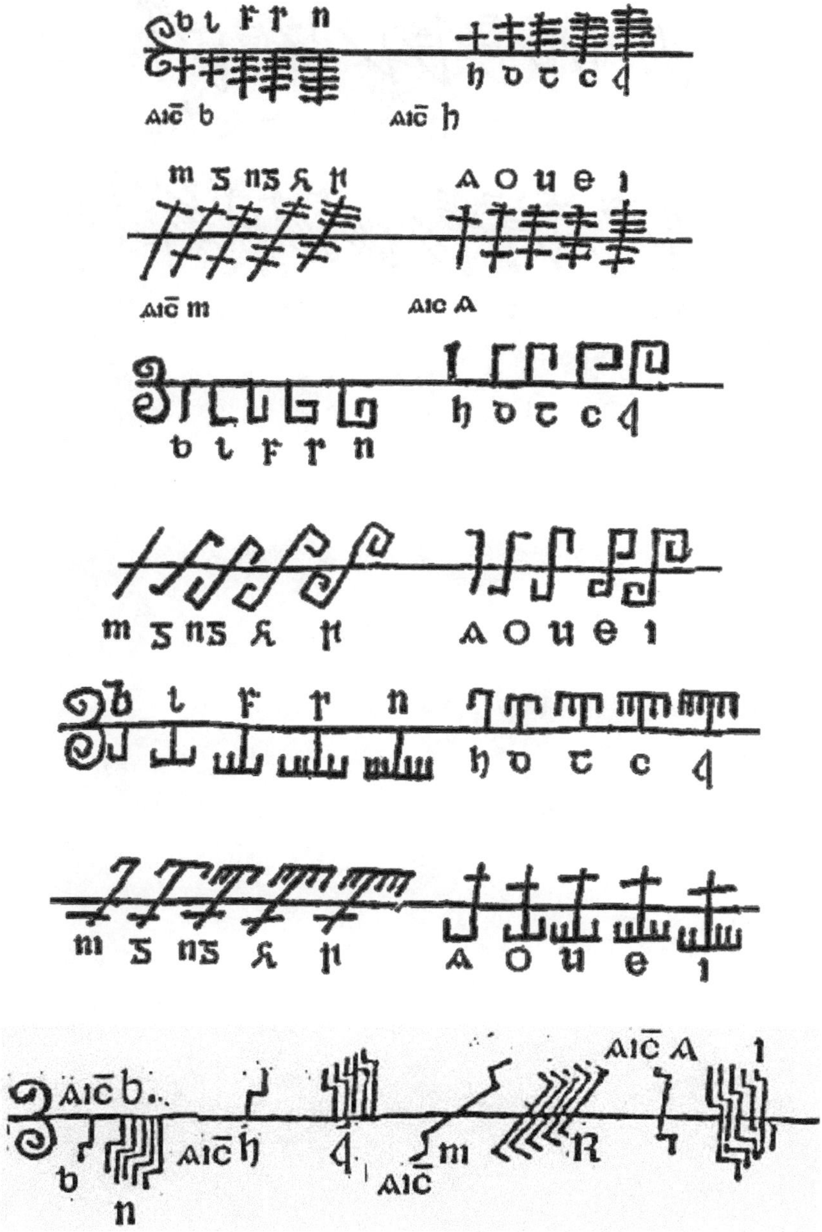
Aic b
Aic h
Aic m
Aic A

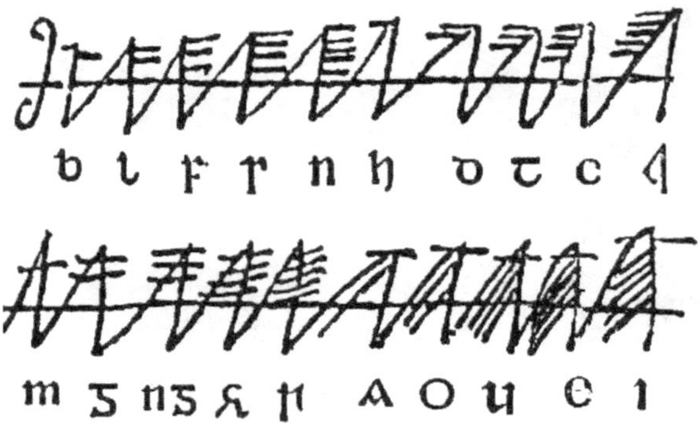
b l f s n h d t c q
m g ng z r a o u e i

Chapter XIX Sylva Druieachd - The Forest Ogham Tract

From Ogham Tract collections

adapted from the 'Book of Elven-Faerie'

and the Book of Ballymote (Auraicept)

as selected by Myrddin Cerrig

Traditional Uses, Divinatory & Energy Expressions

Alder - F - Charcoal, Dye, Housing Foundations, Protection, Guidance, Resistance to water and enchantment. Tree of Resistance. Tree of Power.

"Fearn, Alder, the van of the warrior bands for thereof are the shields."

Apple - Q - Dietary Fruit, beverage (cider), the Silver Branch (bough) or Apple Wand, love, beauty, union of mind and spirit between lovers, eternal life (perpetual youth), abundance, fertility and healing. Tree of Beauty.

"Quiert. Apple, shelter of a wild hind is an Apple Tree."

Ash - N - Spears, May Pole, pool cues, paddles, oars, hockey sticks, baseball bats, Healing Wands, triumph, completion, overview, protection, overcoming mental strife and the World Tree that links the inner and outer worlds. Tree of Strength. Tree of Peace.

"Nion, Ash, a check on peace is NION for it are made the spear-shafts by which the peace is broken."

Aspen / Cottonwood - E - Shapeshifting magic, Divination, shields, overcoming barriers and problems, facing fears, overcoming death, working through emotional distress. Tree of Overcoming.

"Edhadh, Test Tree or Aspen."

Beech - PH - Writing tablets, Book covers, woodcraft, tree communication, archaic/arcane knowledge, writing, communication, runes, victory and letting go of old patterns. Most "human" of all trees. Queen of the Woods.

Birch - B - Wands, Broomsticks, wards, protection for children, new beginnings, renewal, fertility, cleansing, purification, birth. Lady of the Woods. Tree of Beginnings. Initiation Tree.

"Beithe has been named from the Birch owing to its resemblance to the trunk of that tree; of withered trunk, fair-haired the birch."

Blackthorn - ST - Shillelagh (Dark Staff, Thunder and Lightning Staff, cudgel weapons), warding against evil and illness, cleansing, control, operating by force, confusion, restraint, resentment, strife, sudden change or renewal. Tree of Severity.

"Straiph that is Blackthorn, the hedge of a stream is Sraibh."

Cedar - CH - Incense of space purification and home blessings, calling and summoning spirits, height of psychic awareness, spiritual abilities, knowledge of all times and places.

Cherry - DH - "Brown Magic", animals, spirit animals and communication with animals, kindling sacred fires, declaring and ending wars, sweetness, joy, delight, passion/sexuality, love, conflict, competition, attraction.

Elder / Bourtree - R - Exorcisms, Elderberry Wine, banishing, regeneration (healing) magic, completion, self-reflection, self-examination, crossroads, change. NOTE: The Elder Tree is not to be cut for wood. The leaves can be poisonous if ingested. Transformation Tree. Tree of Change.

"Ruis is Elder, the redness of shame."

Elm / Fir / Pine / Redwoods – A – "Green Magic" (Forest Magic), regeneration (healing) magic, kindling sacred fires, earth magic (wands and wards), Elves, ancient knowledge, primal power, high views, objectivity, penetration, strength and the Eternal Earth Memory. The Landmark Tree. Tree of Objectivity.

"Ailm, a Fir tree, a Pine tree."

Furze / Gorse – O – Fertility magic and purification, dietary foodstuffs for animals, wisdom, spiritual fulfillment, optimism, protection, a ray-like projection. Species alternatives (energy signatures): Linden, Basswood and Lime. The Spirit of Wisdom.

"Onn that is Furze."

Hawthorn / Whitethorn – H – love and marriage rites, wands, wards, traditionally grown for its live magical protection, restraint, purity, prosperity, chastity (also love and marriage proper). Note: Wood is only to be collected between April 21 or Beltane and the end of May. Wood is not otherwise taken. Tree of Wild Beauty. Tree of Restraint.

"Huath is Whitethorn, a meet of hounds is hawthorn, its formidable owing to its thorns. "

Hazel – C – Dowsing Rods, divination wands or sticks, Baskets (Thatchwork), Nuts used for love spells and love potions, potions and spells of divination (knowlegde) and sprit vision (flying), manifestation of creativity and intuition. The Poet's Tree. Tree of Creativity.

"Coll, fair wood that is Hazel, everyone is eating of its nuts."

Heather / Mistletoe – U – Heather: perfume and attracting raid. White Heather: purification. Red Heather: passion and sexuality. Mistletoe: All-Heal (healing magic and potions).

"Ur that is Heath."

Holly – T – Spearmaking (combative and protective), Chariot Wheels, charcoal, grown for good fortune and to ward off evil, midwinter (Yule), movement, vigor, consecration (holiness and sacredness). Tree of Balance.

"Tinne, Holly, a third of a wheel is holly because holly is one of the three timbers of the chariot wheel."

Ivy - G - Exorcism rituals, Healing magic, spiral to wrap around wands and wards, the inner spiral of the self and its journey. The icon of growth.

"Gort that is Ivy, greener than pastures is Ivy."

Maple - SH (Shorin) - Binding spells, Maple syrup, unity and strength of family (family life), vibrancy (energy and strength), good fortune.

Oak - D - "Green Magic", Tree Magic, Elven magic, Forest magic, Doors (home protection), Fertility and Prosperity magic (accorns), strength, leadership, endurance, longevity, material gain, absolute truth and the Flaming Door or Doorway / Gateway to the Ancient Mysteries. King of the Woods. Tree of Strength.

"Duir, Oak, higher than bushes is the oak."

Reed / Broom - NG - Writing Pens (scribes), fertility magic, love magic, Brooms, Pipes, harmony, effort applied (direct action), application of will. Spirit of Unity.

"Ngetal, Broom or Fern, a physician's strength is Broom."

Rowen / Mountain Ash - L - Protection against enchantment, personal empowerment (self-control), awareness, the Otherworld, evanescence, nurturance and motherhood. Tree of Inspiration. Tree of Awareness.

"Luis is named from Mountain Ash as it is the old Gaelic name for the tree; Delight of Eye is the Mountain Ash owing to the beauty of its berries."

Vine - M - Dietary (grapes), Beverage (wine), meditation and revealing truths (wine), inner development, self-realization and comprehension. The Meditation Plant.

"Muin is a Vine tree highest of beauty is Muin because it grows aloft."

Willow - S - Wickerwork (baskets, etc.), all lunar and feminine magic (polarity), fertility magic (enchantment and beauty), banishing depression (inner healing), rhythms and cycles. Tree of Comfort. Tree of Intuition.

"Sail, Willow, the color of a lifeless one, owing to the resemblance of its color to a dead person."

Yew - I - Archery bows, poison and poisoned weapons, completion, changes, renewal, transformation, forthcoming rebirth, life and death cycle. Tree of Immortality. Tree of Rebirth.

"Ido, Yew."

Chapter XX Twenty-One Paths of Encounter:

Ascending the Druid's Ladder

Transcribed in the 'Lost Books'

with additional correspondences

Provided by Myrddin Cerrig

The Druids Cabala of the Forest

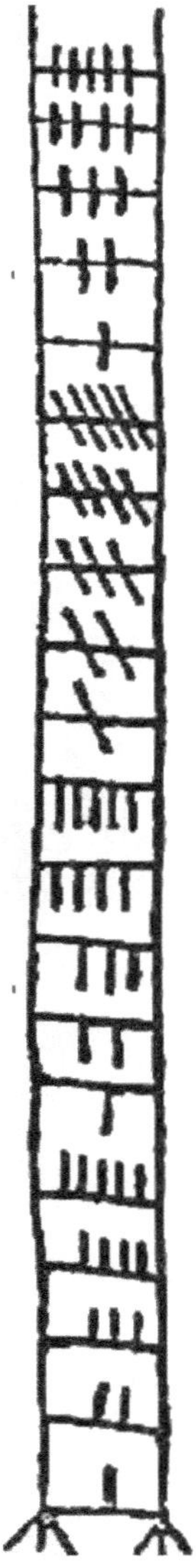

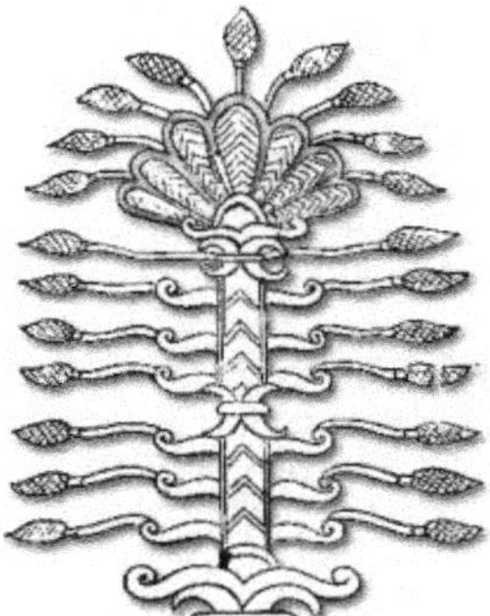

Climbing the Great Tree

The First Path - Birch

New Beginnings, First Realization, Self-Sacrifice, Change to a Higher Level, Deovtion to the Great Work, Awakening onto Your Chosen Spiritual Path.

Color - White

Tarot Pathwork - Star

The Second Path - Rowen

First Action, First Move of a Game, Magical Work Begun, Self-Control, Movement in the Direction of Your Chosen Path.

Color - Grey and Red
Tarot Pathwork - High Priest

The Third Path - Alder

Heated Resistance, Strength to Face the Avoided, Conquering Adversaries, the Material World opposes Your Choice, but Your Aspirations are completely protected.

Color - Crimson
Tarot Pathwork - Strength

The Fourth Path - Willow

New Journeys and Inspiration, Otherworld Contact, Confidence Necessary, Enchantment, Your Path now appears as a Dream on a Moonlit Night.

Color - Bright
Tarot Pathwork - Moon

The Fifth Path - Ash

Personal Resolve, the Resolute Decision, Changing Outlook, the Inner and Outer Worlds meet as One, the Inertia to Break the threshold.

Color - Glass Green
Tarot Pathwork - The Universe

The First Veil Threshold: "Death of the Old"

The Sixth Path - Hawthorn

New Blossoms are Awakening, the First Success or Manifestation is Purified, Protection given as You accept the Bitter and Sweet of the Chosen Path.

Color - Purple
Tarot Pathwork - Judgement

The Seventh Path - Oak

Higher Powers are Experienced and Call to You, the Strong Door to the Inner Mysteries stands closed but beckons, Personal Reflection opens to New Possibilities.

Color - Black and Dark Brown
Tarot Pathwork - Emperor

The Eighth Path - Holly

An Encounter. The Guardian of the Gate. Self-Worth is Tested, A Balance of Opposition, the Challenge is presented, Things may not be what they seem so Dispel All Illusion.

Color - Dark Grey
Tarot Pathwork - Chariot

The Ninth Path - Hazel

The Fruit of Knowledge is Given, Wisdom is now Accessible, Your Encounter yields the straightforward Harvest of Secret Intuitions.

Color - Brown
Tarot Pathwork - High Priestess

The Tenth Path - Apple

Awe and Beauty of the Chosen Path enchants you as New Realizations arise, Awakening to a Higher Purpose, Otherworldly Contact is enhanced, the Fruit of the Chosen Path sends you Traveling anew.

Color - Green
Tarot Pathwork - Empress

The Second Veil Threshold

"Matter Gives Way to Mystery"

The Eleventh Path - Vine

A Meeting of Companions, Fellowship is Born, Hidden Knowledge is Revealed Between Companions, the Strength to Face Destiny as Your Path is Entangled with the Presence, Fate and Prophecy of Others.

Color - Variegated

Tarot Pathwork - Lovers

The Twelfth Path - Ivy

The Steady Spiral of the Path, Self-Reliance, Overcoming Restrictions, Gaining the Confidence and Inner Strength needed to continue and Face the World.

Color - Sky Blue
Tarot Pathwork - Justice

The Thirteenth Path - Blackthorn

Facing the Material, in the Clutches of the World, Transition and Change along the Path, Death and Loss are Cleansing for When All Choices are Taken Away - A Perfect Path Remains.

Color - Purple
Tarot Pathwork - Temperance

The Fourteenth Path - Reed

Experience in the World, Learning from Experience, Understanding the Earth Systems and Material Struggle, knowing Selective Conform and to Yield is to Conquer - Knowing When to Bend with the Wind to Survive.

Color - Grass Green
Tarot Pathwork - Wheel of Fortune

The Fifteenth Path - Elder

Self-Annihilation, Purging the Self of all Artificial, the Darkness before the Dawn (A Dark Night of the Soul), Facing Truth, You Accept the Lesson Given, Seeing Clear Light Ahead.

Color - Red
Tarot Pathwork - Hanged Man

The Third Veil Threshold "Visions of Victory"

The Sixteenth Path - Fir

High Views and Long Sight, Relationships and Experience give rise to a New Range of Vision and Realization, Seeing Past the Illusions of the World reveals a Green Valley in the Distance and a Clear Path is visible.

Color - Light Blue

Tarot Pathwork - The "Devil"

The Seventeenth Path - Furze

The Sweet Smell of Victory, Awareness of the Seeds born from Difficulties, Struggles pass away in Sunstruck Beauty, there is time to Rest as You Collect Yourself anew.

Color - Golden Yellow
Tarot Pathwork - Sun

The Eighteenth Path - Heather

Pause and Reflection while Healing the Spirit, Examination of Actions and Consequences, Rest and Fulfillment make whole Your wounds from the Journey.

Color - Purple
Tarot Pathwork - The Fool

The Nineteenth Path - Aspen

The Rainbow of Spiritual Achievement appears, Protection given on the Rainbow Path, Great Success yields a Rebirth of the Spirit for a New Horizon of Many Colors lies ahead.

Color - Silvery White
Tarot Pathwork - The Tower of Babel

The Twentieth Path - Yew

Completion. Final Realizations, the Ascension, Rising Above the Impermanent, the Product of the Journey, Means (Experience and Struggles) justified by the Ends; the End in the Beginning and the Beginning in the End.

Color - Dark Green
Tarot Pathwork - Death

The Twenty-first Path - Mistletoe

Formless. The Not. The Unknowable that moves beyond All Sense and Prediction, Uncertainty Factors and Observer Effects (quantum), the Manifest Strength of the Future is being Born in the Present. The infinite.

Color - Black
Tarot Pathwork - The Magician (Druid)

Chapter XXI
Godform Evocation:
Awakening the Shades of the Druids

Transcribed in the 'Lost Books'

with additional correspondences and

introduction by Myrddin Cerrig

Shades of the Druid Ancestors

Shades of the Druid Ancestors remain so long as they are remembered. The festival of Samhain (on the eve of October 31) is a time of remembrance and to celebrate the Feast of the Dead.

The Rite of Summoning requires experience and authority in the Spirit World - and the altered states attained by Shamans who walk between the worlds freely. To summon the shade of a Druid Ancestor is to face death.

Conjure a circle in the place most sacred to the deity - a Protective Circle of Heads - Carved from the fruits of the Otherworld (be they Apples, Gourds, Turnip, Squash and the New World Pympin (pumpkin). There should be nine carved heads, lighted and facing outward. An example "evocation incantation" suggested by Douglas Monroe to summon the "Shade of Merlyn" is derived from collected epitaphs for "Stanzas of the Graves" (Chapter XLV).

Herb, Flow'r and Tree is mixed with Mistletoe as an incense burned with Oak.

1 part Wormwood
2 parts Ghostflow'r (Datura)
3 parts Yew (or Juniper or Cypress)

When possible, use wood sacred to the Druidic Deities as provided in the following lists. These deities may also be called to aid in making contact with trees of the related energy. If the Ghostflow'r is not available, Belladonna (Black Nightshade) may be substituted.

The Druidic Pantheon of the Ogham

Bran – "Raven" Blessed King, god of protection and power.

Belinos – Sun god of fire, healing and inspiration.

Barinthus – the "Ferryman", god of teaching and mystery.

Llew – the "Many-Skilled" god of all crafts and trades.

Llyr – God of the sea, rain and waters.

Laighinos – Teacher of battle skills.

Nudd – the "Cloud maker" god of weather, storms and seasons.

Nuada – Chieftain god of wealth, water, power and dominions.

Nwyvre – God of stars and planets.

Fionn – "Great Leader" god of architecture and strategy.

Ffagus – Beech god of forgotten knowledge and lore.

Formorix – God of invention, under-sea and air travel.

Samhann – God of death, Guardian of the Otherworld Gate.

Sucellus – the "Good Striker" god of fighting and assassination.

Silvanus – God of herbalism, plant lore and healing.

Hagfgan – God of gems, precious stones and jewels.

Hesus – God of prophecy.

Heremonix – God of wells and underground rivers.

Dagda – the "Good God" All Father and God of Druidism.

Dian Cecht – Physician-Magician of the Tuatha d'Anu, god of healing.

Dis Pater - Roman god of Pluto (Jupiter).

Taranis - the "Thunderer" who holds up the Empire of the Skies.

Tigeronos - God of hills, mountains and valleys.

Toutorix - "Ruler of the People", the oldest god of war and power.

Cernunnos - the "Horned One" Lord of the Animals and Forests.

Cromm Cruaich - the "Hidden One" God of Darkness and Death.

Camulos - the "Red God" of Mars, War and Blood.

Mabon - the Divine Youth, god of music, poetry and beauty.

Math - God of Shapeshifting and magic.

Myrddin - Sun God and keeper of Stonehenge.

Govannon - the "Divine Smith" god of metal and handicraft.

Gwyn Ap Nudd - Otherworld Mound King, God of the Wild Hunt.

Grannos - Sun God of burnings and corn.

Pwyll - God of Law, Justice and Cunning.

Partholonus - God of Masons, the Architect of the Faeries.

Pryderi - Lord of Dyfed, God of adventure, travel and the open road.

Ronanorix - the "Twice Dead" God of death and old age.

Rhonabwy - God of Dreams, the Unconscious Mind and prophecy.

Ruadanos - God of Crossroads and travel.

Amaethon - God of agriculture.

Arawn - the Otherworld King, God of hunting, hounds and the pursuit.

Albiorix - God of Poetry, Orchards and Streams.

Ogma - "Sun Face" God of Eloquence, literature and scribes.

Ossian – "Beautiful Youth" god of skills and swordsmanship.

Owein Ap Urien – God of leadership and war.

Uath Mach Imoman – "Son of Terror" God of Ancient Magic.

Urias – God of Ancient Wisdom and Supreme Knowledge.

Uaithne Umai – God of pipes, harps and music.

Eochaid Ollathar – "Great Horse Father" God of Animals.

Esus – God of woodcutters and weaponry.

Ethniu – God of Language and Speech.

Ith – God of Towers and Building.

Ialonus – Gaulish God of Cultivated Fields.

Iorix – God of Astronomy, Meteors and Space.

Chapter XXII Dichetal do Channaib: The Hand-Finger Ogham

Derived from the Ogham Tract

with verses by Robert Graves

Recital from the finger-ends

Tree Powers, Fingertips. First pentad of the Four.

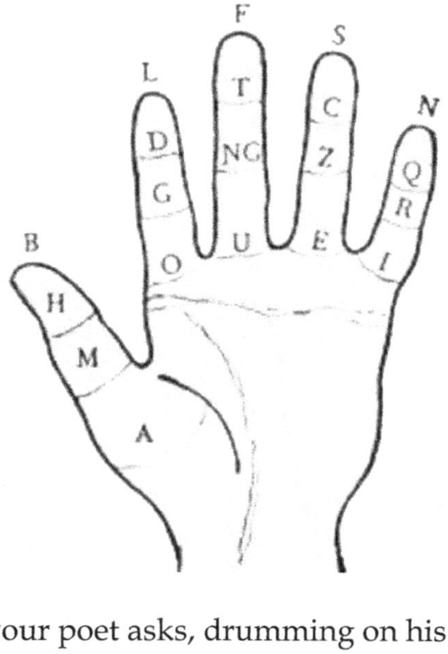

Discover all your poet asks, drumming on his brow.

Birch Peg, Throbbing Thumb, by power of Divination.

Birch, Bring him news of Love; loud the heart knocks.
Rowen rod, forefinger, by power of divination.
Weatherwise, Fool otherwise, mete him out the Winds.
Alder, Physic Finger, by power of divination.
Diagnose all maladies of a doubtful mind.
Willow-wand, Ear Finger, by powers of divination.
Force confessions from the mouth of a mouldering corpse.
Finger-ends, Five Twigs, Trees, true-divining trees.
Discover all your poet asks, drumming on his brow.

Chapter XXIII The Enchanted Forest of Greenwood Magic

From the Book of Elven-Faerie

'Greenwood Forest Grimoire'

Illuminated by Myrddin Cerrig

Walking the Druid Woods

Green is the color of Nature - the Green World. The place of uncovering magic and enchantment of the Forest must be the Green World, that is, the space of Nature that is enveloped by the Green. Wherever you look you should see green or the earth tones of the land and perhaps the azure sky above though treetop canopies may even conceal sky colors.

The Green World is described my Druids as that space in the physical world of Abred that is most synchronous with energies of the four Elemental Kingdoms of Abred. Forest Magic is primarily ruled by Earth and Air Elements.

A "silva" or "sylva" is a treatise or discourse cataloging proper nature and functions of the forests as a system, taking into multifaceted aspects - psychological, spiritual and emotion properties in addition to the physically material. The "Greenwood Grimoire" is based on the "Sylva Druieachd" (given elsewhere in this collection) being the "Treatise of the Sylvan Wizard," writ for those with an inclination to the mysteries of the Deep Woods.

Druids do not practice literal "tree worship" any more than one might worship any of the various symbols used to represent the Divine. Druids see Trees as the perfected symbol of Creation and the Source of All-Being - the All-Absolute. Observation of trees and the way they grow demonstrated the expansiveness of fractal life and all existence.

All life and energy in the Universe is a progression of energy that moves or grows in the same programmed manner as the Tree. This is an important key to the Mysteries.

Trees may not have the same degree of "freedom of movement" like many other creatures living in Nature, however their memory is far older and superior. It is in their nature to take on a charge, to absorb energy, from their natural surroundings - sometimes called Earth Memory.

Trees often live in groups and communities, and by nature, are seldom loners. Awakened Trees will more easily communicate with one another - exchanging energy and information - and if there is a shortage of trees to talk to, they will produce them, through "layrs." The branches or roots will actually re-root to form a new tree.

Dryads of the Trees are like an intelligent spiritual program inhabiting the system that allows its growth. It is a fragmented consciousness connected to the All as an identity - just as is the Druid. In the human being, this tree-like consciousness growth is observed best in "Dendryte" neural formations in the brain.

Spirits within the trees, which have many names in just as many traditions, become a part of any wood taken from it by an experienced Druid for magical purposes. In fact, all of the objects or tools used in Forest Magic and the Ogham are crafted from tree parts (see Chapter XV).

Druids ask permission of the spirits of a Tree, Plant or Animal, before taking away any part of its lifeforce. The same may be seen in practices of true herbalists, hunters and archaic shamans. Permission seeking establishes the relationship shared between you and all life. This is an important part of all Druid work.

There are essentially three main types of wood indexed by the ancient forest loremasters. Wood is a term used to describe a part of the tree that is removable from the Tree like Blood from humans - and both contain the total microcosmic essence of their origins. The three types are:

Deadwood: (dredgwood)
Greenwood: (wickwood)
Livewood: (wizardwood)

Wood found littered throughout the forest floor is Deadwood. It has been broken away from the trees and mixes with the leaves and decaying foliage to form the soil after its decomposition. It is best for kindling standard fires but be sure not to clear it completely away from the forest floor, as it is a necessary part of the ecosystem.

Greenwood or wickwood, when taken from the forest, actually causes the magical spirits of a TREE to retract from it, or emigrate, from survival. This does not occur when removed by an experienced Druid. Wickwood is wood taken from a live Tree by a mortal without asking permission by the code of the Faerie.

Wizardwood or Livewood is wood removed from a living tree by a Druid with authority in Nature or the Master Herbalists after first having asked to remove the piece and giving reason and thanks for its sacrifice.

Chapter XXIV The Wooden Ladder of Authority

From the Ogham Tracts combined with

the 'Greenwood Forest Grimoire'

adapted by Myrddin Cerrig

Tree Groups and Groves

The Elven (Faerie) Triad:

Oak
Ash
Thorn

Seven Noble Trees of the Grove:

Alder
Apple
Birch
Hazel
Holly
Oak
Willow

Nine Sacred Woods of Need-Fire:

Apple
Ash
Ceder
Hazel
Holly
Mistletoe
Oak
Pine
Poplar

Hierarchy of the Forest

Chieftain Trees of

British Druids	Irish Druids
Birch	Oak
Rowen	Hazel
Alder	Holly
Willow	Yew
Ash	Ash
	Pine
	Apple

Peasant Trees of

British Druids	Irish Druids
Hawthorn	Alder
Oak	Willow
Holly	Hawthorn
Hazel	Rowen
Apple	Birch
	Elm
	Pear

Shrub Trees of

British Druids	Irish Druids
Vine	Blackthorn
Ivy	White Hazel
Reed	White Poplar
Blackthorn	Elder
Elder	Arbutis
	Briar
	Ivy

Bramble Trees of

British Druids	Irish Druids
Silver Fir	Fern
Furze	Bog Myrtle
Heather	Golden Pipes
Poplar	Furze
Yew	Heather
	Broom
	Gooseberry

Druids Herbal of the Festival Year

Green World of Winter

Pine
Ceder
Juniper
Sandalwood
Mint
Mead of Winter
Juniper Berries
Wintergreen
Elderflow'r in Freshly Fallen Snow

Green World of Imbolc

Seaweed
Mace
Hops
Cohosh
Elderflow'r
Horehound

Green World of Spring

Lavender
Narcissus
Broom
Crocus

Green World of Beltane

Lilac
Heather
Apple Blossom
Red Clover Blossom
Mead of Beltane
Heather Flowers
Woodruff Sprigs
Meadowsweet Herb in Spring Rain

Green World of Summer

Oak with Mistletoe
St. John's Wort
Fern
Wild Red Rose

Mead of Summer

Oak Leaves
Primrose Flower
Golden Pipes in Morning Dew

Green World of Lughnassadh

Golden Pipes
Chamomile
Furze
Marigold
Sunflow'r

Green World of Autumn

Mugwort
Myrrh
Sage
Balm of Gilead
Iris

Green World of Samhain

Wormwood
Ghostflow'r (Datura)
Nightshade (Belladonna)
Neckweede (Marijuana)

Mead of Samhain

Apple Cider
Wormwood
Pumpkin Blossoms in Deep Well Water

Sacred Incense Smoke for Magic and Ritual

The Celtic-Nine

Rowen
Elder

Pine
Ceder
White Oak Apple
Holly
Juniper
Poplar
Moon-Fire Wood
Juniper
Orris Root
Bay Leaves
Dragon's Blood
Rose Petals
half part Saltpeter

Healing Smoke

Clove
Myrrh
Rosemary

Necromancy

Pepperwort
Musk
Saffron
Red Storax

-or-

Gum Mastic
Balm of Gilead
Dittany of Crete

Flying Fumes

Black Nightshade (Belladonna)
Sweet Flag
Juniper Berries

Astral Projection (Spirit Flight)

Sandalwood
Mugwort
Benzoin Gum
Dittany of Crete

For Academics

Mastic
Rosemary

Summoning Rain

Heather
Fern
Henbane

Prophetic Sight

Mastic
Calamus
Mugwort

-or-

Mastic
Wormwood

-or-

Mastic
Sandalwood
Cinnamon
Patchouli
Juniper

GodForm Evocation

Wormwood
Mugwort
Sandalwood
Willow Bark

Sun-Fire Ceremony

Mistletoe
Oak
Dragon's Blood

-or-

Mace
Saffron
Frankincense

-or-

Sunflower Petals
Dragon's Blood

Merlyn's Wood

Birch Bark
Juniper
Dragon's Blood

Chapter XXV
Guardians of the Grove

Tree Rituals excerpted from the

'Greenwood Forest Grimoire'

of Book of Elven-Faerie

Illuminated by Myrddin Cerrig

The Request and Blessing of the Saplings

Before planting or even breaking ground, go to the future place of the Grove with the trees to be planted. Take any other members of your "spiritual fellowship" with you, if any. All present should enter their Light Body for the remainder of the rites.

The leader stands in the center and says:

Here I [we] have [are] gathered in this place of light. Here I [we] find a place to make a Sacred Space that I wish to honor with the planting and stewardship of a Sacred Grove. May this Holy Nemeton be a place of peace.

Conjure the circle, using stakes to mark the boundary of the circle, where the trees are to be planted. Use the most appropriate liturgy. The forest spirits will not be as concerned about your ritual formalities for these rites.

North: I [we] come forth to this sacred place and call the spirits of the land to join us here. In this Nemeton do I ask permission to raise and tend a Sacred Grove, following the tradition of my ancestors.

East: Here on this sacred spot do I [we] acknowledge my [our] vow[s] as Keeper[s] of the Earth. Here I [we] pledge to be

Guardian of the Grove, a Nemeton that will be ever consecrated as sacred. Here may the sylphs and sylves, 'nature sprits' of the woodlands, come and make holy and enchanted.

South: May the future trees of this Grove, these saplings here, be blessed by the Creatures of Faerie, the Four Elements and the Sun above. May its light strengthen and nourish the trees and offer all life isiting here peace and love.

West: [holding hands over buckets of water]: May the spirits and powers of the Element of Water, Sea and Rain come forth and bless the vessel of water. I apply it now in benediction to these saplings, that they may be blessed by your grace. Be generous in nurturing the Grove with your gentle rains.

Burn incense and carry it thrice about the circle, working clockwise. Feel the energy of the area beginning to equalize to the changes about to take place. Envision the work to be done and project it into the terrain as if you are informing it prior to digging.

Finally, return to the center and say:

By the grace and permission of the Forces of Nature and the Spirits of the Universe, I now break ground in peace, love and compassion. I open this circle now to undertake this work, but the circle is never broken.

Consecration of a Newly Planted Grove

Take the remaining soil and bring it to the center of the circle and say:

May the Spirits of the Earth and Land bless this bit of soil and the region in which it is used. Bless those who use it in their expression of love to nurture newly planted life.

Bring this consecrated soil to each of the trees to be used as topsoil. Wood chips can be used if more appropriate in dryer climates. Feel the love and compassion as you complete the planting stage for each of the trees.

Return to the center and consecrate large vessels of water, saying:

May the Spirits of Water and Sea bless this water and the region in which it soaks. Bless those who use it in their expression of love to nurture newly planted life.

Clean and clear the area before performing a Dedication.

Blessing for the Planting of a Single Tree

Go to the space and ask the spirits of the land for permission before you break ground. Be sure to do all work in your Light Body.

As you dig and plant, say:

I plant this tree in peace, love and compassion. May it be to others and myself a symbol of the same.

When you are almost finished and ready to complete with topsoil or wood-chips, call down and consecrate the soil with Divine energy while saying:

May this earth feed and nourish this sacred life, a symbol of peace, love and compassion.

Complete the planting, and then consecrate the vessel of water and say:

May this water bless and nourish this sacred life, and may the Elemental Spirits of Sea and Water send forth the rains to ever maintain it.

Water the tree healthily with consecrated water and connect with the auric/light field of the tree, saying:

By the Elements of Nature were you sown. By peace and love will you be grown. I am Keeper of the Earth and have overseen your birth. I am a Guardian of Druid Ways and your steward for all my days.

Consecration and Dedication of the Sacred Grove

(Rite of Stewardship)

Before its use as a Nemeton, the Grove should be consecrated to G'ea or Danu, the Earth Morther, the Dagda and/or Cernunnos and to the Source of All Being and Creation. This dedication can be used on the same Grove repeatedly.

North: May the Sacred Grove awaken to the mysteries of the Everlasting Forest. May it grant the Druids, and those who come in peace, the same strength and protection the Sacred Grove offered the Ancients. May the sacred ground on which it stands, be purified and blessed.

East: Here before the Sacred Grove and the 'nature spirits' now awakened and drawn to my work, do I vow stewardship to the Sacred Grove and the mysteries of the Everlasting Forest. I am a Guardian of the Earth Mother, keeper and protector of her ancient ways.

South: I summon forth the energy & power of the Great Sun Father of the Sky. Spirit that grants light and life to the creatures of the Earth, send forth thy Rays of Radiance and instill strength and well-being into th eSacred Grove.

West: May the spirits of the Water and Rain Elements look upon and bless this Holy Nemeton, consecrated and dedicated to the mysteries of the Universe. Nurture and give life while protecting from deluge and fierce storms.

You can also use this rite to dedicate existing groves. You may wish to supplement with individual Tree Awakenings to enchant the region. Doing so repeatedly will turn your Grove (or any space) into a portion of the global Enchanted forest.

Tree Awakening Ritual

(reprise)

Call down the Three Rays and enter your Light Body. Make physical contact with the tree. Speak the Celtic name for the tree three times, followed by the English name, and finally the names "Aldaron," "Daghda" and the Guardian of the particular tree you are working with. Knock three times. As you break contact know that the tree is awakened.

Chapter XXVI The Magic of Language, Persuasion and Communication

Excerpted from the "Book of Druidry"

as written by Myrddin Cerrig

Bard of the Twelfth Chair

The Druid's Voice

Druids were the foremost exponent language and semantics experts in ancient Keltia. Classical accounts refer to the Druid's Voice as a powerful tool of social manipulation and persuasion.

Firstly, communication can be defined as they relay of information, data or energy between a 'sender' and a receiver. The sender must be using clear syntax and semantic language to properly relay the message (information, data, etc.). The receiver must be in an open condition of receiving; they must share the syntax understanding as well as the language being invoked for the communication. It usually best for persuasive acts if the receiver is also in a perceptibly comfortable and safe environment.

Communication is most effective as an exchange; not simply the lecture or dictation of information. The sender should be watching for relays of feedback (the transmission of comprehension cues) from the 'receiver back to the sender. Thus, as many might have guessed, if the receiver is only 'hearing' the sounds, but not truly listening to the semantics, then true communication has not taken place.

Druids were once believed to be able to use sound, speech, voice and music to affect moods and beliefs in the everyday life of the Celtic people.

Persuasion is the communicative or language art of affecting (altering) one's salient (surface) beliefs about some factor. Effective ability to communicate is a prerequisite for effective persuasion. The persuasion intensity is generated by the comprehension level of the influential communication. Therefore, a person is going to be unable to truly persuaded on something that they don't understand. The receiver must be able to understand, comprehend and elaborate the beliefs (or data) for themselves directly and internally for there to be persuasion. There should also be a real (or implied) emotional involvement with the topic or a perceived need to adopt the belief.

The emotional involvement that the receiver has with the message-data and/or belief-topic will affect the intensity of the programming. In short: the message must be shown to be critically relevant. It is most effective to influence beliefs via emotional charge and then allow the internalized processes of the mind to sort the information properly. If the persuasion is effective, the receiver should demonstrate a change in intellectual awareness or behavioral attitude.

Though the actual process of processing and persuasion has not been generally agreed upon by psychologists and academicians, the conclusive knowledge indicates that one's beliefs share a direct relationship with one's behavior.

Behaviors are overt mechanical sequences that represent a person's (or being's) internal perceptions or programming used to process and interact with external stimuli. Perceptions are typically based on beliefs and data stored in the mind. It is logical to assume that behavior can be influenced through belief-persuasion.

Persuasion of a group (or group mind) is not difficult if basic social-condition programming is existent in each participant - meaning that all concerned are wired to be able to be proper receivers. Consider the difference between speaking to a group of your peers versus speaking to an indigenous tribe that not only possesses a different spoken language (or none at all), but also carries different beliefs, values and perceptions of the world-at-large.

It is generally accepted that humans will look to social norms as an indicator or benchmark of what they should believe and how they should behave. When one is unsure about something (for example, experiencing a new life stimulus) there is an almost natural (or programmed) tendency to look toward others for validation, either through the vocalized (verbal) requests for additional information or simply via the observation of existing behaviors.

The human mind is programmed to do this in order to form the most complete assessment (even if inaccurate) to be included in the mental slot that stores experiential knowledge of a particular stimulus. The mind fills-in the gaps of information unconsciously and where inaccurate interpretations of something are born.

The ability to condition or 'program' the mind is a quality based on the mind's already existing 'software' or ability to receive and process information about the perceptibly external world.

Since humans believe themselves to be the product of stimulus-and-response, we can easily see how knowledge of this relationship concerning macrocosmic events in the world around us (as well as in our own minds) will contribute to the knowledge we have of "things" and what we deem true about them. The illusion occurs not when we believe "if p then q", but when the deductions about the p-q relationship are invalid.

Modern psychologists often refer to the infamous case study of classical conditioning used in an experiment known as "Little Albert". Albert was a baby who was consistently introduced to a bunny simultaneously with a frightening noise. The fear generated by the noise was "conditionally displaced" onto the bunny, and a long-standing fear of bunnies then ensued.

One can easily see how the human mind can be tricked into believing in data concerning false causal relationships – even if p and q actually do exist! Neither the bunny or the noise are considered imaginary or illusionary, only our means of processing beliefs and information about them and their affect.

There is also a general social tendency toward compliance - another of the human psychological programs at play, left over from their ancient upgrade into modern man, complete with language and urban civilization.

Being innovators, humans are also more willing to do something, or put forth their energy toward something, if it appears to have been their own idea; has originated within their own psyche. Such democratic processing helps in motivating the population.

The human being, having long since rejected the slave programming from ancient times, is more receptive to a message being delivered by someone they can relate to - one of their own kind - then from a sender who is speaking down to them. Authority still must be executed in order to ensure new information programming, but the relay must fit the circumstances and be made into an exchange as opposed to a dictation.

This information was all a very real part of the Druid body of knowledge, kept and used by the ancients. The Bardic Druids saw this lore as contributory toward the perfection of their creative and expressive arts. The ability to motivate and cull the Celtic tribes into a peaceful world relied on affecting large populations through subtle means, usually cultural and language systems. Therefore strong, but hidden, messages appear throughout the Celtic arts and language use, embedded into the cultural consciousness of people.

Chapter XXVII
The Great Tree Rite

Excerpted from "The Druid Compleat"

as written by Myrddin Cerrig

Bard of the Twelfth Chair

The Great Tree Rite

Lunar orientation of the Great Tree Rite compliments solar orientation of the Druids sacramental, the Druidic Liturgy previously given in Chapter VII of this anthology. Solar observances (like Grove Festivals) are aligned to the Druids sacramental, whereas the lunar cycle, the observation of full and new moons, best applies to the Great Tree Rite. Ritual transcripts from the Druids Sacramental are aligned to day-time ceremonies, whereas lunar celebrations are generally held at night. This present text is elementally aligned and also gives instructions for a leader. As with the Druids Sacramental, the Great Tree Rite can be adapted for either group or solitary practice and either solar or lunar observations.

Note: The performance of the Great Tree Rite begins with the first eleven steps given in the Druids Sacramental ritual formula. The intentions of the rite is proclaimed and then continues with the following text.

Leader: We are here to give witness to the unity and strength of the magick circle, this mandala of love most holy. We, the Druids, the Children of Light, are at one with thee, O Sacred Tree. You, who stands as an eternal symbol of the Circle of Light and Life. You, who represent our eternal link with the ever-present Source. We honor and imitate you as the perfect living specimen of the Source of All Being and Creation. We watch you as you progress through the sacred Earth Year.

North: The beginnings, middles, and ends of the sacred Earth Year.

East: The balance and equinox forces of the sacred Earth Year.

South: Tonight (today) we coven together, man and tree, acknowledging the Sacred Grove.

West: We celebrate the strength, love, and unity of the Sacred Grove, and in that celebration we honor the central icon of its existence: The Great Tree.

East: From the Eastern Winds we are granted a season of growth, as the sun emerges in the spring.

South: From the Southern Flame we are granted a season of fullness, as the sun warms the summer.

West: From the Western Waves we are granted a season of transformation with the shifting tides of autumn.

North: From the Firmness of Northern Ground we are granted a season of stability, self-reflection, and stillness, as the Earth hibernates and is renewed through winter.

Leader: The calendrical month ___, the Oghamic month of the ___ tree in the ancient Druid's calender.

(Trace the Oghamic rune in the air.)

Leader: May the blessing of the ___ tree, and the corresponding energies of ___ be projected forth into our auric light bodies.

Use the following Oghamic Keys to fill in the appropriate information above.

January: Alder Tree, Fearn, protection and power.
February: Willow Tree, Saille, healing and enchantment.
March: Ash Tree, Nuin, protection and peace.
April: Hawthorn Tree, Huatha, love and purity.
May: Oak Tree, Duir, strength and leadership.
June: Holly, Tinne, purification and balance.
July: Hazel Tree, Coll, intuition and creativity.
August: Vine, Muin, meditation and prophecy.
September: Ivy, Gort, protection and growth.
October: Reed, Ngetal, intense energy and direct action.
13th Month*: Elder Tree, Ruis, completion and reflection.
November: Birth Tree, Beith, fertility and growth.
December: Rowan Tree, Luis, strength and insight.

*The 13th month represents the blue moon, or more traditionally, October 29-November 1 – or another observation of a "New Year" period that catches up the lunar and solar calendar synchronization.

East: May the Sacred Grove and the Great Tree grant us the strength of the ancient Druids.

South: We hereby swear (reaffirm) our Guardianship of Gaea, the Sacred Grove, the Great Tree, and all life in Creation.

West: May the gentle rains bless all of Creation, nurturing and giving life, forever and always.

Leader: The entangled roots of the Great Tree shall live deep within our being, offering nourishment and stability to all of its faithful guardians.

North: An in between the roots and branches, we stand as the Guardians, the Keepers of the Earth, we who live in imitation of Oak Trees.

East: Our branches reach into the same sky proving that ascension is the purpose and goal of all life.

South: Great Universal Spirit, beings inhabiting this Sacred Tree, we stand here as your worthy guardians, and Keepers of the Earth and her mysteries.

West: May we grow to become our full potential from the seedlings we now are. May seeds plant in the world, bloom and flourish, spreading the true beauty and love of the Source of All, shared by all those receptive.

Leader: (Knocks three times lightly on the trunk, intoning the name of the tree, perhaps in Celtic, with each knock.) O Great Tree, you are hereby awakened by the Druids of the ancient and ineffable knowledge.

North: May the ground that covers the roots, forever and always be blessed with all that is good and holy. May all of creation grow as the trees in the forest, each beautiful in their own uniqueness, yet still sharing the same Earth in which too spread roots and call home.

Leader: We are united in our strengths, our faith, our love, and our trust. Ours in the bond that must endure all other bonds. The Truth Against the World.

All: The Truth Against The World.

Leader: Through True Knowledge, Power.

All: Through True Knowledge, Power.

Chapter XXVIII Draughts of Inspiration and Oblivion

Collected from The Lost Books

notes on The Book of Pheryllt

as adapted by Myrddin Cerrig

Sacred Libations. Meads and Draughts

Mead of Winter:

Juniper berries
Wintergreen
Elder flowers in Freshly Fallen Snow

Mead of Beltane:

Heather flowers
Woodruff sprigs
Meadowsweet herb in Spring Rain

Mead of Summer:

Oak leaves
Primrose Flower
Golden pipes herb in Morning Dew

Mead of Samhain:

Apple cider
Wormwood
Pumpkin blossoms in Deep Well Water

Alcoholic beverages appear in the ceremonial rites of the Druids. Libation Stones were placed upon the altars of the sacred nemeton as a place of offering to the nature spirits and ancestors.

Draught of Inspiration

The Draught of Ispiration is brewed to enhance the lines of communication between mankind and the Plant Kingdom.

Five tablespoons spring water
+ One pinch of each:
Evening primrose flower
Black willow bark
Thyme

Close away in a glass bottle in the sun for three days, then strain and add one teaspoon of vinegar as a preservative. Also, add one teaspoon of chlorophyll (usually as alfalfa or yellow trefoil).

Three drops may be taken under the tongue before undertaking forest/tree or OGHAM magic.

Draught of Oblivion

The Draught of Oblivion was learned from the Faerie people - the Sidhe residing in the hills and mounds - during the Dark Half of the Year when Elves were seen collecting its main ingredient. It is said they were seen drinking it from a thimble and once the secret of its preparation was known, there were many who called it the Nectar of the Gods.

Smash one gallon of Elder berries into three gallons of good clear well water. Boil together for one hour. Strain and add in three pounds of dark clover honey. Let cool to blood warm, then stir in one ounce of brewer's yeast. Cover and leave to ferment for two weeks.

Final preparations a careful skim and ladle from the top into dark bottles. Cork lightly until the fermentation ceases. Pack in sand in a cool cellar and let age at least one year for the best flavor.

Chapter XXIX
The Herbal Pharmacy of Dian Cecht

& The Physicians of Myddvai

Collected from The Lost Books and

notes from The Book of Pheryllt

as adapted by Myrddin Cerrig

from the files of New Forest

Preparation of Herbs, Tinctures and Extracts

Herbs are prepared from material in a dried powdered form. They may be steeped in hot water as a Tea or tinctured into a water-alcohol base by fermenting with grain.

Take one ounce of the herb in a glass jar with twice its volume in grain alcohol, such as vodka. Leave for two weeks, then strain and filter into amber dropper bottles and label. This tincture may be taken under the tongue. Add one drop of Mistletoe tincture per dose taken.

Pheryllt lore includes references to Coelcerths where Druids burned herb-infused oils in holes of Holey Stones. Place one ounce of herb in five ounces of mineral oil. Store in a cool dark place for two weeks, shaking daily, then strain.

The Sixteen Leeches of Dian Cecht

The Druids herbal garden is marked by stones to represent the Three Circles or Spheres of Existence.

Inside the First Circle; Realm of Earth

Valerian (phu)
Lady slipper (nerveroot)

Skullcap (hoodwort)
Wormwood (absinthe)

Outside the First Circle; Realm of Water

Catnip (catwort)
Hops (beerflow'r)
Black Willow (withe)
Echinacea (coneflow'r)

Outside the Second Circle; Realm of Air

Chamomile (golden pipes)
Marigold (calendula)
Yarrow (earie)
Vervain (brittania)

Outside the Third Circle; Realm of Fire

Goldenseal (goldenruthe)
St. John's Wort (amber)
Buckthorne (sacred bark)
White Oak (quercus)

A Druids Herbal Miscellany

Annointing Oils: Frankincense, Jasmine, Lavender, Lilly of the Valley, Rosemary, Vervain.

Banishing Herbs / Incense: Ceder, Clove, Cypress, Elm, Fern, Mugwort, Rue, St. Johns Wort, Vervain, Yarrow.

Binding Spells: Apple, Cypress, Dragons Blood, Pine, Rowen, Wormwood

Black Willow Bark: one of the herbs of male continence used to decrease sexual drive among Druids, particularly during training, when conservation of sexual energy is most critical.

Catnip, catnep, catmint: chewed by the ancient Celtic warriors for fierceness in battle.

Dragon's Blood, Sanguis Draconis: a mystical substance of greatest antiquity, once common, but now beyond price to those who value such things.

Divination herbs / Incense: Cinnamon, Hazel, Laruel (Bay), Marigold, Mugwort, Nutmeg, Rowen, Wormwood, Yarrow.

Healing Magic: Apple, Cherry, Cinnamon, Clove, hazel, Lavender, Myrrh, Peppermint, Rowen, Sandalwood.

Hops, Beerflow'r: one of the herbs of male continence used to decrease sexual drive among Druids, particularly during training, when conservation of sexual energy is most critical.

Juniper: grove incense for sacred visions.

Love Magic: Apple, Birch, Catnip, Elder, Heather, Honeysuckle, Jasmine, Juniper, Lavender, Marigolg, Mistletoe, Patchouli, Vanilla, Vervain, Wormwood, Yarrow.

Marigold, Holigold, Calendula: called Sun-Bride, it is rubbed on the eye lids to aid in Faery Sight.

Mistletoe, Uchelwydd: called All-Heal, a small amount of the parasitic plant containing the spirit of its host was added to all remedies and magical formulae.

Moonwash: half-ounce Jasmine Flower, half-ounce Eucalyptus Bark, half-ounce Mugwort Herb in amber glass jar with one quart rubbing alcohol for one week, then strain.

Mullein, Velvet Plant: secretly called Graveyard Dust when powdered, used in all types of Necromancy and dark magic.

Narcissus: one of the herbs of male continence used to decrease sexual drive among Druids, particularly during training, when conservation of sexual energy is most critical.

Rue: an anti-magic herb used for defense against spells, purification (exorcism) of a place and sprigs for dispersing bles sed water.

Sunwash: half-ounce Chamomile Flow'r half-ounce Cinnamon bark and half-ounce Oak leaves or bark in amber glass jar with one quart rubbing alcohol for one week, then strain.

Valerian: a powerful sedative used for restgul sleep and lucid dreaming (with Black Willow tree bark). It also appears in love spells.

Vervain, Enchanters Herb: herb found in many Rites and Offerings, warding off attacks, space purification and the acquisition of wealth.

White Pond Lilly: one of the herbs of male continence used to decrease sexual drive among Druids, particularly during training, when conservation of sexual energy is most critical.

Yarrow, Woundwort, Milfoil: an herb of love and unity, found in love spells and used to keep couples together.

Eight Herbs of Elysium

Legend reveals lore of eight sacred herbs which, when mixed togther, threw open the Flaming Door to the Otherworld. The Rite of Elysium invokes the Blood of the Gods, the sacred drink od Eleusis, drunk from the Kernos, where the contents of eight cups is combined in a ninth.

Artemis Herb (mugwort, gwions silver)
Quercus (oak)
Roman Chamomile
Elder Flowers
Dittany of Crete
Laurel (bay leaves)
Rose
Mistletoe

The herbs may be infused in water. As an incense, a mixture of Juniper, Ceder and Yew is burned nearby. Ritual participants (eight) sat in a circle. Each would lift one of the eight Kernos vessels and add it to the central one, while saying:

Nuadh Uile Iceadh meaning in Gaelic: The New All Heal

The Waters of Annwn - Elixir of Sight

European White Pine is of the Ailim Ogham energy current, though traditionally it appears as the Silver Fir. Another hidden Ogham is sometimes given - pingwyddon or Pine. Ogham correspondences indicate that Ailim represents longevity and long or high views. The Druid Council participated in Rites of Elysium and sought Elixirs of Sight and Immortality as a means of preserving the power of the Druids.

Water of Annwn extends life beyond one's allotted years and brings with it the power of Second Sight or Spirit Vision or Prophecy, and so it is too called the Elixir of Sight. It is also said to increase sensibility for a time.

The Pine Needles are gathered on the Sixth Night of the New Moon, made into an elixir by infusing them in hot water - but water drawn from the deepest of wells which has never seen the light of day. It is ingested once every three days.

Pine Resin is gathered from an old tree that is exceeding in age and grace, without steel nor iron. Resin accumulates where branches have broken off by storm damage or lightning.

The Resin is burned upon the coals of a fire bed and breathed in during meditation once every three days, prior and during the drinking of the infusion.

Effectiveness of these techniques increases if observed in early morning before sunrise.

Natural Dye for Druid Cloaks, Robes and Mantles

Druids fashioned their garments from white fabric (linen) that was hand dyed to the proper color by using the necessary plants.

1.

Using once ounce of herb per one pound of fabric weight, bring the dried plant to a boil in three to four gallons of soft water. Strain.

2.

Add one half cup of iodized salt and let to boil for twenty minutes. Add the fabric wetting evenly and return to boil.

3.

Turn off heat and allow to sit until cold.

4.

Rinse briefly in one change of cold water (no more) and air-dry outdoors on a line.

The following herbs may be used to achieve the desired colors.

Dark: Blackthorn, English Oak, Yellow Dock
Violet: Elecampane, Plum, Heather
Purple: Vine (Grape), Elder, Buttercup
Blue: Woad (Indigo), Cornflower, Hollyback
Green: White Canoe Birch, Grass, Coltsfoot
Yellow: Chamomile, Marigold, Sunflower
Orange: Goldenrod, Broom, Aspen, Jewelweed
Red: Alder, Holly, Poinsettia, Ivy, Rue

Chapter XXX The Oracle of the Trees -or- Celtic Tree Oracle

Collected from the Ogham Tracts and
Book of Ballymote with additional
notes from the Book of Pheryllt
and the Book of Elven-Faerie
adapted by Myrddin Cerrig

Druid Ogham Oracle Tools

There are different sets of Ogham tools that are often haphazardly all referred to as "Ogham Sticks." Each set is kept in their own "Crane Bag" or magical pouch.

Ogham Sticks are sticks/twigs of the same type, cut to the same size and polished. An alternate version uses wood-chips as "runic wood-stones." Each of the sticks or chips will have one of the Ogham glyphs burned (preferably) or painted thereon. "Ogham Sticks" are used for high-divination and "cryptomancy."

Ogham Wands range from eight to sixteen inches in length and should be constructed from the correlating tree for each Ogham rune, or a tree of similar energy for the ones you can't find.

The "handle" of the wand should be shaved flat on one side so that you have a surface to put the runic glyph. The other end should be shaved to a stake-like or spear-like point so that it can be pushed several inches into the ground.

The Wizard maintains hold of the handle to complete the circuit. Ogham Wands are used mainly for communication and spiritual communion with Nature.

Ogham Rods are used specifically for divination. They are pieces of dowel or thin wood that are cut to equal lengths, twenty-one in all. Some scholars suggest this ancient tool set is responsible for the children's game "pick-up-sticks," which is what an objective observer might see when they are cast, interpreted and retrieved. They are held in one hand about a foot away from the ground, and then dropped.

Using the rune and Ogham symbols as reference, the Wizard interprets any omens found or "read." When used in conjunction with tree communication, simple acts of divination can become powerful workings of high magic of the forest.

Casting the Woods: Mysteries of Oghamancy

Many types of oracles have existed throughout the ages. The Ogham Oracle as a portable divination system involves a meeting of two axis points - the environment that is fixed and the elements that are variable.

The Spread is the environment that is fixed. It is the manner in which the standard of the cosmos is being seen from the point of the Observer. The Spread is sometimes called a "Lay Out" in the sense that the positions or placements of the variable elements have a fixed consistence so they may be interpreted.

Twenty Ogham Fews are variable elements of the Ogham Oracle system. They are interpreted by seers and oghamancers who are familiar with the energies represented by the Green World of the Forest Trees. Likewise, the system is sometimes called the Celtic Oracle of the Forest Trees.

Any number of Ogham Fews may be drawn, or in the case of the Ogham Rods, the entire pattern is taken into account depending on how they fall. Otherwise, the Ogham Fews are each selected and "read" based on the position or order in which they are drawn. They may be laid out in any way that is predetermined.

Casting the Fifths: Mysteries of Oghamancy

An additional aicme of Ogham appears in the Book of Ballymote, called the Forfedha or Fifths. As the other Ogham aicme, there are five additional Ogham, hence the name fifths.

As an Ogham Oracle spread, the Forfedha are the fixed zones – the background matrix – on which the twenty Ogham Fews are the variable elements. The combination of meaning of the Ogham Fews on the background grid or Forfedha spread determinative positions are what constitute the total "Reading."

The Spread for the Fifths is based on this version of scales from the Book of Ballymote Ogham Tract. Many versions and interpretations of this Oracle exist, but the following one is preferred.

Fifths may be drawn out on the ground before a sacred Oracle Tree or they may be imprinted on a board or Spread Cloth,

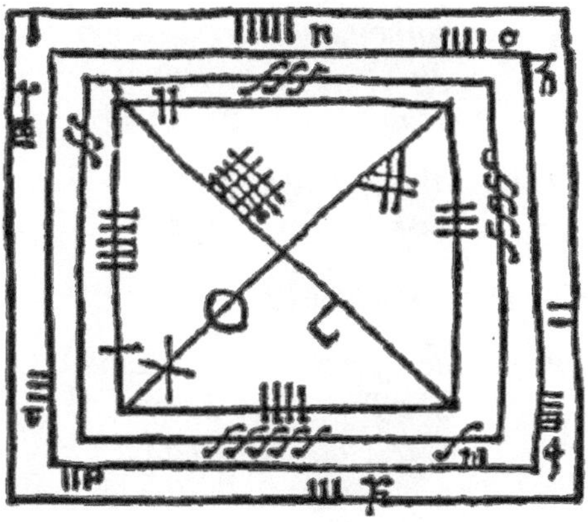

which may be kept in the Crane Bag with Ogham Fews.

Design of the Spread should include a portion for each of the Four Directions and therefore the Four Elements and then also the sacred Center, which represents the Fifth position.

For this method, Druids extract five Ogham Fews placing them in sequence on the Spread for interpretation based on the position they are found in and the nature of the individual Ogham Few itself.

1.) Koad – Grove (center - starfire)
Self, Total Self, God-Self

2.) Oir – Spindle (south - fire)
Harmony, Spiritual Body, Growth

3.) Phagos – Beech (east - air)
Learning, Psychological Body, Beliefs

4.) Uinliean – Honeysuckle (west - water)
Challenge, Emotional Body, Feelings

5.) Peine – Pine (north - earth)
Manifestation, the Physical

The Diviners Invocation to Ogma

Hail to thee, Ogma Sun-face
Eye of the Great God
Eye of the God of Glory
Eye of the Ling of the Living

Pour upon us your Blessing
Pour upon us your Skill
Pour upon us your Power

Hail to thee, thou, Ogma Sun-face
Mask of the God of Life

The Diviner's Branch: The Silver Bough

A Branch of the Apple Tree from Emain I bring
Like Those One Knows,
Silver Twigs are upon it
Crystal Brows with Blossoms

Divination is connected to the Other, thought by some as Divine. The Other is what is hidden from the everyday senses of the Now. Druids have had a long-standing connection to the Other, a domain some have called the Otherworld.

While Hazel and other Ogham trees are best representative of Divination proper, the other connections to the Other may be found with the Ogham tree sacred to Avalonian Druidesses, being the Apple – material used to create a sacred tool called the Silver Branch.

The Silver Branch is an authoritative tool or symbol representing the interconnected aspect of the Druid, the Ogham Fews and the Universe. In essence, the tools become a medium or catalyst for the transmission of energy and information between the Other and the Now.

Branches are traditionally air-element tools, being called the Wand by some. Air is the element of inspiration and the mind, the most important element to the Bards, who called the Silver Branch the Craebh Ciuil or Poets Branch.

Silver Bells are attached to a single branch of Apple wood, twelve to sixteen inches long. It may be a single rod or forked with smaller offshoots left attached. Three Silver Bells are hung from the branch like apples, tied with a blue or white ribbon.

Before performing any divination, the mind and the environment must be purified or cleared to ensure an accurate reading. Ringing the bells from the Silver Branch can "clear the air" prior to any magical work.

Rite of the Flaming Door: The Circle of Ogma

Circles are a traditional symbol of infinity and all existence. They are portals, in and of themselves, representing the combined macrocosm and microcosm all existence. As such they have a long-standing tradition of use among magicians and shamans when performing magical work.

Effectiveness of magical work, including all forms of Forest Magic and Oghamancy is dependent on the Druids awareness of Self and the position of Self and its interconnected nature with the Cosmos.

In the Rite of the Flaming Door, a Druid is seeking to open a gateway of communication between worlds - between the world of Now and the Other, which are one and the same, only perceptibly different and different ranges of perception.

Divination bridges perception allowing an all-encompassing vision of things outside the boundaries of personal belief and perspective - which are wholly relative and will shape the nature of Reality around the expectations of the Observer. Better to be observing in perfect clarity and Self-Honesty.

Druid Tradition observes ritual magic within circles of stones - stones that serve as amplifiers of the energies conjured within. The Circle is long understood to be protective for the Druid or Magician, embodiment of the All and Eternal Presence pervading all existence. During ritual and meditation the Circle serves as a tool to concentrate the universal constant (Universal Agent - Great Magical Agent) at a central point, to be directed by the mind and will of the Druid.

The Circle may be marked with stones, but for this rite, it must be traced into the ground with the knife or sickle. A small trench may be scratched into the dirt two or three inches deep. When ready, pour the prepared Firewater into the circular ditch you dug, lighting it with the words:

Nunc habae emos Lucem – et caloren

Ritual Firewater is prepared from a clean burning grain alcohol - vodka or even rubbing alcohol. One gallon may be mixed with one tablespoon copper sulfate (CuSO4), the "blue crystal that burns blue."

Having first cleared the air and conjured the Circle of Ogma and opened the Flaming Door to the Otherworld, the Oghamancer is ready to invoke the Power of Prophecy from Ogma Sun-face.

Chapter XXXI
The Twenty One Leaves of Ogma Sun-face

Collected from the Ogham Tracts and
Book of Ballymote with additional
notes from the Book of Pheryllt
and the Book of Elven-Faerie
adapted by Myrddin Cerrig

The Original Celtic Tree Oracle

Birch: new start, beginning, cleansing
bardic value: 1 - unity and purity

Rowen: protection vs. enchantment, control of senses
bardic value: 2 - duality, polarity, above and below

Alder: oracular and protective
bardic value: 3 - trinity

Willow: night vision, lunar, female
bardic value: 4 - cosmic cube, the solid

Ash: inner and outer worlds linked, the microcosm/macrocosm
bardic value: 5 - control of the soul

Hawthorn: cleansing, chastity, protection
bardic value: 6 - time

Oak: solid protection, strength, doorway to mysteries
bardic value: 7 - lunar, night, dreams

Holly: best in fight

bardic value: 8 - yearly solar cycle

Hazel: intuition, straight to the source
bardic value: 9 - wisdom and knowledge

Apple: choice of beauty

Vine: prophecy
bardic value: 10 - prophecy

Ivy: the spiral, self-searching
bardic value: 11 - maternity

Reed: direct action
bardic value: 12 - royal or divine purpose

Blackthorn: no choice however unpleasant

Elder: beginnings in the end and ends in the beginning
bardic value: 13 - transformation

Silver Fir: high views and long sight

Furze: good at collecting

Heather: link to inner self

White Poplar: rebirth, illness prevented

Yew: rebirth and everlasting

Colin "Hazel" Murray was one of the first neodruids to devise a coherent revival of the Ogham Tree Oracle. Publication of the kit commercially appeared in 1988, courtesy of his surviving wife Liz Murray. The work set a standard for the 1990's New Age revival of interest in Celtic Magic and the Druidic Ogham. Influence of the Celtic Tree Oracle spread and can be observed in New Age presentations of Celtic Wicca and Druidic Shamanism, such as those given in the works of D.J. Conway since 1990 (in Celtic Magic) that further affected the 'modern standard' for Ogham interpretation.

New Age Ogham Tree Divination

Birch: new beginnings, change, purification

Rowen: control, protection against control from others

Alder: making choices

Willow: guidance, gaining balance

Ash: locked in, bound, choices exist

Hawthorn: being held back for a time

Oak: security and strength

Holly: energy and guidance coming

Hazel: creative energy for projects

Apple: a choice must be made

Vine: relax, inner development needed

Ivy: take time to look out first

Reed: upsets and surprises

Blackthorn: resentment and confusion

Elder: the end of a cycle

Silver Fir: learning from mistakes, a repeat of cycles

Furze: important information

Heather: development

White Poplar: problems, doubts and fears

Yew: a complete change

The Ogam Lochlannach of the Norse

Birch: Jera – fertility, harvest, peace, also "Year" or "Good Year"

Rowen: Perth – assertiveness, karma, initiation, also "Pear Tree"

Alder: Uruz – strength, manifestation, sacrifice, also "Aurochs"

Willow: Laguz – lake life, flow, fertility, also "Water"

Ash: Algiz – life, protection, meta-human, also "Aesir" or "One of the Gods"

Hawthorn: Hagalz – hail, disruption, a framework, also "Precipitation"

Oak: Thurisa – gateway, the door, defense, also "Thor" or "Thunder"

Holly: Ehwaz – movement, soul travel, also "Horse"

Hazel: Othila - property and prosperity, also "Heritage" or "Estate"

Apple: Berkana - birth, life, growth, also "Birch Tree"

Vine: Gebo - partnership, sexuality, lovers, also "Gift"

Ivy: Teiwaz - gods judgment, warrior justice, also "Tiwaz" the god

Reed: Raido - right action and movement, also "Ride" or "Journey"

Blackthorn: Daguz - prosperity, breakthrough, also: "Daylight"

Elder: Isa - concentration, standstill, also "Ice"

Silver Fir: Nauthiz - constraint, persistence, deliverance, also "Need"

Furze: Sowelu - wholeness, victory, also "Sun"

Heather: Mannaz - self, the self on a path, also "Man" or "Humans"

White Poplar: Fehu - physical power, possessions, prosperity, also "Wealth" or "Cattle"

Yew: Eihwaz - life, death, the rebirth cycle, also "Ingwaz" the god

Associations made between the Futhark ("Elven") rune system of the Norse and the Ogham of the Celtic Druids are interpreted for divination purposes only. These very correspondences are intended to demonstrate "semantic" relationships between the oracular systems. As a writing system, the actual appearance of the Ogham alphabet and associated Nordic runes differ greatly - but then, too, we must remember that each was developed for an independent cultural language even if the alphabet may be used to represent each other. It is rumored in lore of the *Coelbren,* however, that the mystical strokes made when writing Norse runes reflect the same "inscribing of rays" found in the Bardic Alphabet. A relationship between the Ogham trees and symbolism of the more Universal Oracle of the Tarot may also be made, following the example provided by Douglas Monroe's interpretation of Tree Personalities:

The Ogham Tarot of Trees Archetypes (Personalities)

Birch: the star

Rowen: high priest

Alder: strength

Willow: the moon

Ash: the universe

Hawthorn: judgment

Oak: emperor

Holly: the chariot

Hazel: high priestess

Apple: empress

Vine: lovers

Ivy: justice

Reed: wheel of fortune

Blackthorn: temperance

Elder: the hanged man

Silver Fir: the devil

Furze: the sun

Heather: the fool

White Poplar: the tower of babel

Yew: death

Volume Three

Chapter XXXII
The Secrets of the Unhewn Dolmen

Interpreted by Robert Graves

from Roebuck in the Thicket

as adapted by Myrddin Cerrig

with additional notes for the

Ritual Zodiac of the Pheryllt

"Who but I can unfold the secrets

of the unhewn dolmen?"

– Song of Amergin

A dolmen is a burial chamber, a Womb of Earth, consisting of a cap-stone supported on two or more uprights, in which a dead hero is buried in a crouched position like a fetus in the womb, awaiting rebirth. In spiral Castle (passage-burial), the entrance to the inner chamber is always narrow and low in representation of the entrance to the womb. But dolmens are used in Melanesia as sacred doors through which the totem-clan initiate crawls in a ceremony of rebirth; it seems likely that they were used for the same purpose in Britain.

"Invoke the poet,

that he may compose a spell for you.

For I, the Druid, who set out letters in Ogham,

I will approach the wrath of the Sidhe to seek a cunning poet that together we may concoct incantations.

I am a wind of the sea."

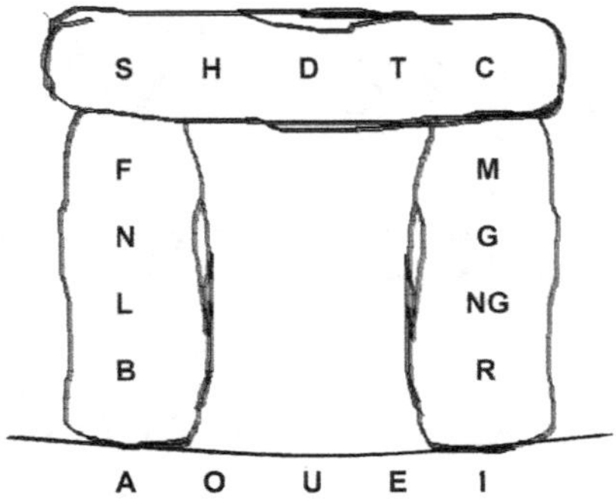

The omission from the (thirteen-letter) Beth-Luis-Nion of the mythically important trees, *Quert*, apple and *Straif*, blackthorn, must be accounted for. The explanation seems to be that though the Beth-Luis-Nion (calendar) is a solar one, in so far as it expresses a year's course of the sun, it is ruled by the White Moon-goddess whose sacred number is thirteen in so far as her courses coincide with the solar year, but fifteen in so far as the full moon falls on the fifteenth day of each lunation. Fifteen letters are needed to present the goddess as both a triad and a pentad (fifteen as a multiple of three and five), and to express the days in a month up to a full moon, and since only thirteen 28-day months can be fitted into a year, two of the months must be shared between pairs of trees.

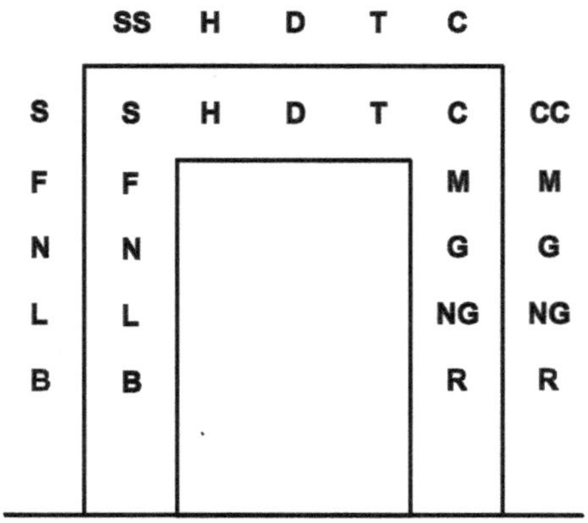

Since Q (*Quert*, apple) was sometimes written CC by the Irish Bards, we may conclude that Z (*Straif*, blackthorn) was similarly written ZZ as it was in Latin during the greater part of the Republic. This is to say that *Quert*, the wild apple, shared a month with *Coll*, the hazel, because the apple and nut harvest coincide, and that *Straif*, the blackthorn, shared a month with *Saille*, the willow, because the White Goddess has to make an appearance in tree form in the Spring - in France (Gaul) the blackthorn is called "the Mother of the Woods."

There is a reference in Amergin's song to the "secrets of the unhewn dolmen." It will be seen that there is room for an extra letter at each corner of the dolmen arch which I constructed to elucidate the reference to the lines of the song: the Oghams being nicked on the edges, not painted on the face, of the stones.

B: I am a stag of seven tines,

L: I am a wide flood on a plain,

N: I am a wind on the deep waters,

F: I am a shining tear of the sun,

S: I am a hawk on a cliff,

H: I am fair among flowers,

D: I am a god who sets fire in the head,

T: I am a battle-waging spear,

C: I am a salmon in the pool,

M: I am a hill of poetry,

G: I am a ruthless boar,

NG: I am a threatening noise of the sea,

R: I am a wave of the sea,

Who but I knows the secrets of the unhewn dolmen?

It will be observed that the seventh to eleventh letters of this alphabet, which follow the same sequence in the Boibel-Loth, are the letters H.D.T.C.Q. These letters, Sir John Rhys has pointed out, form the initials of the Old Goidelic numerals, from one to five – *hoina, duou, ttri, ccetuor, quattuor, quinque* – and this may explain why the inventors of the Boibel-Loth made H.D.T.C.Q. the central five letters of the alphabet and transferred Z to a position between NG and R. Yet the ancientness of the Old Goidelic numerals suggests that in the original Beth-Luis-Nion finger alphabet, the first flight of consonants – the Spring months – numbered only five, not six, to allow H.D.T.C.Q. to form the second or Summer series, and that Z was therefore reckoned to the last series, the Winter series, as a premonitory "blackthorn winter."

Thus:

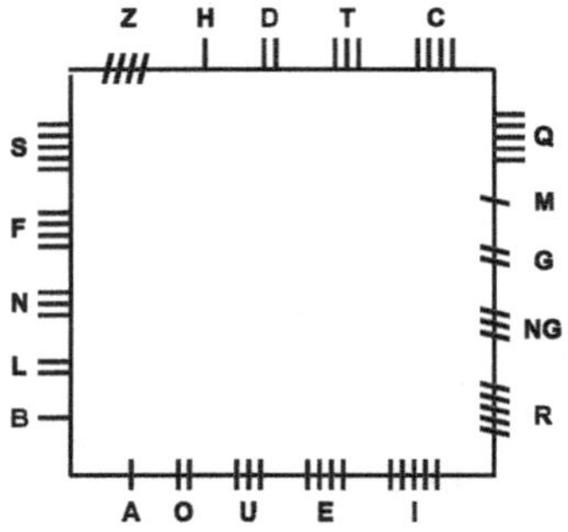

Each series thus has its full five letters, the aggregate number of strokes in each case being fifteen.

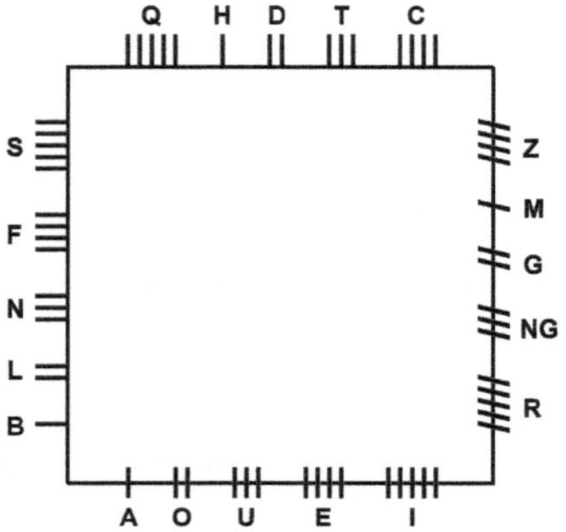

But though this is a logical arrangement, necessitated by the initials of the first five numerals in Latin and Old Goidelic, a sense of mathematical proportion demands that each side of the dolmen should have a single series cut upon it. This would involve a change of places between Z and Q, to make Apple and Willow, Hazel and Blackthorn, share months.

This arrangement makes good seasonal sense, for the wild apple blossoms during the willow month and the sloe is ripe in the hazel month. Poetically it also makes good sense, for the Apple White Goddess is of happier omen than the Blackthorn White Goddess as introducing the summer; and the hostile blackthorn with its mouth-puckering sloe is complementary to apple, in the nut-month, as representing the poet in his satiric capacity. I believe that both these arrangements were used in Ogham, the necessary ambivalence of poetic meaning being thus maintained: it is an axiom that the White Goddess is both lovely and cruel, ugly and kind.

Now it will be noticed that there are two more unoccupied corner positions on the threshold of the dolmen which represents the extra day of the calendar year; and the can be assigned to J (pronounced Y) and to long O: Y as a reduplication of I, the death-vowel; long O as a reduplication of A, the birth-vowel. That only a single character served for both J and I in Latin and Greek is well known; and the close connection between long O (Omega) and A appears both in Ionic Greek, where Omega was often written instead of Alpha - oristos for aristos ('best'); and in Doric Greek where Alpha was often written for Omega - as pratistos for protistos ('first').

Omega (Great O) seems to signify the world-egg of the Orphic mysteries which was split open by the Demiurge to make the universe: for the majuscular Greek character for Omega represents the world-egg laid on the anvil and the the minuscular character shows it already split in halves. The majuscular Omicron (little O) and the minuscular Omicron both show the egg of the year waiting to hatch out. The "*glain*" or "red egg of the sea serpent", which figured in the Druidical mysteries may be identified with the Orphic world-egg: for the creation of the world, according to the Orphics, resulted from the sexual act performed between the Great Goddess and the World-Snake

Ophion. The Great Goddess herself took the form of a snake coupled with Ophion; and the coupling of snakes in archaic Greece was consequently a forbidden sight. The "caduceus" of Hermes, his wand of office, was in the form of coupling snakes. The Goddess then laid the world-egg, which contained infinite potentiality but which was nothing in itself until it was split open by the Demiurge. The Demiurge was Helios, the Sun, with whom the Orphics identified their god Apollo - which was natural, because the Sun does hatch snakes eggs - and the hatching-out of the world was celebrated each year at the Spring festival of the Sun, to which the vowel Omicron is assigned in the alphabet.

But Little-O is not Great-O. Omega, Great-O, must be regarded as an intensification of Alpha, and as symbolizing the birth of birth (requiring a new dolmen figure shown here). Then at last we can complete our Beth-Luis-Nion calendar, with the proper tree accredited to each letter - for the doubled I, or J, letter-tree, the tree belonging to the Day of Liberation which stands apart from the 364 days of the thirteen months (28 times 13 months equals 364 days). When requirements of the tree are put into a bardic riddle, there can only be one answer -

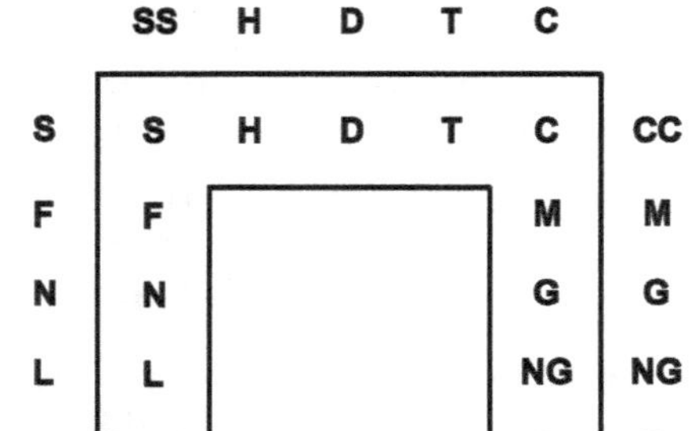

The day that is no day calls for a tree
That is no tree, of low yet lofty growth.
When the pale queen of Autumn casts her leaves
My leaves are freshly tufted on her boughs.
When the wild apple drops her godly fruit
My all-heal fruit hangs ripening on her boughs.
Look, the twin temple-posts of green and gold,
The overshadowing lintel stone of white.
For here with white and green and gold, I shine:
Graft me upon the King when his sap rises
That I may bloom with him at the year's prime,
That I may blind him in his hour of joy.

For the mistletoe, the berries of which were formerly prized both as an all-heal and as an aphrodisiac, is not a tree in the sense that it grows in the earth; it subsists on other trees. There are two sorts of mistletoe: the mistletoe proper and the loranthus. The Greeks distinguished them as, respectively, hypear and ixos or ixias. The loranthus is found in Eastern Europe, but not in Western. It grows on oaks, but also on tamarisks, and its flame-colored leaves may have been the original "burning bush" from which JHVH appeared to Moses. Whether the loranthus was once native to Western Europe, or whether the Celtic Druids brought it with them from the Danube area where their religion was first formulated, or whether they grafted mistletoe proper from poplar, apple, or other host-trees, on their oaks, cannot be determined.

This calendar explains the reference in "Preiddeu Annwn" ("The Spoils of Annwn") to the "ox with seven-score knobs on this collar": the ox is the first flight of the five months, consisting of 140 days; it is presumably followed by a lion of 112 days, and a serpent of the same length, justifying texts from Euripides and the Welsh poet Cynddelw – both appealing that the God of the year appear as a wild bull, a fire-breathing lion and a many-headed snake. The griffon-eagle must be the creature of the extra day, since the god becomes immortal in this form. The year of Bull.

Lion, Serpent and Eagle is Babylonian: a calendar beast, called Sirrush, on the Dragon Gate at Babylon – having the body and horns of a bull; forelegs and mane of a lion; head, scales and tail of a serpent; hindlegs and feet of an eagle.

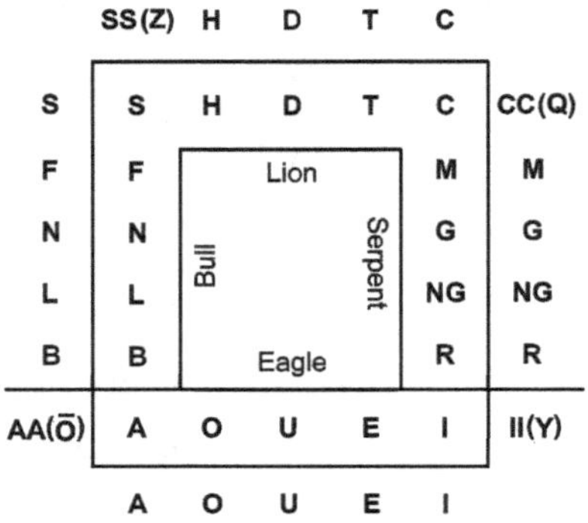

The calendar has several secret qualities. One is that the number of vowels is increased to seven, the Roebuck's own number. Another is that II (double-I or Y) in Ogham makes a ten-stroke letter (that is to say, the I Ogham character twice), and AA (double-A or long-O) makes a two-stroke letter (the A Ogham character twice): thus the aggregate number of letter-strokes for the complete twenty-two letter alphabet is 72, a number constantly recurring in early myth and ritual – 72 is the multiple of nine, the number of lunar wisdom, and eight the number of solar increase. Mr. Clyde Stacey suggests that 72 is also linked to the Goddess, astronomically, by the seventy-two day season during which her planet Venus arcs successively from maximum eastern elongation to inferior conjunction (closest approach to earth) and then to maximum west elongation. A third quality is that the proportion of all the letters in the alphabet to the vowels is 22 to 7, which is the mathematical formula, once secret, for the relation of the circumference of the circle to the diameter – or "pi" as 22 divided by 7.

The most important quality of this calendar requires understanding the poetic relation between Hazel and Apple.

Consider further: that the Roebuck, originally a White Hind, hides in the thicket, and that the thicket is composed of twenty-two sacred trees. The poet naturally asks a further question: But where exactly is the beast lodged in the grove? - "cw-cw" - "Where, where?"

"Where" in English is derived, according to the Oxford English Dictionary, from the interrogative stem - *qua*. Nearly all interrogatives in Indo-European languages begin with Q (except where Q has been, as in Greek, changed into a P or, as in German, into a W), and in Old Scots "where" is spelled *quhair*. Q, in fact, is the letter of perpetual question - but the Muse's promise to the poet is "Seek patiently, and you shall find," so where else should the Wild Hind be hiding except under the Q tree, which is the Wild Apple? The letter Q is from a tree named *Quert,* that is to say an apple tree. As the saying is: "Quert is the shelter of the wild hind" - meaning that the apple tree is so. The Birch is mentioned as very noble in the "*Cad Goddeu*" ("Battle of the Trees"), but the apple-tree was the noblest tree of all, being the tree of immortality - as the poets of Wales have always been aware of its spiritual pre-eminence, and the medieval poem: "Afallenau" (Avalon):

Sweet apple-tree crimson in hue

Which grows concealed in Forest Celyddon...

"Afallenau" is not a poem about the orchard apple-tree but about the apple-tree of the sacred thicket, the tree that is the harbor of the hind - as is written "I fled as a roe to the entangled thicket." And where did King Arthur go to be healed of his grievous wounds? To the Isle of Avalon, the secret island of apple-trees. With what talisman was Bran summoned by the White Goddess to enter the Land of Youth? With a "silver white-blossomed apple branch from Emain in which the bloom and branch were one."

The Roebuck in the Thicket

(Pheryllt Version)

I am a Stag of Seven Tines,
I am a Roebuck in a Thicket,
I am the pursued Messenger of Life...

Five days at Year's End I run,
Five days the Thicket Door stands open.
Five days the Houses of Annwn upon my heels!

Hasten, ready! The Sun awaits us,
Quicken, race! A Son is born,
Burning Yule with Bells at Dawn...
Fly windsong - across the Sunrise!

Past a Winter Sea we sail, far behind us
weep the Birches, bent with ice and branches frail.
Past a cottage bright with candle,
Yellow flame against the night.
Matron Mother, Mabon cradling,
Willow guard by pale moonlight.

Faster, Onward! New year beckons!
Brave Cu Chulainn bests the Spring.
Flocks of Raven circle over,
Blooming boughs of Hawthorn bring!
Hounds, a streak of pink and white,
Follow like a tempest, baying...
Fires of Bel on every hillside,
Math, the Flower-Maiden making.
King of Oak and Summer Lord,
glimpsed along the tables feasting...
Arthur, shining 'mid the hoard
of Dragon Red, and mirth unceasing!

Onward! Faster! Lest they falter
by the side of the Lugh the Long
Arm and Eagle, Vine ensnaring...
Prowess sung in August song!

'Round the ivy path, the Autumn
turns the trees aflame with color.
Taliesin, wise man fleeing
from the wrath of Cauldron Mother.

Final stretch! Hasten, race!
The Head of Bran, a shining face...
Passage through the Blackthorn night,
Chase ahead! Our ending flight!
Looms the Thicket, Mystic Doorway

Forest Elder guards the way...
'Till the next Midwinter's Day.
Ritual Zodiac of the Pheryllt

In this system of the ritual zodiac, based on the Pheryllt version of "The Roebuck in the Thicket," there are eight 45-day Festival constellation periods (composing a 360-day literal "wheel" of the year) plus one 5-day inter-calculatory time; a true Celtic form representative of the eight annual Grove Festivals. As illuminated by Douglas Monroe - "The White Roebuck is chased out of Annwn around the nine star houses" - eight of the stations have 45 days each based on the solar year (8x45=360); the final one, the ninth, lasting 5 days; total: 365 - uniting the numerology of the solar eight with the lunar nine to form a complete luni-solar calendar of the year: 365 solar days.

1.

The Stag of Seven Tines - Bringer of Life through the Thicket-Doorway (barrier of Annwn), arrives at Midwinter bearing the spirit of the Holy Child into the World. Celtic re-birth of the Sun. Ogham: Birch (Birth of the Divine Child). Period: Midwinter, then to Imbolc.

2.

The Flame of Matrona - Divine Mother of Mabon, who carries and protects the child through the darkest dregs of winter. The Celtic Candle Festival. Ogham: Willow (Protectress of the Divine Child). Period: Imbolc, then to Spring Equinox.

3.

Raven of Cu Chulainn - Bringer of destiny into the World. Celtic Festival of the Birds. Ogham: Hawthorn (Fate of the Divine Child). Period: Spring Equinox, then to Beltaine.

4.

The Flowers of Math - Bringer of beauty into the World. Illusions, however pleasant. The Celtic Flower Festival. Ogham: Wild Apple (Instiller of Beauty in the Divine Child). Period: Beltaine, then to Midsummer.

5.

The Red Dragon of Arthur - Bringer of victory and material accomplishment into the World. Celtic Festival of the Oak King. Ogham: Oak (Granter of nobility and bravery in the Divine Child). Period: Midsummer, then to Lughnassadh.

6.

The Eagle of Lleu - Symbol of the fruits of one's labors. Celtic Grain Festival. Ogham: Vine (Granter of rewards to the Divine Child). Period: Lughnassadh, then to Autumn Equinox.

7.

The Cauldron of Taliesin - Bringer of Self-transformation to the World. Celtic Harvest Festival. Growth within the Spiral of Life. Ogham: Ivy (Teacher of self-accomplishment to the Divine Child). Period: Autumn Equinox, then to Samhain.

8.

The Head of Bran - Bringer of safe passage out of the World. Celtic Festival of the Dead, when the Flaming Door between the worlds opens from dusk to dawn. The Roebuck escapes back through the Thicket-Doorway with the Old Year, yet pursued by the Hounds of Annwn. Ogham: Blackthorn (Initiator of the Divine Child beyond the realms of Death). Period: Samhain, then 45 days of Dark Gestation until Cwn Annwn.

9.

The Hounds of Annwn - Cwn Annwn, drivers of fate and destiny before mankind. These dogs arrive back into the World the moment of the Winter Solstice, after a blind, five day chase through the Thicket-Doorway between the worlds in pursuit of the Roebuck. Ogham: Elder (This Otherworld stag bears upon its back the Holy Son of the New Year). Period: "Grove of Five Elders" - the five unnamed days (in which hide the Triple Goddess and the duel God of Light and Dark) before the Solstice hour (approximately December 15-20).

Chapter XXXIII The Celtic Fire Festivals of Agriculture & Astronomy

Interpreted by J.A. MacCullocch with

Selections adapted by Myrddin Cerrig

The Fire Festivals

The Celtic year was not at first regulated by the solstices and equinoxes, but by some method connected with agriculture or with the seasons. Later, the year was a lunar one, and there is some evidence of attempts at synchronizing solar and lunar time. But time was mainly measured by the moon, while in all calculations night preceded day. Thus "*oidhche Samhain*" was the night preceding Samhain (November 1), not the following night. The usage survives in our "sennight" and "fortnight."

In early times the year had two, possibly three divisions, marking periods in pastoral or agricultural life, but it was afterward divided into four periods, while the year began with the winter division, opening at Samhain.

A twofold, subdivided into a fourfold division is found in Irish texts, and may be tabulated as follows:

***Geimredh* (winter half)**

1st Quarter, *Geimredh*, beginning with the festival of Samhain, November 1st.

2nd Quarter, *Earrach,* beginning February 1st. (Sometimes called Oimelc).

***Samhradh* (summer half)**

3rd Quarter, *Samradh,* beginning with the festival of Beltane, May 1st. (Also called Cet-samain, 1st day of Samonos; Welsh Cyntefyn)

4th Quarter, *Foghamhar,* beginning with the festival of Lughnassadh, August 1st (Sometimes called Brontroghain).

These divisions began with festivals, and clear traces of three of them occur over the whole Celtic area, but the fourth has now been merged with St. Brigit's Day. Beltane and Samhain marked the beginning of the two great divisions, and were perhaps at first movable festivals, according as the signs of summer or winter appeared earlier or later. With the adoption of the Roman calendar some of the festivals were displaced, e.g. in Gaul, where the Calends of January took the place of Samhain, the ritual being also transferred.

None of the four fire festivals is connected with the times of equinox and solstice. This points to the fact that the original agricultural Celtic year was independent of these. But Midsummer day was also observed not only by the Celts, but by most European folk, the ritual resembling that of Beltane. The festivals of Beltane and Midsummer may have arisen independently, and entered into competition with each other. Or Beltane may have been an early pastoral festival marking the beginning of summer when the herds went out to pasture, and Midsummer a more purely agricultural or astronomical festival. The Celtic festivals being primarily connected with agricultural and pastoral life, we find in their ritual survivals traces not only of a religious but of a magical view of things, of acts designed to assist the powers of life and growth.

Samhain

Samhain - possibly meaning "summer-end" - beginning the Celtic year, was an important social and religious occasion. The powers of blight were beginning their ascendancy, yet the future triumph of the powers of growth was not forgotten. It bears traces of being a harvest festival, the ritual of the earlier harvest being transferred to the winter feast, as the Celts found themselves in lands where harvest is not gathered before late autumn. The harvest rites may, however, have been associated with threshing rather than in gathering. Samhain also contains in it some of the old pastoral cults, while as a New Year feast its ritual is in great part that of all festivals of beginnings.

New fire was brought into each house at Samhain from the sacred bonfire, itself kindled from the need-fire by the friction of pieces of wood. This preserved its purity, the purity necessary to a festival of beginnings. Putting away of the old fires was connected with various rites for the expulsion of evils, which usual occur among many peoples at the New Year festival. By that process of dislocation which scattered the Samhain ritual over a wider period and gave some of it to Christmas, the kindling of the Yule log at the Winter Solstice may have been originally connected with this festival. Samhain was also a festival of the dead, whose ghosts were fed at this time.

As the powers of growth were in danger and in eclipse in winter, men thought it necessary to assist them. As a magical aid, the Samhain bonfire was chief, and it is still lit in the Highlands. Brands were carried round, and from it the new fire was lit in each house. In North Wales people jumped through the fire, and when it was extinct, rushed away to escape the "black sow" who would take the hindmost. The bonfire represented the sun, and was intended to strengthen it. Having all the sun's force, those who jumped through it were strengthened and purified. The Welsh reference to the hindmost and to the black sow may point to a former human sacrifice, perhaps of any one who stumbled in jumping through the fire. The victim, like the scapegoat, was laden with the accumulated evils of the year, as in similar New Year customs elsewhere.

Beltane

Beltane - "a goodly fire" or derived from "bel-dine," because newly-born cattle ("dine") were offered to the god, Bel - is a festival of life, of the sun shining in his strength. Alternately, its primitive form was "belo-tenid" ("belo-s"), meaning "clear" or "shining" (the root of the names Belenos and Belisama) and "tenos," meaning "fire." Thus the word would mean something like "bright fire," perhaps the sun or the bonfire, or both. Folk-survivals of the Beltane and Midsummer festivals show that both were intended to promote fertility.

One of the chief ritual acts at Beltane was the kindling of bonfires, often on hills. The house-fires in the district were often extinguished, the bonfire being lit by friction from a rotating wheel - the German "need-fire" ("necessity fire"). The fire kept off disease and evil, hence cattle were driven between two fires lit by Druids, in order to keep them in good health during the year. Sometimes the fire was lit beneath a sacred tree, or pole covered with greenery was surrounded by the fuel, or a tree was burned in the fire. These trees survive in the Maypole of later custom, and they represented the vegetation-spirit, to whom the Celts assimilated themselves by dressing in leaves. They danced sunwise round the fire or ran through the fields with blazing branches or wisps of straw, imitating the course of the sun, and thus benefiting the fields. Houses were decked with boughs and thus protected by the spirit of vegetation.

Beltane cakes or bannocks, perhaps made of the grain of the sacred last sheaf from the previous harvest, and therefore sacramental in character, were also used in different ways in folk-survivals. They were rolled down a slope - a magical imitative act, symbolizing and aiding the course of the sun. The cake had also a divinatory character. If it broke on reaching the foot of the slope this indicated the death of its owner. In another custom in Perthshire, part of a cake was thrown over the shoulder with the words, "This I give to thee, preserve thou my horses; this to thee, preserve thou my sheep; this to thee, O fox, preserve thou my lambs; this to thee, O hooded crow; this to thee, O eagle." Here there is an appeal to beneficial and noxious powers, whether this was the original intention of the rite. But if the cakes were made of the last sheaf, they were probably at one time eaten sacramentally (their sacrificial use emerging later).

The bonfire was a sun-charm, representing and assisting the sun. Rain-charms were also used at Beltane. Sacred wells were visited and the ceremony performed with their waters, these perhaps being sprinkled over the tree or the fields to promote a copious rainfall for the benefit of vegetation. The use of such rites at Beltane and at other festivals may have given rise to the belief that wells were especially effective then for purposes of healing. The custom of rolling in the grass to benefit from the May dew was probably connected with magical rites in which moisture played an important part.

The idea that the powers of growth had successfully combated those of blight may have been ritually represented. This is suggested by the mimic combats of Summer and Winter at this time, to which reference has already been made. The May King and Queen represent earlier personages who were regarded as embodying the spirits of vegetation and fertility at this festival, and whose marriage or union magically assisted growth and fertility. Sacred marriage and festival sexuality were an appeal to the forces of nature to complete their beneficial work, as well as a magical aid to them in that work. It may be assumed that a considerable amount of sexual license also took place with the same magical purpose.

Midsummer

Midsummer festival rituals did not materially differ from that of Beltane, and as folk-survivals show, it was practiced not only by the Celts, but by many other European peoples. Midsummer was a nature festival such as would readily be observed by all under similar psychic conditions and in like surroundings. A bonfire was again the central rite of this festival, the communal nature seen in the fact that all must contribute materials to it. Dancing sunwise round the fire to accompanying songs and hymns in honor of the Sun-god - imitating the sun's actions to magically make it more powerful. The more livelier the dance, the better would be the harvest.

The ancient Druidic archetype of the vegetation-spirit in ritual was that of the "tree-spirit," which had power over rain, sunshine, and every species of fruitfulness. For this reason, a tree had a prominent place both in the Beltane and Midsummer feasts. It was carried in procession, imparting its benefits to each house or field. Branches of it were attached to each house for the same purpose. It was then burned, or it was set up to procure benefits to vegetation during the year and burned at the next Midsummer festival. The sacred tree was probably an oak, and the mistletoe rite took place on Midsummer eve, as a preliminary to cutting down the sacred tree and in order to secure the life or soul of the tree, which must first be secured before the tree could be cut down. The life of the tree was in the mistletoe, still alive in winter when the tree itself seemed to be dead.

In the Stone Age, a circle typified the sun, and as soon as the wheel was invented its rolling motion at once suggested that of the sun. Among the Celts the wheel of the sun was a favorable piece of symbolism, and this is seen in various customs at the Midsummer festival. A burning wheel was rolled down a slope or trundled through the fields, or burning brands were whirled round so as to give the impression of a fiery wheel. The intention was primarily to imitate the course of the sun through the heavens, and so, on the principle of imitative magic, to strengthen it. But also, as the wheel was rolled through the fields, it was hoped that the direct beneficial action of the sun upon them would follow.

Lugnasad

Lugnasad – coming midway between Beltane and Samhain – the 1st of August became Lammas in Christian times, but its name still survives in Irish as Lugnasad, in Gaelic as Lunasdal or Lunasduinn, and in Manx as Laa Luanys. It is an important ancient festival among the Celts, in honor of the god Lug (Lugus) long before its Romanized form as the "August feast," or "feast of Augustus," the name having replaced one corresponding to Lugnasad.

As Lammas was a Christian harvest thanksgiving, so also was Lugnasad a pagan harvest feast, part of the ritual of which passed over to Samhain. The people made glad before the sun-god – Lug perhaps having that character – who had assisted them in the growth of the things on which their lives depended. Marriages were also arranged at this feast, probably because men had now more leisure and more means for entering upon matrimony. Some evidence points to the connection of the feast with Lug's marriage, though this has been allegorized into marrying the "sovereignty of Erin (Ireland)."

Due observance of the feast produced abundance of corn, fruit, milk and fish. The ritual observed included the preservation of the last sheaf as representing the corn-spirit, giving some of it to the cattle to strengthen them, and mingling it with next year's corn to impart to it the power of the sacrificed corn-spirit, slain for the feast. In harvest customs of Celtic Scotland and elsewhere, two sheaves of corn were called respectively the Old Woman and the Maiden, the corn-spirit of the past year and that of the year to come. The grain of the Maiden sheaf was mixed with the seed corn, whereas the sheaf of the Old Woman is sacrificed or buried in the earth.

Chapter XXXIV Planetary Astronomy at the Druidical Temples of Merlyn

Illuminated by Rev. E. Duke researching for

Archaeological Institute of Britain & Ireland

With selections adapted by Myrddin Cerrig

Astronomy was the earliest of all sciences, and was the first which brought into exercise the faculties of the mind of man. It probably originated in Chaldaea, and traveled from Babylon in succession to Egypt, Greece, and Rome, and from thence descended to modern times and spread itself throughout all nations. The sciences travel faster than the arts, they may be communicated orally to the many at once, but the knowledge of the arts is transferable alone from man to man. The Ancient Druids developed a complex series of temples forming a magnificent planetarium – on the face of the land, they formed so vast a stationary orrery, constructed on a meridional line of 32 miles in length. The conception was as sublime as its execution was wonderful! It cannot be denied that these worshipers of the planets, were imbued with an intimate knowledge of science of Astronomy.

In the Temple of the Sun at Abury, reference is made to the cycle of the days of the month, to that of the months of the year, and to the year itself; and in a similar manner in the temple of the Moon at Abury, reference is made to the cycle of the days of the month, to that of the months in the year, and to that of the seasons, or early tripartite division of the year. In the Temple within the head of the serpent, at the same place, reference is made to the famous Metonic or lunar cycle. Again, at Stonehenge, reference is made to the cycle of the years of Saturn, to that of the days of the month, to that of the seven planets, and also of the days of the week.

The most early ancients held, that, at the close of an immense period of years, all the heavenly bodies would at a critical period simultaneously arrive at the same places, from whence they originally set out when the impulse of locomotion was imparted to them, and that then this world would be brought to a close and a new world would emerge into existence. This doctrine was called the Platonic Cycle; not that Plato was the inventor of it, for it was known before his time, but that it was embraced within his opinions, and from hence it took his name.

The Platonic Cycle was also called the "magnus annus," the Great Year; it was, in fact, the cycle of the years of the world, and, when we have seen, that the founders were well acquainted with all the minor cycles, and that in the details of these temples, they have demonstrated the cycle of the days of the month—the months of the year—the ancient seasons—the annual lunations—the years of Saturn—the planets—and the zodiacal signs—can we for a moment suppose that their knowledge stopped here? Can we believe, that acquainted as they were with all these cycles, they were ignorant alone of the great year? The Platonic Cycle? The cycle of the years of the world? The cycle of cycles ?—No! To suppose this for a moment would be flagrantly absurd.

The Platonic Cycle is synonymous with what is astronomically denominated the Precession of the Equinoxes, which is thus described by Higgins in his book "Celtic Druids," stating:

"It was well known to ancient astronomers, that a certain slow periodical revolution of the pole of the equator took place round the pole of the ecliptic, and that this periodical revolution was completed in 25,920 years. The fact was known to the Ancients, and has been demonstrated by modern astronomers, by means both of theory and observation, so that it is not at this time a matter of doubt. In consequence of this circular motion of the earth, the equinox, the solstice, or any other fixed moment of the year, takes place a little previously to the time it' took place in the year preceding, on which account this effect is called the Precession of the Equinoxes."

"In viewing the Sun in the belt of the zodiac compared with any other fixed star at the time of the equinox, solstice, etc. he falls every year a little short of the place he occupied in the preceding year, and keeps falling short of it each year an additional equal space, till he gets entirely round the heavens to the same point again. Now as the circle of the heavens is divided into 360 parts or degrees, it is evident that it will take 72 years for the equinox to recede, or precede, for one degree, and 2160 for one sign, or thirty degrees, and 25,920 for the whole twelve signs of the zodiac, or 360 degrees."

My opinion that this majestic and stationary orrery denotes the cycle of cycles, the Platonic year, is borne out as to its correctness by reference to the Temple of Saturn, the modern Stonehenge. Here is in the very centre of the temple an area beautifully assimilating the form of an egg, and caused by the elliptical location of the seven trilithon system, the representatives of the planets. This I regard, with Smith, as denoting the celebrated Ovum Mundi of Universal Nature.

Here, within the only one in this series of temples in which it could with propriety be placed—in the inmost recess of the Temple of Saturn, whose orbit was held to include all time and space—in that inmost recess, which was typically considered as the womb of time, and surrounded by the representatives of the planets, was thus mystically placed the Mundane Egg, the germ of Universal Nature—receiving during the term of this cycle of cycles (that of the years of the world), the daily influence of the rays of the sun, until the lengthened period of incubation being passed—even that of thousands and thousands of years—the old world shall cease to exist, the egg shall burst asunder, and the new world shall spring into being! A more beautiful allegory, a more expressive emblem was never devised by the mind of man, or practically illustrated by the operation of his hand.

In the various ancient systems of the universe, some gave precedence to the Sun, and some to the Earth as the occupant of the centre. In this stationary orrery of the early heathen of our British land, the Earth occupies this distinguished station, in which it follows the Egyptian system, which was espoused by

Macrobius, Vitruvius, etc. and with this system perhaps it more accords than with any other, with the exception that it depicts the Moon as a satellite of the Sun, in which disposition it is unique.

The Earth, then, as the centre of the universe, this terrestrial diagram adequately represented by Silbury Hill, a tumulus of earth, indeed, but not a sepulchral tumulus, neither is there reason to believe that it was a religious temple. The researches of the antiquary have failed to discover any indication that it was in use for either of these purposes. The circumstance that Silbury Hill does not develop itself as a religious temple, or sepulchral tumulus, leaves it admirably at my disposal as the representative of the Earth, the centre of this curious mundane system. I therefore closely connect this vast and interesting mound with the next portion of the system, the ancient works at Abury.

If I leave this representative of the Earth, and proceed on a direct northern course, within the distance of a mile, I arrive at two stone circular temples, surrounded also by a circle of 100 stones, and the whole enclosed within a long narrow trench; and when I inquire the name of this singular place, to my surprise and gratification, I learn that it is in the present day called Abury. Here then we have most obviously the slender corruption of Abiri, signifying in the Hebrew, "Potentes," or the "Mighty Ones," evidently allusive to these two temples as the representatives of the Sun and the Moon.

Thus in the Temple of the Sun, I observe the cycle of the days of the month, the cycle of the months of the year, and a single stone in the centre to denote the entire year – Thus in the temple of the Moon, is again developed the cycle of the days of the month, the cycle of the months of the year, and the cycle of the very early tripartite division of the seasons. Am I asked, how I distinguish the temples of the Sun and Moon, which are here situate respectively north and south of each other? I will answer, by one decided characteristic.

The southern temple is that of the Sun, since, at some distance to the south-east from it, is stationed a stone, evidently a gnomon, from its exact location to take the observation of the rise of the Sun 1 over its apex at the winter solstice, in like manner as Stonehenge has a similar stone to the north-east for observing the rise of the Sun at the summer solstice. But let us move from hence, and proceed to the next connecting link of the chain. What then have we here? What, indeed, but that link which most clearly connects the temples of the Sun and Moon with the Earth, or Silbury Hill.

Behold then, these temples, bounded by their cirque of 100 stones, are located most singularly on the central portion of an immense curved serpent, whose bow is towards the south, and this serpent half surrounds the Earth, or Silbury Hill. In its full curvature it extends upwards of two miles, and its head and tail are sited respectively about half a mile due east and west from the Earth, or Silbury Hill. Here then, in this Serpent, I recognize the northern portion of the ecliptic, and I prove, by quotations from Macrobius and Euripides, that the ancients did portray the ecliptic under the similitude of a serpent. Thus then is proved the decided connection between the temples at Abury, and Silbury Hill; in other words, in this complex system of antiquities, we have the Sun, accompanied by the Moon as a satellite, traversing the northern portion of the sinuous ecliptic, which is depicted as ranging around the Earth, as the centre of the universe, denoted by Silbury Hill.

The body of the Serpent, ranging to the right and left of the temple, is formed of two avenues of stones, composed of 200 in each avenue; and the head of the serpent is composed of 40 stones, enclosing a temple of 19 stones. This temple again is astronomic, and is referable to the famous Metonic or lunar cycle, the basis of the golden number of our own calendar. In this temple it is not improbable that occasional worship was paid to the Serpent, as the vivified path of the Sun. The verification of the Serpent, as the northern portion of the ecliptic, on which is seated the Temple of the Sun, points out the identity of that temple, which is farther corroborated by the accompanying gnomon for taking the observation of the Sun at the winter solstice.

Taking my departure from the holy temple of the Sun and Moon, I proceed three miles to the south of the Earth, or centre of the universe, as represented by Silbury Hill, and there, on the brow of a promontory, impending over the Pewsey vale, I meet with the Temple of Mercury. This is a tumulus of earth, resembling the peculiar kind of long barrow. It stands, as I observed, three miles from the Earth, or Silbury Hill, and is seated on the meridional line from thence. A narrow gorge, passing from the vale to the upland down, separates this promontory, called Walker's Hill, from another at a short distance known by the name of Knap Hill. It is a remarkable circumstance, that by the Egyptians Mercury was known both by the vocative names of Thoth, and Kneph. The corrupted transition from Kneph to Knap is obvious and easy; and the name itself seems to point at the site of the near adjoining temple.

I now leave that temple and I traverse four miles to the north of the Earth, and there, still on the meridional line, I meet with a temple consisting of a single cirque of stones, with another stone at some distance, placed west from the temple. This temple is so dilapidated that the original number of stones could not be recognized, I cannot omit to mention a remarkable circumstance attendant on this temple, which is this, that its gnomon is to the west, to the peculiar point of the heavens most opportune for taking observations of this fair planet as the evening star.

Another most important observation is, that the Temple of Mercury is three miles to the south of the Earth or Silbury Hill, as in the nadir, and that the Temple of Venus is four miles to the north of the Earth, as in the zenith.

Therefore, although the temples are placed seven miles from each other, could locomotion be imparted to this stationary orrery, they would, in their orbits, pass within one mile of each other. Thus, as in the present system of astronomy, the orbits of Mercury and Venus are nearest to each other, so, singularly enough, are they here in this curious terrestrial diagram. In another instance I have to mention a similar astronomic accordance.

Leaving the extreme northern temple, and wending my way again to the south, I again pass the Temples of the Sun and Moon at Abury, and the Earth at Silbury Hill, and I again arrive at the Temple of Mercury, at Walker's Hill. Then, descending the neighboring gorge into the vale of Pewsey, I reach, at the distance of three miles, the Temple of Mars situated at Marden. Here I find an immense mound, inclosed within an area of 51 acres, and surrounded by a trench. This mound, now destroyed, was, in the opinion of Sir R. C. Hoare, decidedly a religious temple. He also says, that "its situation about midway between Stonehenge and Abury, with the vicinity of a British trackway, seems to indicate an immediate connection between those two great sanctuaries."

We trace this trackway, in detached portions, from Stonehenge to the north of the temples at Abury; whence it pursues its course to the north-east, and leaves the county of Wilts, to traverse the high downs of Berks bordering on the vale of White Horse. And we find collateral trackways, from the right and left, which converge into this great way, and were, doubtlessly, to lead the distant hordes, at the stated periods of planetary worship, to and from the various temples to which it was subservient for this purpose. To return to the Temple of Mars. This vast mound was also accompanied by a small tumulus, which most probably served the purpose of a gnomon. I here record too that Marden is derivable from the ancient British words Mars and den; the one signifying the planet Mars, and the other, a cave or residence. What have we then but the Temple of Mars?!

I take my leave of this temple, and pursue my pilgrimage on the meridional line; I ascend the southern ridge of the hill bordering on the vale, and impending over the village of Charlton, and at the distance of another three miles, I meet on the upland down with another religious temple. This I assign to the planet Jupiter, as it is sited, where his temple ought to be. Here is an enclosed area of 60 acres, bounded by a slender ditch. It bears the modem name of Casterley Camp. Since it is at the due distance from the temple of Mars on the north, and the temple of Saturn on the south, I am fully sanctioned in the appropriation of it as the Temple of Jupiter. The even location of the three successive planets, by their temples to the south of the Earth, or Silbury Hill, must not pass unobserved. The Temple of Mars is found three miles' from that of Mercury, and the temple of Jupiter again three miles from that of Mars. The temples, I repeat again, are all located in succession in a right line, and that a meridional line.

Concerning the relative distances of the various temples, representing the orbs of the planets, from the Earth as the centre of the universe. The temples of the Sun and Moon, the Temples of Mercury, Venus, Mars, Jupiter, and Saturn, are located respectively at the distances of 1, 3, 4, 6, 9, 1 6, miles from the Earth. The diameter of their respective orbits, (were the members of this vast planetarium not stationary, but capable of rotatory motion), would be therefore 2, 6, 8, 12, 18, 32 miles. The temples are all placed on a right line, due north and south. As, therefore, the orbit of Saturn in this magnificent planetarium will have a diameter of 32 miles, this is the length of that meridional line, on which the temples are located, the space within which this wonderful work has been performed.

Chapter XXXV Keltic Philosophy & Welsh Mysteries of the Pheryllt

Illuminated by Lewis Spence for the
Secret Traditions of Ancient Britain
as adapted by Bard Myrddin Cerrig

Keltic Philosophy

The mystery of Keltic thought has been the despair of generations of philosophers and aesthetes. The Kelts, that race of artists, poets and aristocrats, appear originally to have formed themselves into a nation in the region between France and Hungary, in all likelihood in the South German plain between Switzerland and Bohemia, and probably developed slowly as a nation from a race known as the "Urn-Field people," a Bronze-Age folk. In the course of generations they became welded into a nation, and as such they were known to the Greeks at least since 500 B.C., their country being spoken of by Hellenic writers as Keltica. They introduced the iron civilization of La Tene into Gaul and Britain - although the name Kelt is rather confusedly applied to mixed races of almost wholly different physical appearance, to Welsh, Irish, Scots and Bretons alike. Despite the intermixture, the ancient leaven of Kelticism triumphs and the peculiar genius of the ancient race - strong being so ancient and so perfectly molded in the matrix of its origin - shines with an almost superhuman radiance through the veils of alien character or idiosyncrasy.

What is the mystical secret of the Kelt, poet, prophet, warrior, aristocrat among aristocrats? It is the memory, the soul-recollection of a former moral and intellectual pre-eminence which he has not lost, for its gifts remain within him, but the arcanum of which he cannot discover. He is like a man with a chest of treasure who has lost the key. In this repository lie the Books of the Secrets of Britain, those most ancient and mysterious volumes containing the lore of the civilizing race of this island in its pristine days. The secrets it holds are of inestimable spiritual concern and importance to the people of a land still overwhelming Keltic. The first task in seeking to recover the secret of the Keltic Grail is, naturally, to review briefly the material that may help us to a true understanding.

The mystical and occult literature of the Brythonic Kelts of South Britain is partly derived from the collection of tales known as the "Mabinogion," which, though existing in a fourteenth century manuscript, was obviously composed at a much earlier date, as its mythological character proves. The "Welsh Triads likewise enshrine similar material, dating, probably, from the twelfth century, but embalming mystical lore greatly more ancient. The "Book of Taliesin," written, or re-written, at some time during the fifteenth century, is on the same footing. The question of the survival of Druidical knowledge in the bardic poetry of Wales is one which has been debated with unusual heat. Opponents indicated not only that the majority of their translations were inexact, but that many of the passages believed to be of a mystical or mythological nature were in reality of a Christian origin.

The truth is that when the Welsh poems in the "Book of Taliesin," the "Red Book of Hergest," the "Black Book of Caermarthen," and in the tales of the "Mabinogion" are sifted and examined properly, they still contain a residual of mystical and mythological material not to be accounted for by the methods of their critics. Moreover, there is nothing inherently impossible in the idea that the ancient British religion and mysticism lingered in Wale and other distant parts of the island for many centuries after the departure of the Romans. Those who adopt the negative position have to explain the presence of hundreds of surviving superstitions in Britain a the present time. The present writer cannot help bur subscribe as partial witness for the preservation of a very considerable body of authentic British lore of Druidic and Keltic origin.

Before examining the mystical material they contain, it will be well to summarize briefly the information we possess regarding the principle divinities of whom these tales and poems reccount the adventures. The first group to attract our attention, is that of Llyr, as alluded to in the "Mabinogion." Llyr is god of the sea, and the histories of his sons Bran and Manawydden, his daughter Branwen, and the half-brothers Nissyen and Evanissyen are recounted in the stories of Branwen and Manawydden. These allude to the invasion of Ireland, to whose king Branwen had been married. Manawydden is Lord of Elysium, and a craftsman and agriculturist. Bran is chiefly famous as the possessor of a magical head which, after death, prophesied and protected the island of Britain from invasion. He presided over poetry and bardic music, and was of titan breed. He seems to have been associated with the world of the hereafter, or rather the underworld of fertility, as is his sister Branwen, as her possession of a magic cauldron reveals.

The Children of Don, another Brythonic group, are Gwydion, Gilvaethwy, Amaethon, Govannon, and Arianrhod, with her sons Dylan and Llew. They resemble the Irish Tuatha De Dannan, and their adventures are described in the "Mabinogi" of Math, which recounts the passion of Gilvaethwy for Math's handmaiden Goewin, and the manner in which Gwydion procures the magical swine of Pryderi, which had been gifted him by Arawn, Lord of Annwn. Math is obviously a territorial and local god of Gwynedd in Wales, a magician par excellence, a "god of Druidism." Gwydion is the patron of poetry, divination and prophecy, the ideal bard, as well as a philosopher and culture-bringer. Amaethon is a husbandman, and Govannon a "smith" or artificer, a species of Keltic Vulcan. Arianrhod, or "Silver Wheel," represented the constellation Corona Borealis, but is also associated with the earth's fertility.

Another group found in the "Mabinogion" is that of Pwyll, Prince of Dyved, his wife Rhuannon, and their son Pryderi. Pwyll changes places for a year with Arawn, King of Annwn, and makes war on his rival Havgan. Still another group is that of

Beli and his sons Llud, Caswallawn, and Llevelys (see Chapter XI in this Pheryllt anthology).

Mysteries of the Pheryllt

In the "Book of Taliesin" we encounter a group still more important from the mystical point of view, that of Keridwen, her hideous son Avagddu, his sister Creirwy, and his brother Morvran. So that Avagddu, the ugly, may be compensated by the possession of supernatural knowledge, Keridwen prepares a cauldron of inspiration which must be brewed for a year, and which produce three drops of divine fluid. She sets a servant, Gwion, to watch it, and the three drops falling on his finger, he conveys it to his mouth and becomes inspired. Keridwen, in her anger, pursues him, and as he assumes various forms, a hare, a fish, and a grain of wheat, in his flight, she takes on the shape of a greyhound, an otter, and at last a hen, in which she swallows the grain, later bearing Gwion as a child, whom she abandons to the sea in a coracle. The child she abandons to the waves becomes, later, Taliesin, the magical bard.

The Druidic bards who lived and sang under the Welsh princes unanimously represent Keridwen as presiding over the hidden mysteries of their ancient cult. Cynddelw, who flourished in the twelfth century, sings: "How mysterious were the ways of the songs of Keridwen! How necessary to understand them in their true sense!" Llywarch ap Llywelyn, wrote between 1160 and 1220, asks for "inspiration as if it were from the Cauldron of Keridwen," and says that he will address his lord "with the dowry of Keridwen, the Ruler of Bardism." It was essential for those bards who aspired to the Chair of Song to have tasted the waters of inspiration from her cauldron, to have been initiated into her mysteries. That the myth of Keridwen is all-important in our quest may be gathered from a passage from the Book of Taliesin:

"Then Keridwen determined, agreeably to the mystery of the Books of Pheryllt, to prepare for her son a cauldron of water of inspiration and knowledge... In the meantime, Keridwen, with due attention to the Books of Astronomy, and to the hours of the planets, employed herself daily in collecting plants of every species, which preserved any rare virtues... She stationed Gwion the Little, the son of Gwreany the Herald of Llanvair, in Powys, the land of rest, to superintend the preparation of the cauldron."

The Pheryllt, according to whose ritual she proceeded, are frequently mentioned by the bards of Wales, and an old chronicle, quoted by Dr. Thomas Williams, states that the Pheryllt had a college at Oxford prior to the foundation of that University. These Pheryllt appear to have been a section of the Druidic brotherhood, teachers and scientists, skilled in all that required the agency of fire, hence the name has frequently been translated "alchemists" or "metallurgists." Indeed, chemistry and metallurgy are known as "*Celvyddydan Pheryllt,*" or "the arts of the Pheryllt," who would seem to have had as their headquarters the city of Emrys in the district of Snowdon, famous for its magical associations, the city of the dragons of Beli.

Somewhere in the district of Snowdon lie the remains of this ancient British city of Emrys, or "the ambrosial city," also known in Welsh tradition as the city of Dinas Affaraon, or "the higher powers." To this mysterious community the poems of the Welsh bards allude so frequently as to place its actual existence beyond all question. Not only is it mentioned in the "Black Book of Caermarthen" and other Cymric manuscripts as the centre of mystical rites, but it is alluded to by one of Camden's commentators as occupying the summit of "the panting cliff" on Snowdon itself. Davies says that it stood "upon the road from the promontory of Lleyn to that part of the coast which is opposite Mona" (Anglesey), and Gibson, in his work on Camden, identifies it with the ruins of an exceedingly strong fortification encompassed by a triple wall on an eminence called Broich y Ddinas, "the ridge of the city," which forms part of the summit of Penmaen, seated on the top of one of the highest mountains of that part of Snowdon which lie toward the sea.

In Emrys were concealed in the time of Bile the solar deity, and in the time of Prydain the son of Aedd the Great, the dragons which are so frequently referred to as harnessed to the car of Keridwen, so it appears not improbable that the city was in some manner associated with her mysteries. Davies believed that the Pheryllt were priests of those mysteries in the ambrosial city of Emrys.

Now what, precisely, is the significance of the goddess Keridwen and her mystical cauldron? Mythically speaking, the vessel in question was designed for the preparation of a brew which induced inspiration and awoke the prophetic and bardic faculties. The myth is an allegory of initiation, of which the tasting of the water was an essential rite.

In the Chair of Taliesin ("Book of Taliesin") a number of ingredients are enumerated which went to compose the mystical elixir brewed in the Cauldron of Keridwen, the Pair Pumwydd, the "Cauldron of the Five Trees," so-called in allusion to the five particular trees or plants requisite to the preparation. Certain Cymric legends represent this Pair as a bath, the water of which conferred immortality, but deprived the bather of utterance - an allusion, perhaps, to the oath of secrecy administered prior to initiation. Elsewhere, Taliesin alludes to it as "the Cauldron of the Lord of the Deep," and states that it will not boil the food of him who is not bound by his oath.

The Welsh Bards made use in their initiatory rites of a decoction of plants or herbs which they believed could bestow certain powers of inspiration, eloquence, prophecy, and song upon those who partook of it. The ingredients of Keridwen's cauldron, which, according to Taliesin, contained berries, the foam of the ocean, cresses, wort and vervain which had grown high and kept apart from the influence of the moon. The residue of the water in the cauldron of Keridwen was, as we have seen, poisonous and accursed, that is, it was symbolically supposed to contain the sins and pollutions of the novitiates, and was cast out.

Chapter XXXVI Naddred - Mysteries of the Druid's Gem

(or Adder's Egg)

Based on the collected writings

researched by Dudley Wright

and additional Celtic Researches

adapted by Myrddin Cerrig

It is said that every Druid wore around his neck, encased in gold, what was known as the anguinum, or Druid's Egg. Pliny, in his "Natural History," gives the following account of it:

"There is a kind of egg held in high esteem by the Druids, unnoticed by the Greek writers. It is called the Serpents' Egg; and, in order to produce it, an immense number of serpents, twisted together in summer, are rolled up in an artificial folding by the saliva of their mouths and the slime of their bodies. The Druids say that this egg is tossed on high with hissings and that it must be intercepted in a cloak before it reaches the ground. The person who seizes it flies on horseback, for the serpents pursue him till they are stopped by the intervention of some river. The proof of this egg is, that, though bound in gold, it will swim against the stream. And, as the magi are very artful and cunning in concealing their frauds, they pretend that this egg can only be obtained at a certain time of the moon, as if this operation of the serpents could be rendered congruous to human determination. I have indeed seen that egg of the size of an ordinary round apple, worn by the Druids in a checkered cover resembling the enormous calculi in the arms of a polypus. Its virtue is highly extolled for gaining lawsuits and procuring access to kings; and it is worn with so great ostentation that I knew a Roman knight by birth, a Vocentian, who was slain by the Emperor Claudius for no cause whatever except wearing one of these eggs on his breast during the dependence of a lawsuit."

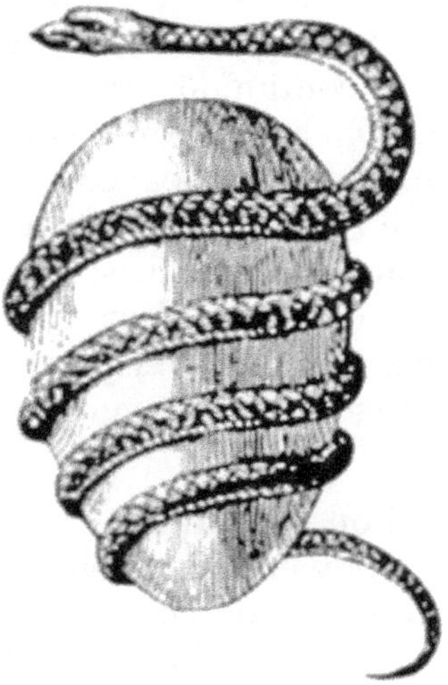

It is not improbable that this egg and the alleged marvelous manner of its production had connection with some primary esoteric dogma which Pliny never fathomed. Hughes, in "Hora Britannica," says that in the writings of the ancient Bards several allusions to what he terms "the mummery" are to be found, one of which he quotes as follows:

"Lively was the aspect of him, who, in his prowess, had snatched over the ford that involved a ball which casts its rays to a distance; the splendid product of the adder, shot forth by serpents."

The Druids themselves were called Nadredd, or snakes [adders], by the Welsh Bards; and the whole of the tale mentioned by Pliny has a mystical reference to the difficulty of attaining Druidical secrets and the danger of disclosing them. There is, of course, no doubt that this famous object of Druidic superstition were manufactured. The art of making these trinkets being known only to the Druids, they availed themselves of the credulity of the common people, to magnify the virtues of them and to give them a mysterious import.

The serpent was a sacred reptile among the Druids. They supposed its spiral coils to represent the eternal existence of the Almighty. Camden tells us that in many parts of Wales and throughout all Scotland and Cornwall it is an opinion held by the people that about Midsummer Eve the snakes meet in company and that by joining heads together and hissing, a kind of bubble is formed, which, by continually being blown upon, passes through the body, when it immediately consolidates and resembles a glass ring, which, whoever finds, shall prosper in all his undertakings. The rings thus generated are called Gleiniau Nadroedd, or snake stones. Wirt Sikes, in "British Goblins," says that the snake stone is a striking Welsh tradition associated with Midsummer Eve, and there is a Welsh saying describing people who lay their heads together in conversation that the talkers are "blowing the gem."

Any water poured on the serpents' eggs is said to have had wonderful life-giving power and become able to produce life. It has also been asserted that the Druids were wont to place live serpents at the foot of the altar during the time of ceremony.

In Scotland, the Druid's Egg was known as an Adder Stone, and it was in great reputation for the foretelling of events, the working of miracles, the curing of disease, and the gaining of law suits. In the Scottish Museum there is a bead of red glass, spotted with white; another of dark brown glass, spotted with yellow; others of pale green and blue glass, plain and ribbed; and two of curiously figured patterns, wrought with various colours interwoven in their surface. It is suggested in several sources that glass beads were also "earned" by apprentices as symbols of achievement when progressing through various levels. These were often hung on a cord as a necklace symbolizing cumulative mastery or "true authority."

These glass baubles were badges and passports that the bearers were initiated, and whoever purloined or carried one without authorization was pursued by the deadly vengeance of the Brotherhood. The amulet was variously shaped. Sometimes it was like a round bead of glass; at others, like a crescent with a glass boat; sometimes it was a glass circle, and sometimes it resembled a glass house. In every case it was regarded as a powerful talisman. Camden has thus described these magical appendages:

"These genuine anguinae are small glass amulets, commonly as wide as our finger rings, but much thicker; of a green color usually, though some of them are blue, and others curiously waved with blue, red, and white."

Specimens have frequently been found in the Isle of Anglesea. Smaller consecrated beads—white for Druids, blue for Bards, and green for Ovates—were carried by the individuals and interred with them at death. A number of these beads were found in an excavation made at Quarrington in 1828. Taliesin, speaking of a warrior's amulet, says: "Beautiful is the circle with its enriched border." The anguinum was not known in Ireland, the reason given by Llhwyd, the antiquarian, being:

"The Druid doctrine about the Glain Neidr obtains very much throughout all Scotland, as well lowlands as highlands; but there is not a word of it in this kingdom (Ireland), where, as there are no snakes, they could not propagate it. Besides snake-stones, the highlanders have their small snail stones, paddock stones, etc., to all which they attribute their special virtues and wear them as amulets."

In another letter, referring to the same subject, he says:

"The Cornish retain a variety of charms, and have still towards the Land's End the amulet of Mael Magal and Gelin Nedir, which latter they call a Milpreu, or Melpreu, and have a charm for the snake to make it, when they have found one asleep and struck a hazel wand in the centre of her spires."

It is supposed that the Welsh Bardic title of Nadredd is to be traced to the belief in transmigration. The serpent, which sheds its skin annually and appears to return to a second youth, may have been regarded by them, as well as by other people of that time, as a symbol of renovation, and this renovation or reincarnation was the great doctrine set forth by the Arkite mysteries and by the symbolical egg. Mason, in Caractacus, has described the ceremony of securing the anguinum in the following words :

"The potent adder stone"

Gendered before the autumnal moon:
When in undulating twine
The foaming snakes prolific join;
When they hiss and when they bear
Their wondrous egg aloof in air,
Thence, before to earth it fall
The Druid, in his hallowed pall.
Receives the prize.
And instant flies,
Followed by the envenomed brood
Till he cross the crystal flood."

Edward Davies illuminates the Serpents Egg in his "Mythology and Rites of British Druids," saying:

"The celebrated efficacy Ovum Anguinum, or Serpent's Egg, of the Celtic priesthood may be easily conceived. The Druids, who were the supreme judges in all litigated causes, may be supposed to have lent a favorable ear to those who produced this credential of their order; and even kings, who stood in awe of their tribunal, would seldom close their gates against them. The Druids, therefore, were the serpents which assembled, at a stated time in the summer, to prepare these emblems of Creirwy - tokens or symbols of the spiritual [sacred] egg which are sacred to Keridwen - and to conceal among them certain discriminative tokens, which probably were kept as a profound secret from the persons who received them." He goes on to explain how Pliny saw one of these eggs, but did not investigate them proper for his writings, or he would have discovered, "that it contained either a lunette of glass, or small ring of the same material; such as those which the Welsh call Gleiniau Nadredd. These were certainly insignia of a very sacred character amongst our ancestors; and they seem to have been intimately connected with the Anguinum."

Many scholars today are of the mind that the Druid's Gem "no larger than an apple" was manufactured from glass - a substance linking the item to both the Motherhood of Avalon, residing on the 'Isle of Apples' (alternatively, the 'Isle of Glas' or "Glastonbury") and the Welsh alchemical Druid fire-workers known in ancient times as the "Pheryllt." It has been further suggested by certain scholars, notably Lady Flavia Anderson in

"The Ancient Secret," that the original serpent's eggs were spheres of clear crystal used to light the Druidic Beltaine "need-fires" via focused sunlight. In addition to friction and lightning, the third type of sacred "coelcerths" [needfires] were caused by a concentration of sunlight through a magnifying crystal, as Douglas Monroe describes: -

"Such crystals varied in color, and were often times embedded in the blades of sacred implements like swords or sickles. The kind most coveted by the Druids, was a peculiar variety called Dragon Stone, (Red Ruby, perhaps Rose Quartz or Garnet), said to have been mined from the slopes of Snowdonia."

In more recent New Age revival traditions, such as those derived from Greer's "Celtic Golden Dawn," the Serpent's Egg as a 'working tool' is "a hollow spherical or egg-shaped container of glass or pottery, no bigger than a hen's egg, that is worn around the neck on a ribbon or cord. It has an opening that is carefully sealed once it is filled. A properly made serpent's egg contains the prepared alchemical salts of vervain, and of [four] additional initiation herbs... It is therefore a unique emblem of your own initiations and serves as a focus and a fount for the magical influences of the whole Druidical tradition. Once made and consecrated, it should be worn whenever you perform magical working, for it will increase in strength with each use."

Herbal Alchemy is at the heart of the Pheryllt tradition; it is the primary element of magic exposed by lore of Ceridwen's Cauldron and it is clear that Vervain, Mistletoe and Oak are among the most sacred of the herbs used by Druids (and ultimately her potion), for which we can only deduce ourselves, since the ingredients are withheld by the author in the "Book of Taliesin." Traditional lore of Druidical herbalism also tend to focus on the Holly and Ivy - so, it is possible that a concentrated reduction of these five elements might be best used to fill or imbue the modern conception of the "Serpent's Egg." However, In the "Chair of Taliesin" verse, berries, ocean foam, water-cresses, wort and vervain are listed, leading some to believe these to be the ingredients. In either case, there is sufficient lore provided within this chapter to actualize multiple versions of crystal gems, sacred eggs and/or stone amulets for the initiate.

Chapter XXVII
The Great Tree Rite

Excerpted from "The Druid Compleat"

as written by Myrddin Cerrig

Bard of the Twelfth Chair

The Great Tree Rite

Lunar orientation of the Great Tree Rite compliments solar orientation of the Druids sacramental, the Druidic Liturgy previously given in Chapter VII of this anthology. Solar observances (like Grove Festivals) are aligned to the Druids sacramental, whereas the lunar cycle, the observation of full and new moons, best applies to the Great Tree Rite. Ritual transcripts from the Druids Sacramental are aligned to day-time ceremonies, whereas lunar celebrations are generally held at night. This present text is elementally aligned and also gives instructions for a leader. As with the Druids Sacramental, the Great Tree Rite can be adapted for either group or solitary practice and either solar or lunar observations.

Note: The performance of the Great Tree Rite begins with the first eleven steps given in the Druids Sacramental ritual formula. The intentions of the rite is proclaimed and then continues with the following text.

Leader: We are here to give witness to the unity and strength of the magick circle, this mandala of love most holy. We, the Druids, the Children of Light, are at one with thee, O Sacred Tree. You, who stands as an eternal symbol of the Circle of Light and Life. You, who represent our eternal link with the ever-present Source. We honor and imitate you as the perfect living specimen of the Source of All Being and Creation. We watch you as you progress through the sacred Earth Year.

North: The beginnings, middles, and ends of the sacred Earth Year.

East: The balance and equinox forces of the sacred Earth Year.

South: Tonight (today) we coven together, man and tree, acknowledging the Sacred Grove.

West: We celebrate the strength, love, and unity of the Sacred Grove, and in that celebration we honor the central icon of its existence: The Great Tree.

East: From the Eastern Winds we are granted a season of growth, as the sun emerges in the spring.

South: From the Southern Flame we are granted a season of fullness, as the sun warms the summer.

West: From the Western Waves we are granted a season of transformation with the shifting tides of autumn.

North: From the Firmness of Northern Ground we are granted a season of stability, self-reflection, and stillness, as the Earth hibernates and is renewed through winter.

Leader: The calendrical month ___, the Oghamic month of the ___ tree in the ancient Druid's calender.

(Trace the Oghamic rune in the air.)

Leader: May the blessing of the ___ tree, and the corresponding energies of ___ be projected forth into our auric light bodies.

Use the following Oghamic Keys to fill in the appropriate information above.

January: Alder Tree, Fearn, protection and power.

February: Willow Tree, Saille, healing and enchantment.

March: Ash Tree, Nuin, protection and peace.

April: Hawthorn Tree, Huatha, love and purity.

May: Oak Tree, Duir, strength and leadership.

June: Holly, Tinne, purification and balance.

July: Hazel Tree, Coll, intuition and creativity.

August: Vine, Muin, meditation and prophecy.

September: Ivy, Gort, protection and growth.

October: Reed, Ngetal, intense energy and direct action.

13th Month*: Elder Tree, Ruis, completion and reflection.

November: Birth Tree, Beith, fertility and growth.

December: Rowan Tree, Luis, strength and insight.

*The 13th month represents the blue moon, or more traditionally, October 29-November 1 - or another observation of a New Year period that catches up the lunar and solar calendar synchronization.

East: May the Sacred Grove and the Great Tree grant us the strength of the ancient Druids.

South: We hereby swear (reaffirm) our Guardianship of Gaea, the Sacred Grove, the Great Tree, and all life in Creation.

West: May the gentle rains bless all of Creation, nurturing and giving life, forever and always.

Leader: The entangled roots of the Great Tree shall live deep within our being, offering nourishment and stability to all of its faithful guardians.

North: An in between the roots and branches, we stand as the Guardians, the Keepers of the Earth, we who live in imitation of Oak Trees.

East: Our branches reach into the same sky proving that ascension is the purpose and goal of all life.

South: Great Universal Spirit, beings inhabiting this Sacred Tree, we stand here as your worthy guardians, and Keepers of the Earth and her mysteries.

West: May we grow to become our full potential from the seedlings we now are. May seeds plant in the world, bloom and flourish, spreading the true beauty and love of the Source of All, shared by all those receptive.

Leader: (Knocks three times lightly on the trunk, intoning the name of the tree, perhaps in Celtic, with each knock.) O Great Tree, you are hereby awakened by the Druids of the ancient and ineffable knowledge.

North: May the ground that covers the roots, forever and always be blessed with all that is good and holy. May all of creation grow as the trees in the forest, each beautiful in their own uniqueness, yet still sharing the same Earth in which too spread roots and call home.

Leader: We are united in our strengths, our faith, our love, and our trust. Ours in the bond that must endure all other bonds. The Truth Against the World.

All: The Truth Against The World.

Leader: Through True Knowledge, Power.

All: Through True Knowledge, Power.

Chapter XXXVIII
Preiddeu Annwn - The Spoils of Annwn

Selections from The Book of Taliesin

Introduced by Myrddin Cerrig

with paraphrased notes and comments and

additional researches by Lewis Spence

describing Arcane Druid Tradition

Following the "*Cad Goddeu*" ("Battle of the Trees") and "*Hanes Taliesen*" ("Ceridwen's Cauldron" and "History of Taliesin"), the third most interesting and instructive pieces of Druidism from the "Book of Taliesin" is entitled "*Preiddeu Annwn,*" usually translated as "The Spoils of Annwn" (although it also appears as "The Victims of the Deep").

Among both scholars and modern druids, "The Spoils of Annwn" is generally considered to overflow with mythology and Druidic lore, although the meaning of such has eluded many revival scholars as 'incomprehensible'. In notes for the "Mabinogion" translated by Lady Charlotte Guest, she calls it "a mystical poem which appears to be full of allusions to traditions now no longer intelligible."

"The Spoils of Annwn" is indicative of an Otherworld journey - meaning an inner journey of the Self. The main setting is "Caer Sidi" (or "Siddi") meaning the mounds or hills for which the Sidhe faerie folk are named for - believing they resided in these hills and/or used them to access the Otherworld (also called the Spirit World or Faerie Realm). "Caer Sidi" is given a new synonym in each of the seven stanzas - and this is our clue into the elusive meaning of the work. The seven "castle-keeps" or "forts" confronted in this Otherworld quest of the Self are reminiscent to the universal sevenfold system found in gatework or pathworking of other ancient traditions, of which an example is most clear in Babylon, where the Self's sevenfold journey of Otherworld initiation requires confronting (or crossing) seven aspects that have been defined throughout the lore of ancient mystics as: veils, levels, layers, light-centres, rays, tones, chakras, colors, planetary frequencies - the seven facets that unify the celestial mysteries on earth.

Following the sequence of the "Book of Taliesin," after the account of "Ceridwen's Cauldron" and the chronicle of Taliesin with the court-bards and Elphin's release from prison - the poet introduces us to one Gwair ap Geirion, lamenting that he cannot escape from Caer Sidi. The background story of Gwair is not given and may be immaterial. The purpose of the poet is clearly to define seven perceived levels or labyrinthine sections of "Annwn" - marking the progression (or dissolution) of the Self on its Otherworld (or "Underworld") journey. The allegorical pursuit of the Otherworld "cauldron" are symbolically identical to the "Grail" quests of Arthur. Few have worked out this cabala in modern practices as it seems too metaphysical for some of the antiquarians to deduce other than literally - which likely led to their difficulties in comprehending the meaning of this poem.

Robert Graves associates "Caer Sidi" with the Castle of Arianrhod (the Welsh Ariadne) and identifies the synonyms for it appearing in the prose as Caer Rigor ('the royal castle') with a pun maybe on the Latin rigor mortis; Caer Colur (the gloomy castle); Caer Pedryvan (four-cornered castle), four times revolving; Caer Vediwid (the castle of the perfect ones); Caer Ochren (the castle of the shelving side), i.e. entered from the side of a slope; Caer Vandwy (the castle on high). The Anglesey Druid Order translates the names thusly: Caer Siddi (the Fort of Necessity or the Fort of the Mound); Caer Feddwit (the Fort of Mead Intoxication); Caer Rigor (the Fort of Hardness and Rigidity); Caer Wydr (the Fort of Glass); Caer Goludd (the Fort of [Guts and] Impediment); Caer Vandwy (the Fort of High Mystery); Caer Ochren (the Fort of Edges); and the additional Caer Pedryfan - the Four-Walled Enclosure - to which no journey is made, for "it is simultaneously interpreted as the island of Britain and as the boundary of Annwn; it is that which contains the experience."

The Spoils of Annwn

(Version One)

1.

Praise to the Lord, Supreme Ruler of the Heavens,
Who has extended his dominion to the shores of the world.
Complete was the prison of Gwair in Caer Sidi;
Through the permission [spite] of Pwyll and Pryderi,
No one before him went to it.
A heavy blue chain firmly held the youth;
And for the spoils of Annwn gloomily he sings,
And till doom shall continue his lay.
Thrice the fullness of Prydwen, we went into it.
Except seven, none returned from Caer Sidi.

2.

Am I not a candidate for fame, to be heard in the song,
In Caer Pedryvan four times revolving?
The first word of from the cauldron, when was it spoken?
By the breath of nine damsels [it is] gently warmed.
Is it not the cauldron of the Chief of Annwn which is social [in its fashion]
With a ridge round its edge of pearls,
It will not boil the food of a coward nor of one excommunicated.
A sword bright flashing to him will be brought,
And left in the land of Llyminawg.
And before the door [portals] of hell [the cold place] a lantern [horns of light] is burning.
And when we went with Arthur in his splendid labors,
Except seven, none returned from Caer Vendiwid.

3.

Am I not a candidate for fame, to be heard in [the] song?
In Caer Pedryfan [the four-cornered enclosure], the island of Pybyrdor [the strong door],
Twilight and darkness [black of night] meet together.
Bright wine was their drink [beverage] in their assembly [of their host].
Thrice the burden [fullness] of Prydwen, we went on the sea.
Except seven, none returned from Caer Rigor.

4.

I will not allow great merit [praise] to the directors [lords] of learning [literature].
Beyond Caer Wydr they have not beheld the prowess of Arthur.
Three score hundred men were placed [stood] upon the wall;
It was difficult to converse with the sentinel.
Thrice the fullness of Prydwen, we went with Arthur.
Except seven, none returned from Caer Golur [Caer Colur].

5.

I will not allow merit [praise] to a multitude trailing on the circuit [men with trailing shields];
They know not on what day, or who caused it,
Not what hour in the splendid day Cwy was born,
Nor who prevented him from going to the vales [dales] of Deowy.
They know not the brindled ox, with this thick head-band,
And seven score knobs in his collar.
And when we went with Arthur of mournful memory,
Except seven, none returned from Caer Vandwy.

6.

I will not allow merit [praise] to the multitude with their weak effusions [drooping courage];
They know not what day the head [chief] was made [arose],
Nor what hour in the fine [splendid] day the owner was born.
What animal they guard [keep] with a silver head.
When we went with Arthur of mournful contention,
Except seven, none returned from Caer Ochren.

The Spoils of Annwn

(Hughes Version)

1.

I praise the Lord, sovereign of the kingly realm
Who extends his leadership across the entire world.
In order was the prison of Gweir in Caer Siddi
Through the course of the tale of Pwyll and Pryderi
None before him went into it.
By the heavy blue-grey chain restraining the loyal lad

And before the spoils of Annwn, bitterly he sang
And until the judgment day our Bardic invocation shall persist.
Three full loads of Prydwen, we went into it;
Except seven, none came back from Caer Siddi.

2.

I am splendid in praise, my song is heard
In Caer Pedryfan fully revolving.
My first words were spoken concerning the cauldron
Which is kindled by the breath of nine maidens.
The cauldron of the head of Annwn; what is its form?
With a dark ridge and pearls around its edge,
It will not boil the food of a coward; it is not destined to do so.
The flashing sword of Lleawg was thrust into it,
And in the hand of Lleminawg it was left.
And before the door of hell lanterns burned,
And when we went with Arthur, resplendent toil,
Except for seven, none came back from Caer Feddwit.

3.

I am splendid in praise, my song greatly heard
In Caer Pedryfan, island of the radiant door,
Fresh water and jet are mixed
Sparkling wine the spirit laid before their host.
Three full loads of Prydwen, we went by sea,
Except for seven, none returned from Caer Rigor.

4.

Those little men of the Lord's scriptures are undeserving of me.
Beyond the walls of Caer Wydr, none saw Arthur's valor.
Six thousand men stood upon its turrets,
It was difficult to discourse with their watchman.
Three full loads of Prydwen, we went with Arthur.
Except for seven, none returned from Caer Goludd.

5.

These pathetic men who trail their shields are undeserving of me.
They know not who was created on what day,
When at midday the god was born,
He who made the one who did not go to the meadows of Defwy;

They do not know the brindled ox and his stout collar,
Seven score links in its fastening,
And when we went with Arthur, a sad journey;
Except for seven, none returned from Caer Vandwy.

6.

These pathetic men with no go in them are undeserving of me.
They know not on what day the lord was created,
What hour of the day the ruler was born,
What beast is it they guard with its silver head.
When we went with Arthur, a sorrowful conflict;
Except for seven, none returned from Caer Ochren.

The Arcane Tradition

If the poem be analyzed, the first verse will be found to refer to the Underworld region of Annwn. "The prison of Gwair in Caer Sidi" may be explained as follows: Gwair ap Geircin had attemped a journey, or essayed the adeptship, had failed, and had been imprisoned in Caer Sidi, which sometimes means the Zodiac, sometimes Annwn itself. He was known as "one of the three supreme prisoners of the isle of Britain," and was held in bondage by Pwyll, Prince of Annwn and Pryderi, his son. The intention of Arthur and his company was probably to rescue him or complete his initiation, and for that purpose thee times a greater number of initiates than could be contained by Arthur's ship Pridwen essayed the task. Annwn is described in the Mabinogion of Pwyll as a palatial dwelling replete with every luxury rather than a darksome abyss, thus showing that the idea of it had become conventionalized.

The second verse alludes to the mystic cauldron of Keridwen, warmed by the breath of the nine damsels, the cauldron of inspiration and the "island of the strong door" mentioned in the fourth verse has reference to some such mysterious island as Sena, where dwelt the nine damsels or Druidesses. The Caer Wydr spoken of in the fifth verse was Arthur's vessel of glass contructed for the special purpose of the exploration of Annwn, and the bard says that he "will not have merit with the multitude in relating the hero's deeds, because they could not see his prowess after he had entered Caer Wydr, or the 'place' or vessel of glass." Merlin made a similar voyage in a similar ship, as did

Alexander the Great, and indeed the latter story is mentioned by Taliesin. The allusion to "the brindled ox with his headband" is obviously to the sacred beast which figured in all such mysteries, the Osirian and the Mithraic as well as the British, the White Bull of the Sun. The place-names which conclude most of the stanzas appear to have reference to various regions in Annwn.

Taken as a whole, this mysterious poem seems to refer to a definite attempt on the part of the initiates of some mystical society to explore the underworld plane of Annwn. Attempts have been made to prove that it really has reference to an expedition of Arthur to Caldedonia, which was euphemistically known as Annwn or Hades, probably by virtue of the old tradition mentioned by Procopius which alluded to the fatal conditions prevailing north of the Roman Wall. But the mystical allusions in the poem readily dispose of such a hypothesis. Elsewhere, Taliesin sings:

> Perfect is my chair in Caer Sidi:
> Plague and age hurt him not who's in it–
> They know, Manawydan and Pryderi.
> Three organs round a fire sing before it,
> And about its points are ocean's streams
> And the abundant well above it–
> Sweeter than white wine the drink in it.

It seems clear that the famous Cauldron tradition served as a prototype of the far more famous Grail. We see, therefore, that the visit to Annwn, the "Astral Plane," as we might call it, was for the purpose of seizing its spoils, its cauldron of mystical wisdom or inspiration. It is certain that a particular ritual must be gone through, a severe initiation, before its portals could be gained, and there was a risk of failure and "imprisonment," even of destruction. The prize was the Grail or cauldron of prophecy, which renewed life and gave health to the soul. That the 'cultus' which guarded the secret was one of select initiates is obvious from the allusion to the multitude who "know not" the ritual of its mysteries.

But what of Arthur's connection with this myth or initiation and of the parallels to the Harrying of Hades? It is plain that he, like Osiris, is the god of a mystical cult who must periodically take a journey through the underworld, not only for the purpose of subduing its evil inhabitants, but of learning their secrets and passwords in order that the souls of the just, the perfected initiates, will be enabled to journey through that plane unharmed. This, Osiris did. [And we can see clear evidence of the same in the Babylonian accounts of the Gates of the Underworld and the Descent epics.] By his agency, through the spells and passwords given in his books, the dead Osirian, the man of his cult, is franked safely through the gloomy region of Amenti, the Egyptian Annwn, to the golden realm of the divinity, so that he may life forever. Archetypes of these myths seem to have a common source. And that Arthur was the god of a mystical Druidic cult, one of whose rites was associated with a real or allegorical passage through a lower plane from which mysterious secrets and treasures might be earned, seems certain enough.

Chapter XXXIX
The Book of Taliesin: A Celtic Miscellany

Selections attributed to Taliesin

in Four Ancient Books of Wales

and in Myvyrian Archaeology

The First Address of Taliesin

A primitive and ingenious address, when thoroughly elucidated.

Which was first, is it darkness, is it light?
Or Adam, when he existed, on what day was he created
Or under the earth's surface, what the foundation?
He who is a legionary will receive no instruction
At once justified in many things,
Will lose the heavenly country, the community of priests.
In the morning no one comes
If they sing of three spheres.
Angles and Gallwydel,
Let them make their war.
Whence come night and day?
Whence will the eagle become gray?
Whence is it that night is dark?
Whence is it that the linnet is green
The ebullition of the sea,
How is it not seen.
There are three fountains
In the mountain of roses,
There is a Caer of defence
Under the ocean's wave
Illusive greeter,
What is the porter's name?

Who was confesso
To the gracious Son of Mary?
What was the most beneficial measure
Which Adam accomplished?
Who will measure Uffern [Hell, cold place]
How thick its veil?
How wide its mouth?
What the size of its stones?
Or the tops of its whirling trees?
Who bends them so crooked?
Or what fumes may be
About their stems?
Is it Lleu and Gwydyon
That perform their arts?
Or do they know books
When they do?
Whence come night and flood?
How they disappear?
Whither flies night from day;
And how is it not seen?
Pater noster ambulo
Gentis tonans in adjuvando
Sibilem signum
Rogantes fortium.
Excellent in every way around the glens
The two skilful ones make inquiries
About Caer Oerindan Oerindydd
For the draught-horses of pector David.
They have enjoyment - they move about -
May they find me greatly expanding.
The Cymry will be lamenting
While their souls will be tried
Before a horde of ravagers.
The Cymry, chief wicked ones,
On account of the loss of holy wafers.
There will long be crying and wailing,And gore will be conspicuous.
There came by sea
The wood-steeds of the strand.
The Angles in council

Shall see signs of
Exultation over Saxons.
The praises of the rulers
Will be celebrated in Sion [Zion].
Let the chief builders be
Against the fierce Ffichti [Picts],
The Morini Brython.
Their fate has been predicted;
And the reaping of heroes
About the river Severn.
The stealing is disguised of Ken and Masswy
Ffls amala, ffur, ffir, sel,
Thou wilt discern the Trinity beyond my age
I implore the Creator, hai
huai, that the Gentile may vanish
From the Gospel Equally worthy
With the retinue of the wall
Cornu ameni dur.
I have been with skilful men,
With Matheu and Govannon,
With Eunydd and Elestron,
In company with Achwyson,
For a year in Caer Gofannon.
I am old. I am young. I am Gwion,
I am universal, I am possessed of penetrating wit.
Thou wilt remember thy old Brython I
and the Gwyddyl [Irish], kiln distillers,
Intoxicating the drunkards.
I am a bard; I will not disclose secrets to slaves;
I am a guide: I am expert in contests.
If he would sow, he would plough; he would plough, he would not reap.
If a brother among brothers,Didactic Bards with swelling breasts will arise
Who will meet around mead-vessels,
And sing wrong poetryAnd seek rewards that will not be,
Without law, without regulation, without gifts.
And afterward will become angry.
There will be commotions and turbulent times,
Seek no peace-it will not accrue to thee.

The Ruler of Heaven knows thy prayer.
From his ardent wrath thy praise has propitiated him
The Sovereign King of Glory addresses me with wisdom
Hast thou seen the dominus fortis?
Knowest thou the profound prediction domini?To the advantage of Uffern
Hic nemo in por progenie
He has liberated its tumultuous multitude.
Dominus virtutum [Virtuous Lord]
Has gathered together those that were in slavery,
And before I existed, He had perceived me.
May I be ardently devoted to God!
And before I desire the end of existence,
And before the broken foam shall come upon my lips,
And before I become connected with wooden boards,
May there be festivals to my soul!
Book-learning scarcely tells me
Of severe afflictions after death-bed;
And such as have heard my bardic books
They shall obtain the region of heaven, the best of all abodes.
The Fold of the Bards
Meditating were my thoughts
On the vain poetry of the bards of Brython.
Making the best of themselves in the chief convention.
Enough, the care of the smith's sledge-hammer.
I am in want of a stick, straitened in song,
The fold of the bards, who knows it not?
Fifteen thousand over it
Adjusting it
I am a harmonious one; I am a clear singer.
I am steel; I am a druid.
I am an artificer; I am a scientific one.
I am a serpent; I am love; I will indulge in feasting.
I am not a confused bard driveling,
When songsters sing a song by memory,
They will not make wonderful cries;
May I be receiving them.
Like receiving clothes without a hand,
Like sinking in a lake without swimming
The stream boldly rises tumultuously in degree.

High in the blood of sea-board towns.
The rock wave-surrounded, by great arrangement,
Will convey for us a defense, a protection from the enemy.
The rock of the chief proprietor, the head of tranquility.
The intoxication of meads will cause us to speak.
I am a cell, I am a cleft, I am a restoration,
I am the depository of song; I am a literary man;
I love the high trees, that afford a protection above,
And a bard that composes, without earning anger;
I love not him that causes contention;
He that speaks ill of the skilful shall
not possess mead.
It is a fit time to go to the drinking,
With the skilful men, about art,
And a hundred knots, the custom of the country,
The shepherd of the districts, support of gates,
Like going without a foot to battle.
He would not journey without a foot.
He would not breed nuts without trees,
Like seeking for ants in the heath.
Like an instrument of foolish spoil,
Like the retinue of an army without a head,
Like feeding the unsheltered on lichen.
Like ridging furrows from the country
Like reaching the sky with a hook,
Like deprecating with the blood of thistles,
Like making light for the blind,
Like sharing clothes to the naked,
Like spreading buttermilk on the sands,
Like feeding fish upon milk,
Like roofing a hail with leaves,
Like killing a tortoise with rods.
Like dissolving riches before a word.
I am a bard of the hail, I am a chick of the chair.
I will cause to loquacious bards a hindrance.
Before I am dragged to my harsh reward,
May we buy thee, that wilt protect us, thou Son of Mary.

The Pleasant Things of Taliesin

A pleasant virtue, extreme penance to an extreme course;

Also pleasant, when God is delivering me.
Pleasant, the carousal that hinders not mental exertion;
Also pleasant, to drink together about horns.
Pleasant is Nudd, the superior wolf-lord;
Also pleasant, a generous one at Candlemas [Imbolc] tide.
Pleasant, berries in the time of harvest;
Also pleasant, wheat upon the stalk.
Pleasant the sun moving in the firmament;
Also pleasant the retaliators of outcries.
Pleasant, a steed with a thick mane in a tangle;
Also pleasant, crackling fuel.
Pleasant, desire, and silver fringes;
Also pleasant, the conjugal ring.
Pleasant, the eagle on the shore of the sea when it flows;
Also pleasant, sea-gulls playing.
Pleasant, a horse with gold-enamelled trappings;
Also pleasant to be honest in a breach.
Pleasant, liquors of the mead-brewer to the multitude;
Also pleasant, a songster generous, amiable.
Pleasant, the open field to cuckoos and the nightingale;
Also pleasant when the weather is serene.Pleasant, right, and a perfect wedding;
Also pleasant, a present that is loved.
Pleasant, a meal from the penance of a priest;
Also pleasant to bring to the altar.
Pleasant, mead in a court to a minstrel,
Also pleasant, the limiting a great crowd.
Pleasant, the catholic clergy in the church,
Also pleasant, a minstrel in the hail.
Pleasant to bring back the divisions of a parish;
Also pleasant to us the time of paradise.
Pleasant, the moon, a luminary in the heavens;
Also pleasant where there is a good rememberer.
Pleasant, summer, and slow long day;
Also pleasant to pass out of chastisement
Pleasant, the blossoms on the tops of the pear-trees;
Also pleasant, friendship with the Creator.
Pleasant, the solitary doe and the fawn;
Also pleasant, the foamy horse-block.
Pleasant, the camp when the leek flourishes;

Also pleasant, the charlock [wild mustard] in the springing corn.
Pleasant, a steed in a leather halter;
Also pleasant, alliance with a king.
Pleasant, the hero that destroys not the yielding;
Also pleasant, the splendid Cymraec language.
Pleasant, the heath when it is green;
Also pleasant, the salt marsh for cattle.
Pleasant, the time when calves draw milk;
Also pleasant, foamy horsemanship.
And what is pleasant to me is no worse.
And the paternal horn by mead-nourished payment.Pleasant, the directing of fish in the pond;
Also pleasant, calling about to play.
Pleasant, the word that utters the Trinity;
Also pleasant, extreme penance for sin.
Pleasant, the summer of pleasantness;
Communion with the Lord, in the day of judgment.

The Chair of Taliesin

I am the agitator
Of the praise of God the Ruler.
With respect to the concerns of song,
The requisites of a profound speaker,
A hard, with the breast of an astrologer.
When he recites
The Awen at the setting in of the evening.
On the fine night of a fine day.
Bards loquacious the light will separate.
Their praise will not bring me to associate,
In the strath, on the course,
With aspect of great cunning.
I am not a mute artist,
Conspicuous among the bards of the people.
I animate the bold,
I influence the heedless;
I wake up the looker on,
The enlightener of bold kings.
I am not a shallow artist,
Conspicuous among kindred bards,
The likeness of a subtle portion,

The deep ocean (is) suitable
Who has filled me with hatred?
A prize in every unveiling.
When the dew is undisturbed,
And the wheat is reaped,
And the bees are gentle,
And myrrh and frankincense,
And transmarine aloes
And the golden pipes of Lleu [an herb],
And a curtain of excellent silver,
And a ruddy gem, and berries.
And the foam of the sea.
Why will the fountain hasten
Water-cresses of purifying juicy quality?
What will join together the common people?
Worth the nobility of liquor.
And a load that the moon separates,
The placid gentleness of Myrddin.
And philosophers of intelligence
Will study about the moon.
And the influence of an order of men,
Exposed to the breeze of the sky.
And a soddening and effusion,
And a portion after effusion,
And the coracle of-glass
In the hand of the pilgrim,
And the valiant one and pitch,
And the honoured Segyrffyg,
And medical plants.
A place of complete benefit,
And bards and blossoms.
And gloomy bushes,
And primroses and small herbs,
And the points of the tree-shrubs.
And deficiency and possession,
And frequent pledging.
And wine overflowing the brim,
From Rome to Rossed.
And deep still water,
Its stream the gift of God.

Or if it will be wood the purifier,
Fruitful its increase.
Let the brewer give a heat,
Over a cauldron of five trees,
And the river of Gwiawn,
And the influence of fine weather,
And honey and trefoil,
And mead-horns intoxicating
Pleasing to a sovereign,
The gift of the Druids.

Song Before the Sons of Llyr

I will adore the love-diffusing Lord of every kindred
The sovereign of hosts manifestly round the universe.
A battle at the feast over joyless beverage,
A battle against the sons of Llyr in Ebyr Henfelyn.
I saw the oppression of the tumult, and wrath and tribulation
The blades gleamed on the glittering helmets,
Against Brochwel of Powys, that loved my Awen.
A battle in the pleasant course early against Urien,
There falls about our feet blood on destruction.
Shall not my chair be defended from the cauldron of Cerridwen?
May my tongue be free in the sanctuary of the praise of Gogyrwen.
The praise of Gogyrwen is an oblation, which has satisfied
Them, with milk, and dew, and acorns.
Let us consider deeply before is heard confession,
That death is assuredly coming nearer and nearer.
And round the lands of Enlli the Dyfi has poured,
Raising the ships on the surface of the plain.
And let us call upon him that has made us,
That he may protect us from the wrath of the alien nation.
When the isle of Mona shall be called a pleasant field,
Happy be the mild ones, the affliciton of the Saxons.
I came to Deganwy to contend
With Maelgwn, the greatest in delinqencies,
I liberated my lord in the presence of the distributor.
Elphin, the sovereign of greatly aspiring ones.
There are to me three chairs regular, accordant,
And until doom they will continue with the singers.

I have been in the battle of Godeu, with Lleu and Gwydion,
They changed the form of the elementary trees and sedges.
I have been with Bran in Ireland.
I saw when Morddwydtyllon [Bran] was killed.
I hears a meeting about the minstrels,
With the Gaels, devils, distillers.
From Penryn Wleth to Loch Reon
The Cymry are of one mind, bold heroes.
Deliver you the Cymry in tribulation.
Three races, cruel from true disposition,
Gael, Briton, and Roman,
Create discord and confusion.
And about the boundary of Prydein, beautiful its towns,
There is a battle against the chiefs above the mead-vessels.
In the festivals of the Distributor, who bestowed gifts upon me.
The chief astrologers received wonderful gifts.
Complete is my chair in Caer Siddi,
No one will be afflicted with disease or old age that may be in it.
Manawyddan and Pryderi know it.
Three utterances, around the fire, will he sing before it,
And around its borders are the streams of the ocean.
And the fruitful fountain is above it,
The liquor Is sweeter than white wine.
And when I shall have worshiped you, Most High, before the sod,
May I be found in the covenant with You.

The Contrived World

He was dexterous that fairly ruled over a country,
He was most generous, with most beautiful queens,
He was a violent poison of woe to his fellow-countrymen.
He broke upon Darius three times in battle.
And he will not be a dwarf shrub in the country of the plumed Darius.
Strenuous, far he conquered, the wood-pushing overtook
Alexander; in the golden fetters of woe he is imprisoned.
He was not long imprisoned; death came.
And where he had moving of armies,
No one before him was exalted,
To go to the grave, rich and prosperous, from the pleasure,

The generous Alexander took him there.
The land of Syr and Siryol, and the land of Syria,
And the land of Dinifdra, and land of Dinitra;
The land of Persia and Mersia, and the land of Canna [Canaan];
And the isles of Pleth and Pletheppa;
And the state of Babylon and Agascia
Great, and the land of Galldarus, little its good.
Until the earth produced, sod was there.
And they do their wills by hunting them.
They render hostages to Europa.
And plunder the countries of the peoples of the earth.
Furiously they pierce women, they impel here,
Before the burned ones there was a devastation of modesty,
Of battles when the sorrow was mentioned.
They satisfy the ravens, they make a head of confused running,
The soldiers of the possessor of multitudes, when they are mentioned.
Nor a country to thy young men, when it is destroyed,
There will not be for thy riddance, a riddance of burden.
From the care of the fetter and its hardship.
A hundred thousand of the army died from thirst:
False their plans with their thousands.
Was poisoned his youth before he came home.
Before this, it would have been better to have been satisfied.
To my lord land-prospering, a country glorious,
One country may the Lord, the best region connect.
May I reform, may I be satisfied. Be 'with thee the fullness,
And as many as hear rue, be mine their unity.
May they satisfy the will of God before the clothing of the sod.

Alexander the Great

I wonder that there is not proclaimed
An acknowledgment of heaven to the earth.
Of the coming of a giant Ruler,
Alexander the Great.
Alexander, possessor of multitudes.
Passionate, iron-gifted,
Eminent for sword-strokes.
He went under the sea,
Under the sea he went,

To seek for science.
Whoever seeks science,
Let him be clamorous in mind.
He wont above the wind,
Between two griffins on a journey,To see a sight.
A sight he saw,
The present was not sufficient.
He saw a wonder.
A superiority of lineage with fishes.
'What he desired in his mind,
He had from the world.
And also at his end
With God, mercy.

Song to the Great World

I will adore my Father,
My God, my strengthener,
Who infused through my head
A soul to direct me.
Who has made for me in perception,
My seven faculties.
Of fire and earth,
And water and air,
And mist and flowers,
And southerly wind.
Other senses of perception
Thy father formed for me.
One is to have instinct
With the second I touch,
With the third I call,
With the fourth I taste,
With the fifth I see,
With the sixth I hear.
With the seventh I smell.
And I foretell,
Seven airs there are,
Above the astronomer,
And three parts the seas.
How they strike on all sides.
How great and wonderful,

The world, not of one form,
Did God make above,
On the planets.
He made Sola,
He made Luna,
He made Marca and Marcarucia,
He made Venus,
He made Venerus,
He made Severus,
And the seventh Saturrnts,
The good God made
Five zones of the earth,
For as long as it will last.
One is cold,
And the second is cold,
And the third is heat,
Disagreeable, unprofitable.
The fourth, paradise,
The people will contain.
The fifth is the temperate,
And the gates of the universe.
Into three it is divided,
In the minstrelsy of perception.
One is Asia,
The second is Africa,
The third is Europa.
The baptism of consolation,
Until doomsday it will continue,
When everything will be judged.
My Awen has caused me
To praise my king.
I am Taliesin,
With a speed flowing as a diviner.
Continuing to the end
In the pattern of Elphin.

Chapter XL
The Songs to Trees by Myrddin the Bard

Verses attributed to Myrddin the Bard

from the Black Book of Carmarthen

Four Ancient Books of Wales

and in Myvyrian Archaeology

Ye Birch Trees

I

Blessed is the birch in the valley of Gwy
Whose branches will fall off one by one, two by two
It will remain when there will be a battle in Ardudwy
And the lowing together of the cattle about the ford of Mochnwy
And spears and shouting at Dyganwy
And Edwin bearing sway in Mona
And youths pale and light
In ruddy clothes commanding them.

II

Blessed is the birch in Pumlumon
Which will see when the front of the stage shall be exalted
and which will see Franks clad in mail
About the hearth food for whelps
And monks frequently riding on steeds.

III

Blessed is the birch in the heights of Dinwythy
Which will know when there shall be a battle in Ardudwy
And spears uplifted around Edrywy
And a bridge in the Taw, and another on the Tawy
And another, on account of a misfortun, on the banks of the Gwy

And the artificer that will make it, let his name by Garwy;
and the principle of Mona have dominion over it.
Women will be under the Gynt, and men in affliction
Happier than I is he who will welcome
The time of Cadwaladyr: a song he may sing!

The Apple Trees

I

Sweet appletree, your branches delight me,
Luxuriantly budding my pride and joy!
I will put before the lord of Macreu,
That on Wednesday, in the valley of Machawy
Blood will flow.
Lloegyr's (England's) blades will shine.
But hear, Oh little pig! on Thursday
The Cymry will rejoice
In their defence of Cymimawd,
Furiously cutting and thrusting.
The Saesons (Saxons) will be slaughtered by our ashen spears,
And their heads used as footballs.
I prophesy the unvarnished truth –
The rising of a child in the secluded South.

II

Sweet and luxuriant appletree,
Great its branches, beautiful its form!
I predict a battle that fills me with far.
At Pengwern, men drink mead,
But around Cyminawd is a deadly hewing
By a chieftain from Eryri - til only hatred remains.

III

Sweet yellow appletree,
Growing in Tal Ardd,
I predict a battle at Prydyn,
In defense of frontiers.
Seven ships will come
Across a wide lake,
Seven hundred men come to conquer.
Of those who come, only seven will return
According to my prophecy.

IV

Sweet appletree of luxuriant growth!
I used to find food at its foot,
When because of a maid,
I slept alone in the woods of Celyddon,
Shield on shoulder, sword on,
Hear, Oh little pig! listen to my
As sweet as birds that sing on Monday
When the sovereigns come across the sea,
Blessed by the Cymry [Welsh], because of their strength.

V

Sweet appletree in the glade,
Trodden is the earth around its base.
The men of Rhydderch see me not,Gwendyyd no longer loves nor greets me
I am hated by Rhydderch's strongest scion.
I have despoiled both his son and daughter:
Death visits them all - why not me?
After Gwnddoleu no one shall honour me,
No diversions attend me,
No fair women visit me.
Though at Arderydd, I wore a golden torque
The swan-white woman despises me now.

VI

Sweet appletree, growing by the river,
Who will thrive on its wondrous fruit?
When my reason was intact
I used to lie at its foot
With a fair wanton maid, of slender form.
Fifty years the plaything of lawless en
I have wandered in gloom among spirits
After great wealth, and gregarious minstrels,
I have been here so long not even sprites
Can lead me astray. I never sleep, but tremble at the thought
Of my Lord Gwenddoleu, and y own native people.
Long have I suffered unease and longing-
May I be given freedom in the end.

VII

Sweet appletree, with delicate blossom,
Growing concealed, in the wind!
At the tale was told to me
That my words had offended the most powerful minister,
Not once, not twice, but thrice in a single day.
Christ! that my end has come
Before the killing of Gwndydd's son
Was upon my hands!

VIII

Sweet appletree with your delicate blossom,
Growing amid the thickets of trees!
Chwyfleian foretells,
A tale that will come to pass
A staff of gold, signifying bravery
Will be given by the glorious Dragon Kings.
The grateful one will vanquish the profaner,
Before the child, bright and bold,
The Saesons shall fall, and bards will flourish

IX

Sweet appletree of crimson colour,
Growing, concealed in the wood of Celyddon:
Though men seek your fruit, their search is vain
Until Cadwaladyr comes from Cadfaon's meeting
To Teiwi river and Tywis lands,
Till anger and anguish come from Arawynion,
And the long-hairs are tamed.

X

Sweet appletree of crimson colour,
Crowing, concealed, in the wood of Celyddon
Though men seek your fruit, their search is vain,
Till Cadwalad comes from Rhyd Rheon's meeting,
And with Cynon advances against the Saeson.
Victorious Cymry, glorious their leaden,All shall how their rights again,
All Britons rejoice, sounding joyful horns.
Chanting songs of happiness and peace!

Chapter XLI The Mystic Life of Merlyn - Vita Merlini

Authored by Geoffrey of Monmouth in 1150

for his Historia Regum Britanniae series.

Selections adapted by Myrddin Cerrig

After many years had passed under many kings, Merlin the Briton was held famous in the world. He was a king and prophet; to the proud people of the South Welsh he gave laws, and to the chieftains he prophesied the future. Meanwhile it happened that a strife arose between several chiefs of the kingdom, and throughout the cities they wasted innocent people with fierce war. Peredur, king of North Wales, made war on Gwenddoleu, who ruled the realm of Scotland; and already the day fixed for the battle was at hand, and the leaders were ready in the field, and the troops were fighting, falling on both sides in a miserable slaughter. Merlin had come to the war with Peredur and so had Rhydderch, king of the Cumbrians, both savage men. They slew the opposing enemy with their hateful swords, and three brothers of the prince who had followed him through his wars, always fighting, cut down and broke the battle lines. Thence they rushed fiercely through crowded ranks with such an attack that they soon fell killed. At this sight, Merlin grieved and poured out sad complaints throughout the army, and cried out in these words, "Could injurious fate be so harmful as to take from me so many and such great companions, whom recently so many kings and so many remote kingdoms feared? O dubious lot of mankind! O death ever near, which has them always in its power, and strikes its hidden goad and drives out the wretched life from the body! O glorious youths, who now will stand by my side in arms, and with me will repel the chieftains coming to harm me, and the hosts rushing in upon me? Bold young men your audacity has taken from you your pleasant years and pleasant youth! You who so recently were rushing in arms through the troops, cutting down on every side those who resisted you, now are beating the ground and are red with red blood!" So among the hosts he lamented with flowing tears, and mourned for the men, and the savage battle was unceasing. The lines rushed together, enemies were slain by enemies, blood flowed everywhere, and people died on both sides. But at length the Britons assembled their troops from all quarters and all together rushing in arms they fell upon the Scots and wounded them and cut them down, nor did they rest until the hostile battalions turned their backs and fled through unfrequented ways.

Merlin called his companions out from battle and bade them bury the brothers in a richly colored chapel; and he bewailed the men and did not cease to pour out laments, and he strewed dust on his hair and rent his garments, and prostrate on the ground rolled now hither and now thither. Peredur strove to console him and so did nobles and princes, but he would not be comforted nor put up with their beseeching words. He had now lamented for three whole days and had refused food, so great was the grief that consumed him. Then when he had filled the air with so many and so great complaints, new fury seized him and he departed secretly, and fled to the woods not wishing to be seen as he fled. He entered the wood and rejoiced to lie hidden under the ash trees; he marveled at the wild beasts feeding on grass of the glades; now he chased after them and again he flew past them; he lived on roots of grasses and on the grass, on fruit of the trees and on mulberries of the thicket. He became a silvan man just as though devoted to the woods. For a whole summer after this, hidden like a wild animal, he remained buried in the woods, found by no one and forgetful of himself and of his kindred. But when winter came and took away all the grass and the fruit and he had nothing to live on, he poured out the following lament in a wretched voice.

"Christ, God of heaven, what shall I do? In what part of the world can I stay, since I see nothing here I can live on, neither grass on the ground nor acorns on the trees? Here once there stood nineteen fruit-bearing apple trees; now they are not standing. Who has taken them away from me? Where have they gone all of a sudden? Now I see them - now I do not! Thus the fates fight against me and for me, since they both permit and forbid me to see. Now I lack the apples and everything else. The trees stand without leaves, without fruit; I am afflicted by both circumstances since I cannot cover myself with leaves or eat the fruit. Winter and the south wind with its falling rain have taken them all away. If by chance I find some turnips deep in the ground the hungry swine and the voracious boars rush up and snatch them away from me as I dig them up from the turf. You, O wolf, dear companion, accustomed to roam with me through the secluded paths of the woods and meadows, now can scarcely get across fields; hard hunger has weakened both you and me. You lived in these woods before I did and age has whitened your hairs first. You have nothing to put into your mouth and do not know how to get anything, at which I marvel, since the wood abounds in so many goats and other wild beasts that you might catch. Now, as the only thing left to you, you fill the air with howling, and stretched out on the ground you extend your wasted limbs."

These words he was uttering among shrubs and dense hazel thickets when the sound reached a certain passer-by who turned his steps to the place whence the sounds were rising in the air, and found the place and found the speaker. As soon as Merlin saw him he departed, and the traveler followed him, but was unable to overtake the man as he fled. Thereupon he resumed his journey and went about his business, moved by the lot of the fugitive. Now this traveler was met by a man from the court of Rhydderch, king of the Cumbrians, who was married to Ganieda and happy in his beautiful wife. She was sister to Merlin and, grieving over the fate of her brother, she had sent her retainers to the woods and the distant fields to bring him back. One of these retainers came toward the traveler and the latter at once went up to him and they fell into conversation; the one who had been sent to find Merlin asked if the other had seen him in the woods or the glades. The latter admitted that he had seen such a man among the bushy glades of the Calidonian forest, but, when he wished to speak to him and sit down with him, the other had fled away swiftly among the oaks. These things he told, and the messenger departed and entered the forest; he searched the deepest valleys and passed over the high mountains; he sought everywhere for his man, going through the obscure places.

On the very summit of a certain mountain there was a fountain, surrounded on every side by hazel bushes and thick with shrubs. There Merlin had seated himself, and thence through all the woods he watched the wild animals running and playing. The messenger climbed, and with silent step went on up the heights seeking the man. At last he saw the fountain and Merlin sitting on the grass behind it. He heard the words of Merlin:

"You who rules all things, how does it happen that the seasons are not all the same, distinguished only by their four numbers? Now spring, according to its laws, provides flowers and leaves; summer gives crops, autumn ripe apples; icy winter follows and devours and wastes all the others, bringing rain and snow, and keeps them all away and harms with its tempests. And it does not permit the ground to produce variegated flowers, or the oak trees acorns, or the apple trees dark red apples. If only there were no winter or white frost! That it were spring or summer, and that the cuckoo would come back singing, and the nightingale who softens sad hearts with her devoted song, and the turtle dove keeping her chaste vows, and that in new foliage other birds should sing in harmonious measures, delighting me with their music, while a new earth should breathe forth odors from new flowers under the green grass; that the fountains would also flow on every side with their gentle murmurs, and nearby, under the leaves, the dove would pour forth her soothing laments and incite to slumber."

The messenger heard the prophet and broke off his lament with songs brought that he might attract and soften the madman. Making plaintive sounds with his fingers and striking the strings in order, he lay hidden behind him and sang in a low voice of Ganieda weeping for her lost brother And the messenger sang thus to his plaintive lyre, and with his music soothed the ears of the prophet that he might become more gentle and rejoice with the singer. Quickly the prophet arose and addressed the young man with pleasant words, and begged him to touch once more the strings with his fingers and to sing again his former song. The latter therefore set his fingers to the lyre and played over again the song that was asked for, and by his playing compelled the man, little by little, to put aside his madness, captivated by the sweetness of the lute. So Merlin became mindful of himself, and he recalled what he used to be, and he wondered at his madness and he hated it. His former mind returned and his sense came back to him, and, moved by affection, he groaned at the names of his sister and of his wife, since his mind was now restored to him, and he asked to be led to the court of King Rhydderch. The other obeyed him, and straightway they left the woods and came, rejoicing together, to the city of the king. So the queen was delighted by regaining her brother and the wife became glad over the return of her husband. They vied with each other in kissing him and they twined their arms about his neck, so great was the affection that moved them. The king received him with honor, and the chieftains who thronged the palace rejoiced throughout the city.

But when Merlin saw such great crowds of men present he was not able to endure them; he went mad again, and, filled anew with fury, he wanted to go to the woods, and he tried to get away by stealth. Then Rhydderch ordered him to be restrained and a guard posted over him, and his madness be softened with music; and he stood about him grieving, and with imploring words begged the man to be sensible and to stay with him, and not to long for the grove or to live like a wild beast, or to want to abide under the trees when he might hold a royal sceptre and rule over a warlike people. After that he promised that he would give him many gifts, and he ordered people to bring him clothing and birds, dogs and swift horses, gold and shining gems, and cups that Wayland had engraved in the city of Segontium. Every one of these things Rydderch offered to the prophet and urged him to stay with him and leave the woods.

The prophet rejected these gifts, saying, "Let the dukes who are troubled by their own poverty have these, they who are not satisfied with a moderate amount but desire a great deal. To these gifts I prefer the groves and broad oaks of Calidon, and the lofty mountains with green pastures at their feet. Those are the things that please me, not these of yours - take these away with you, King Rhydderch. My Calidonian forest rich in nuts, the forest that I prefer to everything else, shall have me."

Finally since the king could not retain the sad man by any gifts, he ordered him to be bound with a strong chain lest, if free, he might seek the deserted groves. The prophet, when he felt the chains around him and he could not go as a free man to the Calidonian forests, straightway fell to grieving and remained sad and silent, and took all joy from his face so that he did not utter a word or smile.

Meanwhile the queen was going through the hall looking for the king, and he greeted her as she came and took her by the hand and bade her sit down, and, embracing her, pressed her lips in a kiss. In so doing he turned his face toward her and saw a leaf hanging in her hair; he reached out his fingers, took it and threw it on the ground, and jested joyfully with the woman he loved. The prophet turned his eyes in that direction and smiled, and made the the men standing about look at him in wonder since he was not in the habit of smiling. The king too wondered and urged the madman to tell the cause of his sudden laugh, and he added to his words many gifts. More and more Rhydderch continued to urge him with riches until eventually the prophet, vexed at him, said in return for his gift, "A miser loves a gift and a greedy man labors to get one; these are easily corrupted by gifts and bend their minds in any direction they are bidden to. What they have is not enough for them, but for me the acorns of pleasant Calidon and the shining fountains flowing through fragrant meadows are sufficient. I am not attracted by gifts; let the miser take his, and unless liberty is given me and I go back to the green woodland valleys, I shall refuse to explain my laughter."

When Rhydderch realized that he could not influence the prophet by any gift, and he could not find out the reason for the laughter, straightway he ordered the chains to be loosed and gave him permission to seek the deserted groves, that he might be willing to give the desired explanation. Then Merlin, rejoicing that he could go, said, "This is the reason I laughed, Rhydderch. You were by a single act both praiseworthy and blameworthy. When just now you removed the leaf that the queen had in her hair without knowing it, you acted more faithfully toward her than she did toward you when she went under the bush where her lover met her and lay with her; and while she was lying there with her hair spread out, by chance there caught in it the leaf that you, not knowing all this, removed."

Rhydderch became sad at this accusation and turned his face from her and cursed the day he had married her. But she, not at all moved, hid her shame behind a smiling face and said to her husband, "Why are you sad, my love? Why do you become so angry over this thing and blame me unjustly, and believe a madman who, lacking sound sense, mixes lies with the truth? The man who believes him becomes many times more a fool than he is. Now then, watch, and if I am not mistaken I will show you that he is crazy and has not spoken the truth."

There was in the hall a certain boy, one of many, and the ingenious woman catching sight of him straightway thought of a novel trick by which she might convict her brother of falsehood. So she ordered the boy to come in and asked her brother to predict by what death the lad should die. He answered, "Dearest sister, he shall die a grown man falling from a high rock." Smiling at these words, she ordered the boy to go away and take off the clothes he was wearing and put on others and to cut off his long hair; she bade him come back to them thus that he might seem to them a different person. The boy obeyed her, for he came back to them with his clothes changed as he had been ordered to do. Soon the queen asked her brother again, "Tell your dear sister what the death of this boy will be like." Merlin answered, "This boy when he grows up shall, while out of his mind, meet with a violent death in a tree." When he had finished she said to her husband, "Could this false prophet lead you so far astray as to make you believe that I had committed so great a crime? Notice with how much sense he has spoken about the boy, and you would believe that the things he said about me were made up so that he might get away to the woods. Far be it from me to do such a thing! I shall keep my bed chaste, and chaste shall I always be while the breath of life is in me. I convicted him of falsehood when I asked him about the death of the boy. Now I shall do it again; pay attention and judge."

When she had said this she told the boy in an aside to go out and put on woman's clothing, and to come back as such. Soon the boy left and did as he was bid, for he came back in woman's clothes just as though he were a woman, and stood in front of Merlin to whom the queen said banteringly, "Say brother, tell me about the death of this girl." And her brother said, "Girl or not she shall die in the river." This made King Rhydderch laugh;

since when asked about the death of a single boy Merlin had predicted three different kinds. Therefore Rhydderch thought he had spoken falsely about the queen, and did not believe him, but grieved, and hated the fact that he had trusted him and had condemned his beloved. The queen, seeing this, forgave him and kissed and caressed him and made him joyful.

Meanwhile Merlin planned to go to the woods, and he left his dwelling and ordered the gates to be opened; but his sister stood in his way and with rising tears begged him to remain with her for a while and to put aside his madness. Since no one could hold him back when he wanted to go, the queen quickly ordered Guendoloena, who was absent, to come to make him desist. She came and on her knees begged him to remain; but he spurned her prayers and would not stay, nor would he, as he was accustomed to do, look upon her with a joyful face. She grieved and dissolved in tears and tore her hair, and scratched her cheeks with her nails and rolled on the ground as though dying. The queen seeing this said to him, "This Guendoloena who is dying for you, what shall she do? Shall she marry again or do you bid her remain a widow, or go with you wherever you are going? For she will go, and with you she will joyfully inhabit the groves and the green woodland meadows provided she has your love." To this the prophet answered, "Sister, I do not want a cow that pours out water in a broad fountain like the urn of the Virgin in summer-time, nor shall I change my care as Orpheus once did when Eurydice gave her baskets to the boys to hold before she swam back across the Stygian sands. Freed from both of you I shall remain without the taint of love. Let her therefore be given a proper opportunity to marry and let him whom she shall choose have her. But let the man who marries her be careful that he never gets in my way or comes near me; let him keep away for fear lest if I happen to meet him he may feel my flashing sword. But when the day of the wedding comes, I shall be present in person, furnished with seemly gifts, and I shall profusely endow Guendoloena when she is given away." When he had finished he said farewell to each of them and went away, and with no one to hinder him he went back to the woods he longed for.

Guendoloena remained sadly in the door watching him and so did the queen, both moved by what had happened to their friend, and they marveled that a madman should be so familiar with secret things and should have known of the love affair of his sister. Nevertheless they thought that he lied about the death of the boy since he told of three different deaths when he should have told of one. Therefore his speech seemed for long years to be an empty one until the time when the boy grew to manhood; then it was made apparent to all and convincing to many. For while he was hunting with his dogs he caught sight of a stag hiding in a grove of trees and he loosed the dogs. He urged on his horse with his spurs and followed after, urging on the huntsmen to go more quickly. There was a high mountain surrounded on all sides by rocks with a stream flowing through the plain at its foot. The animal came to the river and sought refuge in hiding in the manner of its kind. The young man pressed on and passed straight over the mountain, hunting for the stag among the rocks lying about. Impetuously pushing on , his horse slipped from a high rock and the man fell over a precipice into the river, but so that one of his feet caught in a tree, and the rest of his body was submerged in the stream. Thus he fell, and was drowned, and hung from a tree, and by his threefold death made the prophet a true one.

Merlin had returned to the woods and was living like a wild beast, subsisting on frozen moss, in the snow, in the rain, in the cruel blasts of the wind. This pleased him more than administering laws throughout his cities and ruling over fierce people. Meanwhile Guendoloena, since her husband was leading a life like this with his woodland flock through the passing years, was married in accordance with her husband's permission.

It was night and the horns of the bright moon were shining, and all the lights of the vault of heaven were gleaming; the air was clearer than usual, for cruel, frigid, Boreas had driven away the clouds and had made the sky serene again and had dried up the mists with his arid breath. From the top of a lofty mountain the prophet was regarding the courses of the stars, speaking to himself out in the open air. "What does this ray of Mars mean? Does its fresh redness mean that one king is dead and that there shall be another? So I see it, for Constantine has died and his nephew Conan, through an evil fate and the murder of his uncle, has taken the crown and is king. And you, highest Venus, who slipping along within your ordered limits beneath the zodiac are accompanying the sun in his course, what about this double ray of yours that is cleaving the air? Does not its division indicate a severing of my love? Such a ray indeed shows that loves are divided. Perhaps Guendoloena has left me in my absence and now clings to another man and rejoices in his embraces. So I lose; so another enjoys her. So my rights are taken away from me while I dally. So it is surely, for a slothful lover is beaten by one who is not slothful or absent but is right on hand. But I am not jealous; let her marry now under favorable auspices and let her enjoy her new husband with my permission. And when tomorrow's sun shall shine I will go and take with me the gift I promised her when I left." So he spoke and went about all the woods and groves and collected a herd of stags in a single line, and the deer and she-goats likewise, and he himself mounted a stag. And when day dawned he arrived and commanded the stags to stand patiently outside the gates while he cried aloud, "Guendoloena! Guendoloena! Come! Your presents are looking for you!" Guendoloena came quickly, smiling and marveling that the man was riding on the stag and that it obeyed him, and that he could get together so large a number of animals and drive them before him.

The bridegroom stood watching from a lofty window and marveling at the rider on his seat, and he laughed. But when the prophet saw him and realized who he was, he immediately wrenched the horns from the stag he was riding and threw them at the man, completely smashing his head in, killing him. With a quick blow of his heels he set the stag flying and was on his way back to the woods. At these happenings the servants rushed out from all sides and quickly followed the prophet through the fields. But he ran ahead so fast that he would have reached the woods untouched if a river had not been in his way; while his beast was hurriedly leaping over the torrent Merlin slipped from his back and fell into the rapid waves. The servants lined the shore and captured him as he swam, and bound him and took him home and gave him to his sister.

The prophet, captured in this way, became sad and wanted to go back to the woods, and he fought to break his bonds and refused to smile or to take food or drink, and by his sadness he made his sister sad. Rhydderch, seeing him drive all joy from him and refuse to taste of the banquets that had been prepared for him, took pity on him and ordered him to be led out into the city, through the market place among the people, in the hope that he might be cheered up by going and seeing the novelties that were being sold there.

After he had been taken out and was going away from the palace he saw before a door a servant of a poor appearance, the doorkeeper, asking with trembling lips of all the passers-by some money with which to get his clothes mended. The prophet thereupon stood still and laughed, wondering at the poor man. When he had gone on from here he saw a young man holding some new shoes and buying some pieces of leather to patch them with. Then he laughed again and refused to go further through the market place to be stared at by the people he was watching. But he yearned for the woods, toward which he frequently looked back, and to which, although forbidden, he tried to direct his steps.

The servants returned home and told that he had laughed twice and also that he had tried to get away to the woods. Rhydderch, who wished to know what he had meant by his laughter, quickly gave orders for his bonds to be loosed and gave him permission to go back to his accustomed woods if only he would explain why he laughed. The prophet, now quite joyful, answered, "The doorkeeper was sitting outside the doors in well worn clothing and kept asking those who went by to give him something to buy clothes with, just as though he had been a pauper, and all the time he was secretly a rich man and had under him hidden piles of coins. That is what I laughed at; turn up the ground under him and you will find coins preserved there for a long time. From there they led me further toward the market place and I saw a man buying some shoes and also some patches so that after the shoes were worn out and had holes in them he might mend them and make them fit for service again. This too I laughed at since the poor man will not be able to use the shoes nor the patches, since he is already drowned in the waves and is now floating toward the shore; go and you will see." Rhydderch, wishing to test the man's sayings, ordered his servants to go quickly along the bank of the river, so that if they should chance to find such a man drowned by the shore they might at once bring him word. They obeyed the king's orders, for going along the the river they found a drowned man in a waste patch of sand, and returned home and reported the fact to him. But the king meanwhile, after sending away the doorkeeper, had dug and turned up the ground and found a treasure placed under it, and laughingly he praised the prophet.

After these things had happened the prophet was making haste to go to the woods he was accustomed to, hating the people in the city. The queen advised him to stay with her and to put off his desired trip to the woods until the cold of white winter, which was then at hand, should be over, and summer should return again with its tender fruits on which he could live while the weather grew warm from the sun. He refused, desiring to depart and scorning the winter he said to her, "Dear sister, why do you try to hold me back? Winter with his tempests cannot frighten me, nor icy Boreas when he rages with his cruel blasts and suddenly injures the flocks of sheep with hail; neither does it disturb me when rain clouds shed their waters. Why should I not seek the deserted groves and the green woodlands? Content with little, I can endure the frost. There under the leaves of the trees among the odorous blossoms I shall take pleasure in lying through the summer; but lest I lack food in winter you might build me a house in the woods and have servants in it to wait on me and prepare me food when the ground refuses to produce grain or the trees fruit. Before the other buildings build me a remote one with seventy doors and as many windows through which I may watch fire-breathing Phoebus and Venus and the stars gliding from the heavens by night, all of whom shall show me what is going to happen to the people of the kingdom. And let the same number of scribes be at hand, trained to take my dictation, and let them be attentive to record my prophecy on their tablets. You too are to come often, dear sister, and then you can relieve my hunger with food and drink." After he had finished speaking he departed hastily for the woods.

His sister obeyed him and built the place he had asked for, and the other houses and whatever else he had bid her. But while the apples remained and Phoebus was ascending higher through the stars, he rejoiced to remain beneath the leaves and to wander through the groves with their soothing breezes. Then winter came, harsh with icy winds, and despoiled the ground and the trees of all their fruit, and Merlin lacked food because the rains were at hand, and he came, sad and hungry, to the aforesaid place. There the queen often came and rejoiced to bring her brother both food and drink. After he had refreshed himself with various kinds of edibles, would arise and express his approval of his sister. Then wandering about the house he would look at the stars while he prophesied things like these which he knew were going to come to pass.

"O madness of the Britons whom a plenitude, always excessive, of riches exalts more than is seemly. They do not wish to enjoy peace but are stirred up by the Fury's goad. They engage in civil wars and battles between relatives. The nephews of the Boar of Cornwall cast everything into confusion, and setting snares for each other engage in a mutual slaughter with their wicked swords. They do not wish to wait to get possession of the kingdom lawfully, but seize the crown. The fourth from them shall be more cruel and more harsh still; him shall a wolf from the sea conquer in fight and shall drive defeated beyond the Severn through the kingdoms of the barbarians. This latter shall besiege Cirencester with a blockade and with sparrows, and shall overthrow its walls to their very bases. He shall seek the Gauls in his ship, but shall die beneath the weapon of a king. Rhydderch shall die, after whom long discord shall hold the Scots and the Cumbrians for a long time until Cumbria shall be granted to his growing tusk. The Welsh shall attack the men of Gwent, and afterward those of Cornwall and no law shall restrain them. Wales shall rejoice in the shedding of blood; O people always hateful to God, why do you rejoice in bloodshed? Wales shall compel brothers to fight and to condemn their own relatives to a wicked death. The troops of the Scots shall often cross the Humber and, putting aside all sentiment, shall kill those who oppose them. Not with impunity, however, for the leader shall be killed; he shall have the name of a horse and because of that fact shall be fierce. His heir shall be expelled and shall depart from our territories. Scots, sheathe your swords which you bare too readily; your strength shall be unequal to that of our fierce people. The city of Dumbarton shall be destroyed and no king shall repair it for an age until the Scot shall be subdued in war. Carlisle, spoiled of its shepherd, shall lie vacant until the sceptre of the Lion shall restore its pastoral staff. Segontium and its towers and mighty palaces shall lament in ruins until the Welsh return to their former domains. Porchester shall see its broken walls in its harbour until a rich man with the tooth of a wolf shall restore it. The city of Richborough shall lie spread out on the shore of its harbor and a man from Flanders shall re-establish it with his crested ship. The fifth from him shall rebuild the walls of St David's and shall bring back to her the pall lost for many years. The City of the Legions shall fall into thy bosom, O Severn, and shall lose her citizens for a long time, and these the Bear in the Lamb shall restore to her when he shall come.

Saxon kings shall expel the citizens and shall hold cities, country, and houses for a long time. From among them thrice three dragons shall wear the crown. Two hundred monks shall perish in Leicester and the Saxon shall drive out her ruler and leave vacant her walls. He who first among the Anglos shall wear the diadem of Brutus and shall repair the city laid waste by slaughter. A fierce people shall forbid the sacrament of confirmation throughout the country, and in the house of God shall place images of the gods. Afterward Rome shall bring God back through the medium of a monk and a holy priest shall sprinkle the buildings with water and shall restore them again and shall place shepherds in them. Thereafter many of them shall obey the commands of the divine law and shall enjoy heaven by right. An impious people full of poison shall violate that settlement and shall violently mix together right and wrong. They shall sell their sons and their kinsmen into the furthest countries beyond the sea and shall incur the wrath of the Thunderer. O wretched crime! that man whom the founder of the world created with liberty, deeming him worthy of heaven, should be sold like an ox and be dragged away with a rope. You miserable man who turned traitor to your master when first you came to the throne, you shall yield to God. The Danes shall come upon you with their fleet and after subduing the people shall reign for a short time and shall then be defeated and retire. Two shall rule over them whom the serpent forgetful of his treaty shall strike with the sting in his tail instead of with the garland of his sceptre.

Then the Normans, sailing over the water in their wooden ships, bearing their faces in front and in back, shall fiercely attack the Anglos with their iron tunics and their fierce swords, and shall destroy them and possess the field. They shall subjugate many realms to themselves and shall rule foreign peoples for a time until the Fury, flying all about, shall scatter her poison over them Then peace and faith and all virtue shall depart, and on all sides throughout the country the citizens shall engage in battles. Man shall betray man and no one shall be found a friend. The husband, despising his wife, shall draw near to harlots, and the wife, despising her husband, shall marry whom she desires. There shall be no honor kept for the church and the order shall perish. Then shall bishops bear arms, and armed camps shall be built. Men shall build towers and walls in holy ground, and they shall give to the soldiers what should belong to the needy. Carried away by riches they shall run along on the path of worldly things and shall take from God what the holy bishop shall forbid. Three shall wear the diadem after whom shall be the favor of the newcomers. A fourth shall be in authority whom awkward piety shall injure until he shall be clothed in his father, so that girded with boar's teeth he shall cross the shadow of the helmeted man. Four shall be anointed, seeking in turn the highest things, and two shall succeed who shall so wear the diadem that they shall induce the Gauls to make war on them. The sixth shall overthrow the Irish and their walls, and pious and prudent shall renew the people and the cities. All these things I formerly predicted more at length to Vortigern in explaining to him the mystic war of the two Dragons when we sat on the banks of the drained pool. But you, dear sister, go home to see the king dying and bid Taliesin come, as I wish to talk over many things with him; for he has recently come from the land of Brittany where he learned sweet philosophy of Gildas the Wise."

Ganieda returned home and found that Taliesin had returned and the prince was dead and the servants were sad. She fell down lamenting among her friends and tore her hair and cried, "Women, lament with me the death of Rhydderch and weep for a man such as our earth has not ever produced in our age so far as we know. He was a lover of peace, for he so ruled a fierce people that no violence was done to any one by anyone else. He treated the holy priest with just moderation and permitted the highest and the lowest to be governed by law. He was generous, for he gave away much and kept scarcely anything. He was all things to all men, doing whatever was seemly; flower of knights, glory of kings, pillar of the kingdom. Woe is me! I leave you, nobles, and lofty walls, household gods, sweet sons, and all the things of the world. In company with my brother I shall dwell in the woods and shall worship God with a joyful heart, clothed in a black mantle." So she spoke, giving her husband his due, and she inscribed on his tomb this verse, "Rhydderch the Generous, than whom there was no one more generous in the world, a great man rests in this small urn."

Meanwhile Taliesin had come to see Merlin the prophet who had sent for him to find out what wind or rain storm was coming up, for both together were drawing near and the clouds were thickening. He drew the following illustrations under the guidance of Minerva his associate.

"Out of nothing the Creator of the world produced four elements that they might be the prior cause as well as the material for creating all things when they were joined together in harmony: the heaven which He adorned with stars and which stands on high and embraces everything like the shell surrounding a nut; then He made the air, fir for forming sounds, through the medium of which day and night present the stars; the sea which girds the land in four circles, and with its mighty influence so strikes the air as to generate the winds which are said to be four in number; as a foundation He placed the earth, standing by its own strength and not lightly moved, which is divided into five parts, whereof the middle one is not habitable because of the heat and the two furthest are shunned because of their cold. To the last two He gave moderate temperature and these are inhabited by men and birds and herds of wild beasts. He added clouds to the sky so that they might furnish sudden showers to make the fruits of the trees and of the ground grow with their gentle sprinkling. With the help of the sun these are filled like water skins from the rivers by a hidden law, and then, rising through the upper air, they pour out the water they have taken up, driven by the force of the winds. From them come rain storms, snow, and round hail when the cold damp wind breathes out its blasts which, penetrating the clouds, drive out the streams just as they make them. Each of the winds takes to itself a nature of its own from its proximity to the zone where it is born. Beyond the firmament in which He fixed the shining stars He placed the ethereal heaven and gave it as a habitation to troops of angels whom the worthy contemplation and marvelous sweetness of God refresh throughout the ages. This also He adorned with stars and the shining sun, laying down the law by which the star should run within fixed limits through the part of heaven entrusted to it. Afterward He placed beneath this the airy heavens, shining with the lunar body, which throughout their high places abound in troops of spirits who sympathize or rejoice with us as things go well or ill. They are accustomed to carry the prayers of men through the air and to beseech God to have mercy on them, and to bring back intimations of God's will, either in dreams or by voice or by other signs, through doing which they become wise. The space beyond the moon abounds in evil demons, who are skilled to cheat and deceive and tempt us; often they assume a body made of air and appear to us and many things often follow. They even hold intercourse with women and make them pregnant, generating in an unholy manner. So therefore He made the heavens to be inhabited by three orders of spirits that each one might look out for something and renew the world from the renewed seed of things.

The sea too He distinguished by various forms that from itself it might produce the forms of things, generating throughout the ages. Indeed, part of it burns and part freezes and the third part, getting a moderate temperature from the other two, ministers to our needs. That part which burns surrounds a gulf and fierce people, and its divers streams, flowing back, separate this from the orb of the earth, increasing fire from fire. Here descend those who transgress the laws and reject God; whither their perverse will leads them they go, eager to destroy what is forbidden to them. There stands the stern eyed judge holding his equal balance and giving to each one his merits and his deserts. The second part, which freezes, rolls about the foreshore sands which it is the first to generate from the nearby vapor when it is mingled with the ray from the star of Venus. This star, the Arabs say, makes shining gems when it passes through Pisces while its waters look back at the flames. These gems by their virtues benefit the people who wear them, and make many well and keep them so. These too the Creator distinguished by their kinds (as He did all things), that we might discern from their forms and from their colors of what kinds they are and of what manifest virtues. The third form of the sea which circles our orb furnishes us many good things owing to its proximity. For it nourishes fishes and produces salt in abundance, and bears back and forth ships carrying our commerce, by the profits of which the poor man becomes suddenly rich. It makes fertile the neighboring soil and feeds the birds who, they say, are generated from it along with the fishes and, although unlike, are moved by the laws of nature. The sea is dominated by them more than by the fishes, and they fly lightly up from it through space and seek the lofty regions. But its moisture drives the fishes beneath the waves and keeps them there, and does not permit them to live when they get out into the dry light. These too the Creator distinguished according to their species and to the different ones gave each his nature, whence through the ages they were to become admirable and healthful to the sick.

For men say that the barbel restrains the heat of passion but makes blind those who eat it often. The thymallus, which has its name from the flower thyme, smells so that it betrays the fish that often eats of it until all the fishes in the river smell like itself. They say the the muraenas, contrary to all laws, are all of the feminine sex, yet they copulate and reproduce and multiply their offspring from a different kind of seed. For often snakes come together along the shore where they are, and they make the sound of pleasing hissing and, calling out the muraenas, join with them according to custom. It is also remarkable that the remora, half a foot long, holds fast the ship to which it adheres at sea just as though it were fast aground, and does not permit the vessel to move until it lets go; because of this power it is to be feared. And that which they call the swordfish because it does injury with its sharp beak, people often fear to approach with a ship when it is swimming, for if it is captured it at once makes a hole in the vessel, cuts it in pieces, and sinks it suddenly in a whirlpool. The serra makes itself feared by ships because of its crest; it fixes to them as it swims underneath, cuts them to pieces and throws the pieces into the waves, wherefore its crest is to be feared like a sword. And the water dragon, which men say has poison under its wings, is to be feared by those who capture it; whenever it strikes it does harm by pouring out its poison. The torpedo is said to have another kind of destruction, for if any one touches it when it is alive, straightway his arms and his feet grow torpid and so do his other members and they lose their functions just as though they were dead, so harmful is the emanation of its body.

To those and other fishes God gave the sea, and He added to it many realms among the waves, which men inhabit and which are renowned because of the fertility which the earth produces there from its fruitful soil. Of these Britain is said to be the foremost and best, producing in its fruitfulness every single thing. For it bears crops which throughout the year give the noble gifts of fragrance for the use of man, and it has woods and glades with honey dripping in them, and lofty mountains and broad green fields, fountains and rivers, fishes and cattle and wild beasts, fruit trees, gems, precious metals, and whatever creative nature is in the habit of furnishing. Besides all these it has fountains healthful because of their hot waters which nourish the sick and provide pleasing baths, which quickly send people away cured with their sickness driven out. So Bladud established them when he held the sceptre of the kingdom, and he gave them the name of his consort Alaron. These are of value to many sick because of the healing of their water, but most of all to women, as often the water has demonstrated. Near to this island lies Thanet which abounds in many things but lacks the death-dealing serpent, and if any of its earth is drunk mixed with wine it takes away poison. Our ocean also divides the Orkneys from us. These are divided into thirty three islands by the sundering flood; twenty lack cultivation and the others are cultivated. Thule receives its name "furthest" from the sun, because of the solstice which the summer sun makes there, turning its rays and shining no further, and taking away the day, so that always throughout the long night the air is full of shadows, and making a bridge congealed by the benumbing cold, which prevents the passage of ships.

The most outstanding island after our own is said to be Ireland with its happy fertility. It is larger and produces no bees, and no birds except rarely, and it does not permit snakes to breed in it. Whence it happens that if earth or a stone is carried away from there and added to any other place it drives away snakes and bees. The island of Gades lies next to Herculean Gades, and there grows there a tree from whose bark a gum drips out of which gems are made, breaking all laws. The Hesperides are said to contain a watchful dragon who, men say, guards the golden apples under the leaves. The Gorgades are inhabited by women with goats' bodies who are said to surpass hares in the swiftness of their running. Argyre and Chryse bear, it is said, gold and silver just as Corinth does common stones. Sri Lanka blooms pleasantly because of its fruitful soil, for it produces two crops in a single year; twice it is summer, twice spring, twice men gather grapes and other fruits, and it is also most pleasing because of its shining gems. Tiles produces flowers and fruits in an eternal spring, green throughout the seasons.

The island of apples which men call "The Fortunate Isle" gets its name from the fact that it produces all things of itself; the fields there have no need of the plows of the farmers and all cultivation is lacking except what nature provides. Of its own accord it produces grain and grapes, and apple trees grow in its woods from the close-clipped grass. The ground of its own accord produces everything instead of merely grass, and people live there a hundred years or more. There nine sisters rule by a pleasing set of laws those who come to them from our country. She who is first of them is more skilled in the healing art, and excels her sisters in the beauty of her person. Morgen is her name, and she has learned what useful properties all the herbs contain, so that she can cure sick bodies. She also knows an art by which to change her shape, and to cleave the air on new wings like Daedalus; when she wishes she is at Brest, Chartres, or Pavia, and when she will she slips down from the air onto your shores. And men say that she has taught mathematics to her sisters, Moronoe, Mazoe, Gliten, Glitonea, Gliton, Tyronoe, Thitis; Thitis best known for her music. Here after the battle of Camlan we took the wounded Arthur, guided by Barinthus to whom the waters and the stars of heaven were well known. With him steering the ship we arrived there with the prince, and Morgen received is with fitting honor, and in her chamber she placed the king on a golden bed and with er own hand she uncovered his honorable wound and gazed at it for a long time. At length she said that health could be restored to him if he stayed with her for a long time and made use of her healing art. Rejoicing, therefore, we entrusted the king to her and returning spread our sails to the favoring winds."

Merlin said in answer, "Dear friend, since that time how much the kingdom has endured from the violated oath, so that what it once was it no longer is! For by an evil fate the nobles are roused up and turned against each other's vitals, and they upset everything so that the abundance of riches has fled from the country and all goodness has departed, and the desolated citizens leave their walls empty. Upon them shall come the Saxon people, fierce in war, who shall again cruelly overthrow us and our cities, and shall violate God's law and his temples. For He shall certainly permit this destruction to come upon us because of our crimes that He may correct the foolish." Merlin had scarcely finished when Taliesin exclaimed, "Then the people should send someone to tell the chief to come back in a swift ship if has recovered his strength, that he may drive off the enemy with his accustomed vigor and re-establish the citizens in their former peace."

"No," said Merlin, "never shall these people depart when once they have fixed their claws on our shores. For at first they shall enslave our kingdom and our people and our cities, and shall dominate them with their forces for many years. Nevertheless three from among our people shall resist with much courage and shall kill many, and in the end shall overcome them. But they shall not continue thus, for it is the will of the highest Judge that the Britons shall through weakness lose their noble kingdom for a long time, until Conan shall come in his chariot from Brittany, and Cadwalader the venerated leader of the Welsh, who shall join together Scots and Cumbrians, Cornishmen and men of Brittany in a firm league, and shall return to their people their lost crown, expelling the enemy and renewing the times of Brutus, and shall deal with the cities in accordance with their consecrated laws. And the kings shall begin again to conquer remote peoples and to subjugate their own realms to themselves in mighty conflict."

"No one shall then be alive of those who are now living," said Taliesin, "nor do I think that any one has seen so many savage battles between fellow citizens as you have."

"That is so," said Merlin, "for I have lived a long time, seeing many of them, both of our own people among themselves and of the barbarians who disturb everything. And I remember the crime when Constans was betrayed and the small brothers Uther and Ambrosius fled across the water. At once wars began in the kingdom which now lacked a leader, for Vortigern of Gwent, the consul, was leading his troops against all the nations so that he might have the leadership of them, and was inflicting a wretched death upon the harmless peasants. At length with sudden violence he seized the crown after putting to death many of the nobles and he subdued the whole kingdom to himself. But those who were allied to the brothers by blood relationship, offended at this, began to set fire to all the cities of the ill-fated prince and to perturb his kingdom with savage soldiery, and they would not permit him to possess it in peace. Disquieted therefore since he could not withstand the rebellious people, he prepared to invite to the war men from far away with whose aid he might be able to meet his enemies. Soon there came from divers parts of the world warlike bands whom he received with honor. The Saxon people, in fact, arriving in their curved keels had come to serve him with their helmeted soldiery. They were led by two courageous brothers, Horsus and Hengist, who harmed the people and the cities with wicked treachery afterward. Then, by serving the king with industry, they won him over to themselves and seeing the people moved by a quarrel that touched them closely they were able to subjugate the king; then turning their ferocious arms upon the people they broke faith and killed the princes by a premeditated fraud while they were sitting with them after calling them together to make peace and a treaty with them, and the prince they drove over the top of the snowy mountain. These are the things I had begun to prophesy to him would happen to the kingdom. Next roaming abroad they set fire to the houses of the nation, and strove to make everything subject to themselves. But when Vortimer saw how great was the peril of his country, and saw his father expelled from the hall of Brutus, he took the crown, with the assent of the people, and attacked the savage tribes that were crushing them, and by many battles forced these to return to Thanet where the fleet was that had brought them. But in their flight fell the warrior Horsus and many others, slain by our men. The king followed them and, taking his stand before Thanet besieged it by land and sea, but without success, for the enemy suddenly got possession of their fleet and with violence broke out and, led over the sea, they regained their own country in haste. Therefore, since he had conquered the enemy in victorious war, Vortimer became a ruler to be respected in the world, and he treated his kingdom with just restraint. But Hengist's sister, Rowena, seeing with indignation these successes, and protected by deceit, mixed poison, becoming on her brother's account a malignant step-mother, and she gave it to Vortimer to drink, and killed him. At once she sent across the water to her brother to tell him to come back with so many and such great multitudes that he would be able to conquer the warlike natives. This therefore he did, for he came with such force against our army that he took booty from everybody until he was loaded with it, and he thoroughly destroyed by fire the houses throughout the country.

"While these things were happening Uther and Ambrosius were in Breton territory with King Biducus and they had already girded on their swords and were proved fit for war, and had associated with themselves troops from all directions so that they might seek their native land and put to flight the people who were busy wasting their patrimony. So they gave their boats to the wind and the sea, and landed for the protection of their subjects; they drove Vortigern through the regions of Wales and shut him up in his tower and burned both him and it. Then they turned their swords upon the Anglos and many times when they met them they defeated them, and on the other hand they were often defeated by them. At length in a hand to hand conflict our men with great effort attacked the enemy and defeated them decisively, and killed Hengist, and by the will of Christ triumphed.

"After these things had been done, the kingdom and its crown were with the approval of clergy and laity given to Ambrosius, and he ruled justly in all things, but after the space of four times four years had elapsed he was betrayed by his doctor, and died from drinking poison. His younger brother Uther succeeded him, and at first was unable to maintain his kingdom in peace, for the perfidious people, accustomed by now to return, came and laid waste everything with their usual phalanx. Uther fought them in savage battles and drove them conquered across the water with returning oars. Soon he put aside strife and re-established peace and begat a son who became so eminent that he was second to none in uprightness. Arthur was his name and he held the kingdom for many years after the death of his father Uther, and this he did with great grief and labour, and with the slaughter of many men in many wars. For while the aforesaid chief lay ill, from Anglia came a faithless people who with sword subdued all the country and the regions across the Humber. Arthur was a boy and on account of his youth he was not able to defeat such a force. Therefore after seeking the advice of clergy and laity he sent to Hoel, king of Brittany, and asked him to come to his aid with a swift fleet, for they were united by ties of blood and friendship, so that each was bound to relieve the distresses of the other. Hoel therefore quickly collected for the war fierce men from every side and came to us with many thousands, and joining with Arthur he attacked the enemy often, and drove them back and made terrible slaughter. With his help Arthur was secure and strong among all the troops when he attacked the enemy whom at length he conquered and forced to return to their own country, and he quieted his own kingdom by the moderation of his laws.

"Soon after this struggle he changed the scene of the war, and subdued the Scots and Irish and all these warlike countries by means of the forces he had brought. He also subjugated the Norwegians far away across the broad seas, and the Danes whom he had visited with his hated fleet. He conquered the people of the Gauls after killing Frollo to whom the Roman power had given the care of that country; the Romans, too, who were seeking to make war on his country, he fought against and conquered, and killed the Procurator Hiberius Lucius who was then a colleague of Legnis the general, and who by the command of the Senate had come to bring the territories of the Gauls under their power.

Meanwhile the faithless and foolish custodian Modred had commenced to subdue our kingdom to himself, and was making unlawful love to the king's wife. For the king, desiring, as men say, to go across the water to attack the enemy, had entrusted the queen and the kingdom to him. But when the report of such a great evil came to his ears, he put aside his interest in the wars and, returning home, landed with many thousand men and fought with his nephew and drove him flying across the water. There the traitor, after collecting Saxons from all sides, began to battle with his lord, but he fell, betrayed by the unholy people confiding in whom he had undertaken such big things. How great was the slaughter of men and the grief of women whose sons fell in that battle! After it the king, mortally wounded, left his kingdom and, sailing across the water with you as you have related, came to the court of the maidens. Each of the two sons of Modred, desiring to conquer the kingdom for himself, began to wage war and each in turn slew those who were near of kin to him. Then Duke Constantine, nephew of the king, rose up fiercely against them and ravaged the people and the cities, and after having killed both of them by a cruel death ruled over the people and assumed the crown. But he did not continue in peace since Conan his relative waged dire war on him and ravaged everything and killed the king and seized for himself those lands which he now governs weakly and without a plan."

While Merlin was speaking all this, the servants hurried in and announced to him that a new fountain had broken out at the foot of the mountains and was pouring out pure waters which were running through all the hollow valley and swirling through the fields as they slipped along. Both therefore quickly rose to see the new fountain, and having seen it Merlin sat down again on the grass and praised the spot and the flowing waters, and marveled that they had come out of the ground in such a fashion. Soon afterward, becoming thirsty, he leaned down to the stream and drank freely and bathed his temples in its waves, so that the water passed through the passages of bowels and stomach, settling the vapors within him, and at once he regained his reason and knew himself, and all his madness departed and the sense which had long remained torpid in him revived, and he remained what he had once been - sane and intact with his reason restored. Therefore, praising God, he turned his face toward the stars and uttered devout words of praise. "O King, through whom the machine of the starry heavens exists, through whom the sea and the land with its pleasing grass give forth and nourish their offspring and with their profuse fertility give frequent aid to mankind, through whom sense has returned and the error of my mind has vanished! I was carried away from myself and like a spirit I knew the acts of past peoples and predicted the future. Then since I knew the secrets of things and the flight of birds and the wandering motions of the stars and the gliding of the fishes, all this vexed me and denied a natural rest to my human mind by a severe law. Now I have come to myself and I seem to be moved with a vigor such as was wont to animate my limbs. Therefore, highest Father, ought I to be obedient to Thee, that I may show forth Thy most worthy praise from a worthy heart, always joyfully making joyful offerings. For twice Thy generous hand has benefited me alone, in giving me the gift of this new fountain out of the green grass. For now I have the water which hitherto I lacked, and by drinking of it my brains have been made whole. But what of this virtue, O dear companion, that this new fountain breaks out thus, and makes me myself again who up to now was as though insane and beside myself?"

Taliesin answered, "The opulent Regulator of things divided the rivers according to their kinds, and added moreover to each a power of its own, that they might often prove of benefit to the sick. For there are fountains and rivers and lakes throughout the world which by their power cure many, and often do so. There is another fountain, called Cicero's, which flows in Italy, which cures the eyes of all injuries. The Ethiopians also are said to have a pool which makes a face on which it is poured shine just as though from oil. Africa has a fountain, commonly called Zama, a drink from it produces melodious voices by its sudden power. The fountain of Cyzicus drives away lust and the love of Venus. In the region of Campania there flow, it is said, rivers which when drunk of make the barren fruitful, and the same ones are said to take away madness from men. The land of the Ethiopians contains a fountain with a red stream; whoever drinks of this will come back demented. The fountain of Leinus never permits miscarriages. There are two fountains in Sicily, one of which makes girls sterile and the other makes them fruitful by its kindly law. There are two rivers in Thessaly of the greatest power; a sheep drinking of one turns black and is made white by the other, and any one drinking of both spends its life with a variegated fleece. There is a lake called Clitumnus in the Umbrian land which is said at times to produce large oxen, and in the Reatine Swamp the hooves of horses become hard as soon as they cross its sands. In the Asphalt Lake of Judaea bodies can never sink while life animates them, but on the other hand the land of India has a pool called Sida in which nothing floats but sinks at once to the bottom. And there is a Lake Aloe in which nothing sinks but all things float even if they are pieces of lead. The fountain of Marsida also compels stones to float. The River Styx flows from a rock and kills those who drink of it; the land of Arcadia bears testimony to this form of destruction. The fountain of Idumea, changing four times throughout the days, is said to vary its color by a strange rule; for it becomes muddy, then green, then the order changes and it turns red and then becomes clear with a beautiful stream. It is said to retain each of these colors for three months as the years roll around. There is also a Lake Trogdytus whose waves flow out, three times in the day bitter, and three times sweet with a pleasant taste. From a fountain of Epirus torches are said to be lighted, and if extinguished to resume their light again. The fountain of the Garamantes is said to be so cold in the day time, and on the other hand so hot all night, that it forbids approach on account of its cold or its heat. There are also hot waters that threaten many because of the heat which they get when they flow through alum or sulphur which have a fiery power, pleasant for healing. God endowed the rivers with these powers and others so that they might be the means of quick healing for the sick, and so that they might make manifest with what power the Creator stands eminent among things while He works thus in them. I think that these waters are healthful in the highest degree and I think that they could afford a quick cure through the water that has thus broken out. They have up to now been flowing about through the dark hollows under the earth like many others that are said to trickle underground. Perhaps their breaking out is due to an obstacle getting in their way, or to the slipping of a stone or a mass of earth. I think that, in making their way back again, they have gradually penetrated the ground and have given us this fountain. You see many such flow along and return again underground and regain their caverns."

While they were doing these things a rumor sprung out all about that a new fountain had broken out in the woods of Calidon, and that drinking from it had cured a man who had for a long time been suffering from madness and had lived in these same woods after the manner of the wild beasts. Soon therefore the princes and the chieftains came to see it and to rejoice with the prophet who had been cured by the water. After they had informed him in detail of the status of his country and had asked him to resume his sceptre, and to deal with his people with his accustomed moderation, he said, "Young men, my time of life, drawing on toward old age, and so possessing my limbs that with my weakened vigor I can scarce pass through the fields, does not ask this of me. I have already lived long enough, rejoicing in happy days while an abundance of great riches smiled profusely upon me. In that wood there stands an oak in its hoary strength which old age, that consumes everything, has so wasted away that it lacks sap and is decaying inwardly. I saw this when it first began to grow and I even saw the fall of the acorn from which it came, and a woodpecker standing over it and watching the branch. Here I have seen it grow of its own accord, watching it all, and, fearing for it in these fields, I marked the spot with my retentive mind. So you see I have lived a long time and now the weight of age holds me back and I refuse to reign again. When I remain under the green leaves the riches of Calidon delight me more than the gems that India produces, or the gold that Tagus is aid to have on its shore, more than the crops of Sicily or the grapes of pleasant Methis, more than lofty turrets or cities girded with high walls or robes fragrant with Tyrian perfumes. Nothing pleases me enough to tear me away from my Calidon which in my opinion is always pleasant. Here shall I remain while I live, content with apples and grasses, and I shall purify my body with pious fasting that I may be worthy to partake of the life everlasting."

While Merlin was speaking all this, the chiefs caught sight of long lines of cranes in the air, circling through space in a curved line in the shape of certain letters. Marveling at these they asked Merlin to tell why it was that they were flying in such manner. Merlin presently said to them, "The Creator of the world gave to the birds as to many other things their proper nature, as I have learned by living in the woods for many days. It is therefore the nature of the cranes, as they go through the air, if many are present, that we often see them in their flight form a figure in one way or another. One, by calling, warns them to keep the formation as they fly, lest it break up and depart from the usual figure; when he becomes hoarse another takes his place. They post sentries at night and the watchman holds a pebble in his claws when he wishes to drive away sleep, and when they see any one they start up with a sudden clamor. The feathers of all of them grow black as they grow older. But the eagles, who get their name from the sharpness of their sight, are said to be of such keen vision, beyond all others, that they are able to gaze at the sun without flinching. They hang up their young in its rays wishing to know by his avoidance of them whether their exists among them one of inferior breeding. They remain on their wings over waters as high as the top of a mountain and they spy their prey in the lowest depths; straightway they descend rapidly through the void and seize the fish swimming as their inheritance demands. The vulture, thinking little of the commerce of the sexes, often conceives and bears (strange to say) without any seed of her spouse. Flying about on high in the manner of the eagle she scents with distended nostrils a dead body far across the water. This she has no horror of approaching in her flight, although she is slow, so that she may satiate herself with the prey she wishes for. This same bird also lives vigorous for a hundred years. The stork with its croaking voice is a messenger of spring; it is said to nourish its young so carefully that it takes out its own feathers and denudes its own breast. When winter comes men say it avoids the storms and approaches the shores of Asia, led by a crow. Its young feed it as it grows old because it fed them when it owed them this care. The swan, a bird most pleasing to sailors, excels all others in the sweetness of its music when it dies. Men say that in the country of the Hyperboreans it comes up close by being attracted by the sound of a zither played loudly along the shore. The ostrich deserts her eggs which she places under the dust that they may be taken care of there when she herself neglects them. Thence the birds come into the world hatched by the sun instead of their mother. The heron, when it fears the rain and the tempests, flies to the clouds to avoid such a peril; hence sailors say that it portends sudden rainstorms when they see it high up in the air. The phoenix by divine dispensation always lives as an unique bird, and in the land of the Arabs rises with a renewed body. When it grows old it goes to a place very warm from the heat of the sun and gets together a great heap of spices and builds itself a pyre, which it lights with rapid movements of its wings, and it settles down upon this and is completely consumed. The ashes of its body produce a bird, and in this way the phoenix is again renewed throughout the ages. The cinnamolgus when it wishes to build a nest brings cinnamon, and builds of that because of its undoubted strength. From this men are in the habit of driving it away with arrows, after which they remove the heap and sell it. The halcyon is a bird that frequents sea pools and builds its nest in time of winter; when it broods the seas are calm for seven days and the winds cease and the tempests, relaxed, hold off, furnishing placid quiet for the bird. The parrot is thought to utter human speech as its own call when no one is looking directly at it, and it mixes "ave" and "chaire" with jocose words. The pelican is a bird accustomed to kill its young and to lament for three days confused with grief. Then it tears its own body with its beak and, cutting the veins, lets out streams of blood with which it sprinkles the birds and brings them back to life. The Diomedae when they resound with tearful noise and make lament are said to portend the sudden death of kings or a great peril to the realm. And when they see anyone they know at once what he is, whether barbarian or Greek; for they approach a Greek with beatings of the wings and with caresses and they make a joyful noise but they fly about the others on hostile wings and approach them with a horrible sound as though they were enemies. The Memnonides are said to go on a long flight every fifth year to the tomb of Memnon, and to lament the prince killed in the Trojan war. The shining Hercynia has a marvelous feather which gleams on a dark night like a lighted lamp, and shows the way if it is carried in front of a traveler. When the woodpecker makes a nest he pulls out of the tree nails and wedges that no one else can get out and the whole neighborhood resounds with his blows."

After Merlin had finished speaking, a certain madman came to them, either by accident or led there by fate; he filled the grove and the air with a terrific clamor and like a wild boar he foamed at the mouth and threatened to attack them. They quickly captured him and made him sit down by them that his remarks might move them to laughter and jokes. When the prophet looked at him more attentively he recollected who he was and groaned from the bottom of his heart, saying, "This is not the way he used to look when we were in the bloom of our youth, for at that time he was a fair, strong knight and one distinguished by his nobility and his royal race. Him and many others I had with me in the days of my wealth, and I was thought fortunate in having so many good companions, and I was. It happened one time while we were hunting in the lofty mountains of Arwystli that we came to an oak which rose in the air with its broad branches. A fountain flowed there, surrounded on all sides by green grass, whose waters were suitable for human consumption; we were all thirsty and we sat down by it and drank greedily of its pure waters. Then we saw some fragrant apples lying on the tender grass of the familiar bank of the fountain. The man who saw them first quickly gathered them up and gave them to me, laughing at the unexpected gift. I distributed to my companions the apples he had given to me, and I went without any because the pile was not big enough. The others to whom the apples had been given laughed and called me generous, and eagerly attacked and devoured them and complained because there were so few of them. Without any delay a miserable sadness seized this man and all the others; they quickly lost their reason and like dogs bit and tore each other, and foamed at the mouth and rolled on the ground in a demented state. Finally, they went away like wolves filling the vacant air with howling. These apples I thought were intended for me and not for them, and later I found out that they were. At that time there was in that district a woman who had formerly been infatuated with me, and had satisfied her love for me during many years. After I had spurned her and had refused to cohabit with her she was suddenly seized with an evil desire to do me harm, and when with all her plotting she could not find any means of approach, she placed the gifts smeared with poison by the fountain to which I was going to return, planning by this device to injure me if I should chance to find the apples on the grass and eat them. But my good fortune kept me from them, as I have just said. I pray you, make this man drink of the healthful waters of this new fountain so that, if by chance he get back his health, he may know himself and may, while his life lasts, labor with me in these glades in service to God." This, therefore, the leaders did, and the man who had come there raging drank the water, recovered, and, cured at once recognized his friends.

Then Merlin said, "You must now go on in the service of God who restored you as you now see yourself, you who for so many years lived in the desert like a wild beast, going about without a sense of shame. Now that you have recovered your reason, do not shun the bushes or the green glades which you inhabited while you were mad, but stay with me that you may strive to make up in service to God for the days that the force of madness took from you. From now on all things shall be in common between you and me in this service so long as either lives." At this, the man, named Maeldinus, said, "Reverend father, I do not refuse to do this, for I shall joyfully stay in the woods with you, and shall worship God with my whole mind, while that spirit, for which I shall render thanks to your ministry, governs my trembling limbs." "And I shall make a third with you, and shall despise the things of the world," said Taliesin. "I have spent enough time living in vain, and now is the time to restore me to myself under your leadership. But you, lords, go away and defend your cities; it is not fitting that you should disturb beyond measure our quiet with your talk. You have applauded my friend enough."

The chiefs went away, and the three remained, with Ganieda, the prophet's sister, making a fourth, she who at length had assumed and was leading a seemly life after the death of the king who so recently had ruled so many people by the laws he administered. Now with her brother there was nothing more pleasant to her than the woods. She too was at times elevated by the spirit so that she often prophesied to her friends concerning the future of the kingdom. Thus on a certain day when she stood in her brother's hall and saw the windows of the house shining with the sun she uttered these doubtful words from her doubtful breast.

"I see the city of Oxford filled with helmed men, and the holy men and the holy bishops bound in fetters by the advice of the Council, and men shall admire the shepherd's tower reared on high, and he shall be forced to open it to no purpose and to his own injury. I see Lincoln walled in by savage soldiery and two men shut up in it, one of whom escapes to return with a savage tribe and their chief to the walls to conquer the cruel soldiers after capturing their leader. O what a shame it is that the stars should capture the sun, under whom they sink down, compelled neither by force nor by war! I see two moons in the air near Winchester and two lions acting with too great ferocity, and one man looking at two and another at the same number, and preparing for battle and standing opposed. The others rise up and attack the fourth fiercely and savagely but not one of them prevails, for he stands firm and moves his shield and fights back with his weapons and as victor straightway defeats his triple enemy.

Two of them he drives across the frozen regions of the north while he gives to the third the mercy that he asks, so that the stars flee through all portions of the fields. The Boar of Brittany, protected by an aged oak, takes away the moon, brandishing swords behind her back. I see two stars engaging in combat with wild beasts beneath the hill of Urien where the people of Gwent and those of Deira met in the reign of the great Coel. O with what sweat the men drip and with what blood the ground while wounds are being given to the foreigners! One star collides with the other and falls into the shadow, hiding its light from the renewed light. Alas what dire famine shall come, so that the north shall inflame her vitals and empty them of the strength of her people. It begins with the Welsh and goes through the chief parts of the kingdom, and forces the wretched people to cross the water. The calves accustomed to live on the milk of the Scottish cows that are dying from the pestilence shall flee. Normans depart and cease to bear weapons through our native realm with your cruel soldiery. There is nothing left with which to feed your greed for you have consumed everything that creative nature has produced in her happy fertility. Christ, aid thy people! restrain the lions and give to the country quiet peace and the cessation of wars." She did not stop with this and her companions wondered at her, and her brother, who soon came to her, spoke approvingly with friendly words in this manner, "Sister, does the spirit wish you to foretell future things, since he has closed up my mouth and my book? Therefore this task is given to you; rejoice in it, and under my favor devoted to him speak everything."

I have brought this song to an end, furthering an account of the "History of British Kings." So, therefore, ye Britons, give a wreath to Geoffrey of Monmouth. He is indeed yours for once he sang of your battles and those of your chiefs, which are celebrated throughout the world.

Chapter XLII Prophetic Dreams with Myrddin the Bard

Interpreted in the 16th Century

Chronicles by Elis Gruffudd

with additional verses from

The Red Book of Hergest

The Story of Myrddin Wyllt

According to the narrative of some authors there was about this time within one which is called Nanconwy a man who was called Morfryn. But others show this was Morfryn Frych, prince of Gwynedd - which he could not be according to the tenor of his songs. Nevertheless the writing shows that a man of this name had a son who was called Mryddin son of Morfryn, and a daughter who was called Gwenddydd as the story shows, the son was unstable in his senses; for at one time he would be witless and out of mind and reason, and at another time he would be in his mind at which time he would be wise and discreet and prompt in his answers and good counsels concerning everything that would be asked of him. To him God had given the of prophecy, which prophecies he would declare in poetry in metre, when he wool in his mind, and especially to Gwenddydd his sister, who, as my copy shows, was wise and learned and who wrote a great book of his utterances, especially about prophecies as related to this island. Some of these follow hereafter in this vein although there is hardly any profitable meaning to be gathered from any of them. Nevertheless, in order to ward off sloth, with God's help I will write down all that I have been able to see in writing.

The books show that this Myrddin was so unstable in mind and senses that he would not live within dwelling houses, especially during the three months of summer, but in caves in the rocks and in harbours of his own work in the glens and the woods on either side of the river Conway. To these parts and plaçes Gwenddydd his sister would come many a time with his food, which she would set in a place so that he could take his nourishment when he came to his senses.

And at a certain time, as the narrative shows, it happened that Gwenddydd saw certain rare dreams on various nights. All these she carefully retained in her memory until she should find a place and time to relate them to Myrddin her brother. Against that time Gwenddydd prepared bread and butter on a herb cake of wheaten bread with various drinks in various vessels, every drink in its grade as its nature demanded, as wine in silver, and mead in a horn, and the beer in sycamore, and the milk in a white jug, and the water in an earthen jug. All these she placed in order besides the bread and butter inside the harbour to which Myrddin was wont to come, when he was in his senses, to take his nourishment.

To this part and place he came soon thereafter, as the writing shows. At which time Gwenddydd hid herself within the harbour or cell to listen to his declamations. At which time, as Gwenddydd shows at length, Myrddin took the finely wrought cake and the bread and butter upon it, to which he composed many songs. Of it he said:

England will not muster hosts to every place;
It is not from its centre that bread and butter is eaten.

And after he had eaten a portion of his bread and butter he complained to himself about drink. Thereupon Gwenddydd revealed herself to her brother, to whom she showed the drinks in order, as she had placed them in order. At which time, as [the story] shows, Myrddin asked his sister what kind of drink stood in the bright shining vessel. To which Gwenddydd answered saying, 'This drink, which is called wine, has been made from the fruit of the trees of the earth." "Aha!" said Myrddin, "verily this drink is not suitable for me or for my people , for it is the nature of this drink to make such as are wont to drink it in these regions poor from being rich". And after this he asked Gwenddydd what kind of drink was in the horn. To which answered Gwenddydd, who spoke thus: "This drink, which is called mead amongst our people, has been made from water and honey." "Aha!" said Myrddin, "much of this drink is not healthy for me or for anyone, for its nature is to make ill the healthy". And afterwards he asked his sister what kind of drink was in the many coloured wood, to which Gwenddydd answered saying, "This drink, which is called beer, has been made from water and from grains of barley." "Aha!" said Myrddin, "this drink is not at all good for me, for its nature is to deprive the prudent of their senses."

And then Myrddin asked Gwenddydd what kind of drink was in the white jug. To which she answered saying, "This drink is made from the produce of animals and is called milk." Then Myrddin said thus: "Verily this drink is good for me and my people, for this is natural to nurture the weak and to help the feeble and to strengthen the wretched and to increase energy for the strong." And after this he asked what kind of drink stood in the earthen vessel. To which Gwenddydd answered saying, "This is one of the four elements and it is called water, which God from Heaven has sent for the benefit of mankind." Then Myrddin said thus, "All thou hast said is true, and verily this is the one best drink till the Day of judgement. Of this I will drink my fill to slake my thirst."

And after this she begged of him to listen to her relating to him certain dreams which she had seen certain times previously, begging him to interpret them and to show clearly to her what they represented. Upon which Myrddin asked her to them, and she spoke as follows written in this work.

The First Dream-

My true brother and friend, of a night in my sleep I thought for certain within myself that I was standing on a great wide field which I saw full of stone cairns small in and a few big cairns amongst the small ones. And I could see great numbers of people gathering the stones from the small cairns and casting them into the big ones with a pause. And yet in spite of this I could not see either the small cairns becoming smaller, however much I could see the peoples gathering from them, or the big one becoming bigger, however great the assiduity with which I could see the peoples collecting the stones from the small cairns and casting them into the big cairns. And the marvel of the dream I awoke; but verily I cannot let the marvel of the dream out of my memory.

How Myrddin Interpreted the First Dream to his Sister–

Gwenddydd and my dearest sister, do not marvel too much at thy vision, for no harm will come to thee from it. And be it known to thee that the field thou sawest represents this island. And the small cairns represent the husbandmen of the kingdom and it's labourers of each and every grade who live lawfully and win their livelihood by labour of their bodies, and who place their trust in God alone. And the big cairns represent the chiefs of the kingdom of each and every grade. And the peoples whom thou sawest gathering the stones from the small cairns and casting them into the big ones represent the servants of noblemen who are and always will be ready to keep their servants to take the wealth of the labourers and the husbandmen without ceasing for ever, sometimes under pretence or semblance of the offices of the law, sometimes by force sometimes by stealth. And in as much as thou sawest not the big cairns increasing however much the load thou sawest the peoples carrying from the small cairns to the big ones, that shows God's wrath and displeasure, for God does not allow the wealth that is wrongfully amassed to multiply with the gatherers and their descendants. And in as much as thou sawest not the small cairns smaller however much thou sawest people taking away from them, that represents the grace of God, for it is certain the noblemen of each and every grade oppress the common husbanding people their worldly goods. And yet in spite of this, however much goods the noblemen; their peoples take from the husbandmen by oppression, the latter will not be the worse or the poorer; for as much as they may lose the one way God will send them twice as much another way, especially if they will take such oppression forbearingly with patience and restraint and by entrusting the punishment and vengeance to the Fat of Heaven to Whom it is meet and rightful to punish all iniquity; for He ordained weak and the strong. And verily, however much an innocent man may lose in world, God will not allow him to want any wordly thing in this world, and an abundance of all goodness in the world that is to come. And verily this is what thy dream represents.

And after this she showed him the Second Dream–

Myrddin the wise and my true brother, I saw the second dream, that is, in my sleep thought that I was standing in an alder grove of the straightest and fairest trees which the heart of man could think of or imagine. Whither I saw great hosts of men coming with axes in their hands, and with these they were cutting the alder grove and felling them all to the ground from their trunks. And forthwith I saw the straightest and fairest yew trees which man could imagine, growing on the trunks of the alders. And with the marvel of the vision I awoke from my sleep, and from that to this day I cannot let it out of my memory.

How Myrddin Interpreted the Second Dream–

Gwenddydd, my counsel to thee is that thou marvel not at the dream, for no harm or hurt will come to thee from it, for the alder grove thou sawest represents this island and its ancestral peoples, which [island] will be greatly impoverished, especially of its noblemen, whom the alder trees represent. All of them will be destroyed even as thou sawest the alders destroyed. Yet in spite of this, in the same way as thou sawest the yews growing forthwith on the trunks of the alders, so noblemen will again grow from the remnants of their lineage. At which time no wealth will remain in the hands of the noblemen, who will betroth their children to men of low rank, from whom there will grow mighty noblemen who will continue in that mode and state for a long time thereafter. And verily this is what thy dream represents.

After this she showed him the Third Dream–

My true brother, I saw the third dream, for as I was sound asleep I could see myself standing on a level circular strand upon which I could see a great number of high green hills or mounds. And to my mind and thought I could see the earth quaking so that the mounds subsided into level land. In place of these, to my mind and thought, there forthwith arose heaps of dung. And on these dunghills I could see various kinds of flowering scented herbs growing. There is a great marvel in my heart at the- dream from that to this day.'

How Myrddin Interpreted the Third Dream-

Fair Gwenddydd, feel no worry in the matter, for the vision will do thee no harm; for the strand represents this island, and the mounds represent the chiefs of the island. And the quaking of the earth denotes that there will come war by which all the nobles will be destroyed in the same way as thou sawest the mounds destroyed. And the heaps thou sawest arising forthwith in their place denote that their dominions will be given to ignoble men. And the flowers denote that from these churls there will grow mighty noblemen. And yet it will be rare for the fifth descendant from the stock of these to possess the hearth of his father and grandfather and great-grandfather, for they will disappear like dung shoots. And this is the meaning of this dream.

And after this she declared to him how she saw the Fourth Dream-

Myrddin my brother, I thought at night in my sleep that I was standing in a park of the fairest wheat which a man could see with the sight of his eyes. The ears of the wheat I could see drily ripe and the stalks quite green. And I could see a mighty plague of swine coming and breaking down the hedge and coming into the park, where they caused grievous damage and destruction to the wheat so that the corn was level with the ground. At which time I saw coming into the wheat field a troop of white greyhounds, which forthwith ran at the swine and killed them nearly all. Because of the sight there is still a great marvel in my heart.

How Myrddin Interpreted the Fourth Dream-

Fair Gwenddydd, feel no worry in the matter, for the wheat field represents this kingdom, and the wheat represents the people. And the ripe ears and the sappy stalks denote that men young in age will be whiteheaded at this time, which verily will h rare a sight as seeing an ear of wheat quite ripe and the stalk quite green. And the swine thou sawest breaking into the wheat field denote that there will come to this kingdom a plague of foreigners who will destroy the people in the same way as sawest the swine destroying the wheat. And the greyhounds denote that then come men who will avenge the whiteheaded people upon the swine; such of these as will have been left their lives the greyhounds will drive to flight out of the kingdom. And this is thy dream in full.

And after this she declared to him the Fifth Dream-

My brother, I saw the fifth dream, that is, I thought that I was standing in the middle of a grave-yard of exceeding size, which I could see full of girls or maidens of the age. All these I could see pregnant and near the time of their delivery. And I though myself that the children were conversing with one another from their mothers' won which is a great marvel in my heart when I think of this vision.

Then Myrddin said-

Let there be no worry upon thee because of the dream. For this graveyard represents this island. And the girls or maidens denote that there will come a world and time when betrothals and marriage will be made between children under their snoods. Aye, and verily almost everyone of that age and generation will be married very young; the children and offspring which will be begotten between them will be full of evil cunning. And inasmuch as thou wert imagining that the children were speaking from their mothers' wombs, that denotes that a fifteen years old youth of this age will wiser in that age than a man of sixty years at this time.

Thus end the dreams.

A Fugitive Poem of Myrddin from the Grave

(The Book of Hergest)

He who speaks from the grave
Knows that before seven years
March of Eurdein will die.

I have drunk from a bright cup
With fierce and warlike lords;
My name is Myrddin, son of Morvryn.

I have drunk from a goblet
With powerful warlords;

Prophetic Dreams with Myrddin the Bard

Myrddin is my given name.

When the black wheel of oppression
Comes to destroy exhausted Llogres
Defence will be bitter and sustained.
The White Mount will see sorrow
A long regret to the people of the Cymry.

Protection won't be found
From the Boar of the Hosts,
Even in the heights of Ardudwy

When the red one of Normandy will come
To charge the Lloegrians with enormous expense,
There will be a tax upon every prediction
And a castle at Aber Hodni.

When the Freckled One comes
As far as Ryd Bengarn, men will face disgrace,
Their sword-hilts will break,
The new King of Prydain will be their judge.

Henri comes to claim
Mur Castell on Eryri's border
Trouble across the sea will call him.

When the Pale One comes to London
Upon ugly horses
He will call out the lords of Caergain.

Scarce the acorns, thick the corn
When a young king appears
Who will cause men to tremble.

A youth of great renown
Conqueror of a hundred cities -
Tender and frail will be his life.

Strong to the weak will he be
Weak towards the strong of the upland—
One whose coming will bring dark days.

Wantonness will rule,
Women will be easy prey -
Even children will need to confess.

A time of order will follow
When even churls will do good deeds;
Maidens will be lovely, youths resolute.
A time will follow, towards the end of the age,
When the young will fail from adversity
And cuckoos die of cold in Maytime.

There will be a time of great hunting dogs,
And buildings in secret places,
When even a shirt will cost a fortune.

There will be a time of great profanity,
When vices are active, and churches empty.
Words and relics will be broken–
Truth will vanish, falsehood spread
Faith will grow weak, and disputes abound.

There will be a time when everyone delights in clothing
When the lord's counsellors become like vagrants;
Bards will go empty-handed, though happy the priest;
Men will be despised, and frequently selfish.

There will be the time of windless days, without rain,
With little ploughing and less food,
One acre of land worth nine.

Men will be weak and unmanly
And corn grown under trees –
Though feasts will still occur.

When trees are held in high estate
There will be a new spring
There will be after the chief of mischeif –
The cowhouse worse than a single stake.

On Wednesday, a time of violence,
Blades will wear out,
Who will be bloodied at Cynghen.

At Aber Sor there will be a council
Of men following on the battle,
A bright ruler ruling the camp.

In Aber Avon the host of Mona congregate
Angles gather at Hinwedon;

Moryon's valour will be long remembered.

In Aber Dwyver the leader will fail
When the actions of Gwidig occur
After the battle of Cyvarllug.

A battle will be on the River Byrri,
Where Britons will have victory;
Gwhyr's men will be heroes.

An Aber Don a battle will occur
And the spears be unequal.
Blood on the brows of Saxons.
Servile you are today, Gwenddydd
The mountain ghosts come to me
Here in Aber Carav.

Chapter XLIII Merlyn & Vortigern - A Tale of Two Dragons

Chronicled by Geoffrey of Monmouth in

History of the British Kings (1138)

adapted by Myrddin Cerrig

Book VI

XVII

Vortigern, after consultation with magicians, orders a youth to be brought that never had a father

At last Vortigern had recourse to magicians for their advice, and commanded them to tell him what course to take in which to solidify his power. They advised him to build a very strong tower for his own safety, since he had lost all his other fortified places. Accordingly, he made a progress about the country, to find out a convenient situation, and came at last to Mount Erir, where he assembled workmen from several countries, and ordered them to build the tower. The builders, therefore, began to lay the foundation; but whatever they did one day the earth swallowed up the next, so as to leave no appearance of their work.

Vortigern being informed of this again consulted with his magicians concerning the cause of it, who told him that he must find out a youth that never had a father, and kill him, and then sprinkle the stones and cement with his blood; for by those means, they said, he would have a firm foundation. Hereupon messengers were dispatched away over all the provinces, to inquire out such a man.

In their travels they came to a city, called afterward, Kaermerdin, where they saw some young men, playing before the gate, and went up to them; but being weary with their journey, they sat down in the ring, to see if they could meet with what they were in quest of.

Towards evening, there happened on a sudden quarrel between two of the young men, whose names were Merlin and Dabutius. In the dispute, Dabutius said to Merlin: "You fool, do you presume to quarrel with me? Is there any equality in our birth? I am descended of royal race, both by my father and mother's side. As for you, nobody knows what you are, for you never had a father." At that word the messengers looked earnestly upon Merlin, and asked the bystanders who he was. They told him, it was not known who was his father; but that his mother was daughter to the king of Dimetia, and that she lived in St. Peter's church among the nuns of that city.

XVIII

Vortigern inquires of Merlin's mother concerning her conception of him.

Upon this the messengers hastened to the governor of the city, and ordered him, in the king's name, to send Merlin and his mother to the king. As soon as the governor understood the occasion of their message, he readily obeyed the order, and sent them to Vortigern to complete his design. When they were introduced into the king's presence, he received the mother in a very respectful manner, on account of her noble birth; and began to inquire of her by what man she had conceived. "My sovereign lord," said she, "by the life of your soul and mine, I know nobody that begot him of me. Only this I know, that as I was once with my companions in our chambers, there appeared to me a person in the shape of a most beautiful young man, who often embraced me eagerly in his arms, and kissed me; and when he had stayed a little time, he suddenly vanished out of my sight. But many times after this he would talk with me when I sat alone, without making any visible appearance. When he had a long time haunted me in this manner, he at last lay with me several times in the shape of a man, and left me with child. And I do affirm to you, my sovereign lord, that excepting that young man, I know no body that begot him of me."

The king full of admiration at this account, ordered Maugantius to be called, that he might satisfy him as to the possibility of what the woman had related. Maugantius, being introduced, and having the whole matter repeated to him, said to Vortigern: "In the books of our philosophers, and in a great many histories, I have found that several men have had the like original. For, as Apuleius informs us in his book concerning the Demon of Socrates, between the moon and the earth inhabit those spirits, which we will call incubuses. These are of the nature partly of men, and partly of angels, and whenever they please assume human shapes, and lie with women. Perhaps one of them appeared to this woman, and begot that young man of her."

XIX

Merlin's speech to the king's magicians, and advice about the building of the tower.

Merlin in the meantime was attentive to all that had passed, and then approached the king, and said to him, "For what reason am I and my mother introduced into your presence?" — "My magicians," answered Vortigern, "advised me to seek out a man that had no father, with whose blood my building is to be sprinkled, in order to make it stand." — "Order your magicians," said Merlin, "to come before me, and I will convict them of a lie."

The king was surprised at his words, and presently ordered the magicians to come, and sit down before Merlin, who spoke to them after this manner: "Because you are ignorant what it is that hinders the foundation of the tower, you have recommended the shedding of my blood for cement to it, as if that would presently make it stand. But tell me now, what is there under the foundation? For something there is that will not suffer it to stand."

The magicians at this began to be afraid, and made him no answer. Then said Merlin, who was also called Ambrose, "I entreat your majesty would command your workmen to dig into the ground, and you will find a pond which causes the foundations to sink." This accordingly was done, and then presently they found a pond deep under ground, which had made it give way.

Merlin after this went again to the magicians, and said, "Tell me ye false sycophants, what is there under the pond." But they were silent. Then said he again to the king, "Command the pond to be drained, and at the bottom you will see two hollow stones, and in them two dragons asleep." The king made no scruple of believing him, since he had found true what he said of the pond, and therefore ordered it to be drained: which done, he found as Merlin had said; and now was possessed with the greatest admiration of him. Nor were the rest that were present less amazed at his wisdom, thinking it to be no less than divine inspiration.

Book VIII

I

Vortigern asks Merlin concerning his own death.

Merlin, by delivering these and many other prophecies, caused in all that were present an admiration at the ambiguity of his expressions. But Vortigern above all the rest both admired and applauded the wisdom, and prophetical spirit of the young man: for that age had produced none that ever talked in such a manner before him. Being therefore curious to learn his own fate, he desired the young man to tell him what he knew concerning that particular.

Merlin answered: —"Fly the fire of the sons of Constantine, if you are able to do it: already are they fitting out their ships: already are they leaving the Armorican shore: already are they spreading out their sails to the wind. They will steer towards Britain: they will invade the Saxon nation: they will subdue that wicked people; but they will first burn you being shut up in a tower. To your own ruin did you prove a traitor to their father, and invite the Saxons into the island. You invited them for your safeguard; but they came for a punishment to you. Two deaths instantly threaten you; nor is it easy to determine, which you can best avoid. For on the one hand the Saxons shall lay waste your country, and endeavor to kill you: on the other shall arrive the two brothers, Aurelius Ambrosius and Uther Pendragon, whose business will be to revenge their father's murder upon you. Seek out some refuge if you can: to-morrow they will be on the shore of Totness. The faces of the Saxons shall look red with blood, Hengist shall be killed, and Aurelius Ambrosius shall be crowned. He shall bring peace to the nation; he shall restore the churches; but shall die of poison. His brother Uther Pendragon shall succeed him, whose days also shall be cut short by poison. There shall be present at the commission of this treason your own issue, whom the boar of Cornwall shall devour." Accordingly the next day early, arrived Aurelius Ambrosius and his brother, with ten thousand men.

II

Aurelius Ambrosius, being anointed king of Britain, burns Vortigern besieged in his tower.

As soon as the news of his coming was divulged, the Britons, who had been dispersed by their great calamities, met together from all parts, and gaining this new accession of strength from their countrymen, displayed unusual vigor. Having assembled together the clergy, they anointed Aurelius king, and paid him the customary homage. And when the people were urgent to fall upon the Saxons, he dissuaded them from it, because his desire was to pursue Vortigern first. For the treason committed against his father so very much affected him, that he thought nothing done till that was first avenged. In pursuance therefore of this design, he marched with his army into Cambria, to the town of Genoreu, whither Vortigern had fled for refuge. That town was in the country of Hergin, upon the river Gania, in the mountain called Cloarius. As soon as Ambrosius was arrived there, bearing in his mind the murder of his father and brother, he spake thus to Eldol, duke of Gloucester.

"See, most noble duke, whether the walls of this city are able to protect Vortigern against my sheathing this sword in his bowels. He deserves to die, and you cannot, I suppose, be ignorant of his desert. Oh most villainous of men, whose crimes deserve inexpressible tortures! First he betrayed my father Constantine, who had delivered him and his country from the inroads of the Picts; afterward my brother Constans whom he made king on purpose to destroy him. Again, when by his craft he had usurped the crown, he introduced pagans among the natives, in order to abuse those who continued steadfast in their loyalty to me: but by the good providence of God, he unwarily fell into the snare, which he had laid for my faithful subjects. For the Saxons, when they found him out in his wickedness, drove him from the kingdom; for which nobody ought to be concerned. But this I think matter of just grief, that this odious people, whom that detestable traitor invited over, has expelled the nobility, laid waste a fruitful country, destroyed the holy churches, and almost extinguished Christianity over the whole kingdom. Now, therefore, my countrymen, show yourselves men; first revenge yourselves upon him that was the occasion of all these disasters; then let us turn our arms against our enemies, and free our country from their brutish tyranny."

Immediately, therefore, they set their engines to work, and labored to beat down the walls. But at last, when all other attempts failed, they had recourse to fire, which meeting with proper fuel, ceased not to rage, till it had burned down the tower and Vortigern in it.

Chapter XLIV The Prophecies of Merlyn

Chronicled by Geoffrey of Monmouth in

History of the British Kings (1138)

adapted by Myrddin Cerrig

Book VII

III

The Prophecy of Merlin.

As Vortigern, king of the Britons, was sitting upon the bank of the drained pond, the two dragons, one of which was white, the other red, came forth, and, approaching one another, began a terrible fight, and cast forth fire with their breath. But the white dragon had the advantage, and made the other fly to the end of the lake. And he, for grief at his flight, renewed the assault upon his pursuer, and forced him to retire. After this battle of the dragons, the king commanded Ambrose Merlin to tell him what it portended. Upon which he, bursting into tears, delivered what his prophetical spirit suggested to him, as follows:—

Woe to the red dragon, for his banishment hastens on. His lurking holes shall be seized by the white dragon, which signifies the Saxons whom you invited over; but the red denotes the British nation, which shall be oppressed by the white. Therefore shall its mountains be leveled as the valleys, and the rivers of the valleys shall run with blood.

The exercise of religion shall be destroyed, and churches be laid open to ruin. At last the oppressed shall prevail, and oppose the cruelty of foreigners. For a boar of Cornwall shall give his assistance, and trample their necks under his feet. The islands of the ocean shall be subject to his power, and he shall possess the forests of Gaul. The house of Romulus shall dread his courage, and his end shall be doubtful. He shall be celebrated in the mouths of the people; and his exploits shall be food to those that relate them. Six of his posterity shall sway the sceptre, but after them shall arise a German worm. He shall be advanced by a sea-wolf, whom the woods of Africa shall accompany. Religion shall be again abolished, and there shall be a translation of the metropolitan sees.

The dignity of London shall adorn Dorobernia, and the seventh pastor of York shall be resorted to in the kingdom of Armorica. Menevia shall put on the pall of the City of Legions, and a preacher of Ireland shall be dumb on account of an infant growing in the womb.

It shall rain a shower of blood, and a raging famine shall afflict mankind. When these things happen, the red one shall be grieved; but when his fatigue is over, shall grow strong. Then shall misfortunes hasten upon the white one, and the buildings of his gardens shall be pulled down. Seven that sway the sceptre shall be killed, one of whom shall become a saint. The wombs of mothers shall be ripped up, and infants be aborted. There shall be a most grievous punishment of men, that the natives may be restored. He that shall do these things shall put on the brazen man, and upon a brazen horse shall for a long time guard the gates of London.

After this, shall the red dragon return to his proper manners, and turn his rage upon himself. Therefore shall the revenge of the Thunderer show itself, for every field shall disappoint the husbandmen. Mortality shall snatch away the people, and make a desolation over all countries. The remainder shall quit their native soil, and make foreign plantations. A blessed king shall prepare a fleet, and shall be reckoned the twelfth in the court among the saints. There shall be a miserable desolation of the kingdom, and the floors of the harvests shall return to the fruitful forests. The white dragon shall rise again, and invite over a daughter of Germany. Our gardens shall be again replenished with foreign seed, and the red one shall pine away at the end of the pond. After that, shall the German worm be crowned, and the brazen prince buried. He has his bounds assigned to him, which he shall not be able to pass. For a hundred and fifty years he shall continue in trouble and subjection, but shall bear sway three hundred.

Then shall the north wind rise against him, and shall snatch away the flowers which the west wind produced. There shall be gilding in the temples, nor shall the edge of the sword cease. The German dragon shall hardly get to his holes, because the revenge of his treason shall overtake him. At last he shall flourish for a little time, but the decimation of Neustria shall hurt him. For a people in wood and in iron coats shall come, and revenge upon him his wickedness. They shall restore the ancient inhabitants to their dwellings, and there shall be an open destruction of foreigners.

The seed of the white dragon shall be swept out of our gardens, and the remainder of his generation shall be decimated. They shall bear the yoke of slavery, and wound their mother with spades and plows. After this shall succeed two dragons, whereof one shall be killed with the sting of envy, but the other shall return under the shadow of a name.

Then shall succeed a lion of justice, at whose roar the Gallican towers and the island dragons shall tremble. In those days gold shall be squeezed from the lily and the nettle, and silver shall flow from the hoofs of bellowing cattle. The frizzled shall put on various fleeces, and the outward habit denote the inward parts. The feet of barkers shall be cut off; wild beasts shall enjoy peace; mankind shall be grieved at their punishment; the form of commerce shall be divided; the half shall be round. The ravenousness of kites shall be destroyed, and the teeth of wolves blunted. The lion's whelps shall be transformed into sea-fishes; and an eagle shall build her nest upon Mount Aravius. Venedotia shall grow red with the blood of mothers, and the house of Corineus kill six brethren. The island shall be wet with night tears; so that all shall be provoked to all things. Woe to thee, Neustria, because the lion's brain shall be poured upon thee; and he shall be banished with shattered limbs from his native soil.

Posterity shall endeavor to fly above the highest places; but the favor of new comers shall be exalted. Piety shall hurt the possessor of things got by impiety, till he shall have put on his Father: therefore, being armed with the teeth of a boar, he shall ascend above the tops of mountains, and the shadow of him that wears a helmet. Albania shall be enraged, and, assembling her neighbors, shall be employed in shedding blood. There shall be put into her jaws a bridle that shall be made on the coast of Armorica. The eagle of the broken covenant shall gild it over, and rejoice in her third nest.

The roaring whelps shall watch, and, leaving the woods, shall hunt within the walls of cities. They shall make no small slaughter of those that oppose them, and shall cut off the tongues of bulls. They shall load the necks of roaring lions with chains, and restore the times of their ancestors. Then from the first to the fourth, from the fourth to the third, from the third to the second, the thumb shall roll in oil. The sixth shall overturn the walls of Ireland, and change the woods into a plain. He shall reduce several parts to one, and be crowned with the head of a lion. His beginning shall lay open to wandering affection, but his end shall carry him up to the blessed, who are above. For he shall restore the seats of saints in their countries, and settle pastors in convenient places.

Two cities he shall invest with two palls, and shall bestow virgin-presents upon virgins. He shall merit by this the favor of the Thunderer, and shall be placed among the saints. From him shall proceed a lynx penetrating all things, who shall be bent upon the ruin of his own nation; for, through him, Neustria shall lose both islands, and be deprived of its ancient dignity. Then shall the natives return back to the island; for there shall arise a dissension among foreigners. Also a hoary old man, sitting upon a snow-white horse, shall turn the course of the river Periron, and shall measure out a mill upon it with a white rod. Cadwallader shall call upon Conan, and take Albania into alliance.

Then shall there be a slaughter of foreigners; then shall the rivers run with blood. Then shall break forth the fountains of Armorica, and they shall be crowned with the diadem of Brutus. Cambria shall be filled with joy; and the oaks of Cornwall shall flourish. The island shall be called by the name of Brutus: and the name given it by foreigners shall be abolished. From Conan shall proceed a warlike boar, that shall exercise the sharpness of his tusks within the Gallic woods. For he shall cut down all the larger oaks, and shall be a defense to the smaller. The Arabians and Africans shall dread him; for he shall pursue his furious course to the farther part of Spain.

There shall succeed the goat of the Venereal castle, having golden horns and a silver beard, who shall breathe such a cloud out of his nostrils, as shall darken the whole surface of the island. There shall be peace in his time; and corn shall abound by reason of the fruitfulness of the soil. Women shall become serpents in their gait, and all their motions shall be full of pride. The camp of Venus shall be restored; nor shall the arrows of Cupid cease to wound. The fountain of a river shall be turned into blood; and two kings shall fight a duel at Stafford for a lioness. Luxury shall overspread the whole ground; and fornication not cease to debauch mankind.

All these things shall three ages see; till the buried kings shall be exposed to public view in the city of London. Famine shall again return; mortality shall return; and the inhabitants shall grieve for the destruction of their cities. Then shall come the board of commerce, who shall recall the scattered flocks to the pasture they had lost. His breast shall be food to the hungry, and his tongue drink to the thirsty. Out of his mouth shall flow rivers, that shall water the parched jaws of men.

After this shall be produced a tree upon the Tower of London, which, having no more than three branches, shall overshadow the surface of the whole island with the breadth of its leaves. Its adversary, the north wind, shall come upon it, and with its noxious blast shall snatch away the third branch; but the two remaining ones shall possess its place, till they shall destroy one another by the multitude of their leaves; and then shall it obtain the place of those two, and shall give sustenance to birds of foreign nations.

It shall be esteemed hurtful to native fowls; for they shall not be able to fly freely for fear of its shadow. There shall succeed the ass of wickedness, swift against the goldsmiths, but slow against the ravenousness of wolves. In those days the oaks of the forests shall burn, and acorns grow upon the branches of teil trees. The Severn sea shall discharge itself through seven mouths, and the river Uske burn seven months. Fishes shall die with the heat thereof; and of them shall be engendered serpents. The baths of

Badon shall grow cold, and their salubrious waters engender death. London shall mourn for the death of twenty thousand; and the river Thames shall be turned into blood. The monks in their cowls shall be forced to marry, and their cry shall be heard upon the mountains of the Alps.

IV

The continuation of the prophecy.

Three springs shall break forth in the city of Winchester, whose rivulets shall divide the island into three parts. Whoever shall drink of the first, shall enjoy long life, and shall never be afflicted with sickness. He that shall drink of the second, shall die of hunger, and paleness and horror shall sit in his countenance. He that shall drink of the third, shall be surprised with sudden death, neither shall his body be capable of burial. Those that are willing to escape so great a surfeit, will endeavor to hide it with several coverings: but whatever bulk shall be laid upon it, shall receive the form of another body.

For earth shall be turned into stones; stones into water; wood into ashes; ashes into water, if cast over it. Also a damsel shall be sent from the city of the forest of Canute to administer a cure, who, after she shall have practiced all her arts, shall dry up the noxious fountains only with her breath. Afterward, as soon as she shall have refreshed herself with the wholesome liquor, she shall bear in her right hand the wood of Caledon, and in her left the forts of the walls of London. Wherever she shall go, she shall make sulfurous steps, which will smoke with a double flame. That smoke shall rouse up the city of Ruteni, and shall make food for the inhabitants of the deep. She shall overflow with rueful tears, and shall fill the island with her dreadful cry. She shall be killed by a hart with ten branches, four of which shall bear golden diadems; but the other six shall be turned into buffalo's horns, whose hideous sound shall astonish the three islands of Britain.

The Daneian wood shall be stirred up, and breaking forth into a human voice, shall cry: Come, O Cambria, and join Cornwall to thy side, and say to Winchester, the earth shall swallow thee up. Translate the seat of thy pastor to the place where ships come to harbor, and the rest of the members will follow the head. For the day hastens, in which thy citizens shall perish on account of the guilt of perjury. The whiteness of wool has been hurtful to thee, and the variety of its tinctures. Woe to the perjured nation, for whose sake the renowned city shall come to ruin. The ships shall rejoice at so great an augmentation, and one shall be made out of two. It shall be rebuilt by Eric, laden with apples, to the smell whereof the birds of several woods shall flock together. He shall add to it a vast palace, and wall it round with six hundred towers. Therefore shall London envy it, and triply increase her walls. The river Thames shall encompass it round, and the fame of the work shall pass beyond the Alps. Eric shall hide his apples within it, and shall make subterranean passages.

At that time shall the stones speak, and the sea towards the Gallic coast be contracted into a narrow space. On each bank shall one man hear another, and the soil of the island shall be enlarged. The secrets of the deep shall be revealed, and Gaul shall tremble for fear. After these things shall come forth a hern from the forest of Calaterium, which shall fly round the island for two years together. With her nocturnal cry she shall call together the winged kind, and assemble to her all sorts of fowls. They shall invade the tillage of husbandmen, and devour all the grain of the harvests.

Then shall follow a famine upon the people, and a grievous mortality upon the famine. But when this calamity shall be over, a detestable bird shall go to the valley of Galabes, and shall raise it to be a high mountain. Upon the top thereof it shall also plant an oak, and build its nest in its branches. Three eggs shall be produced in the nest, from whence shall come forth a fox, a wolf, and a bear. The fox shall devour her mother, and bear the head of an ass. In this monstrous form shall she frighten her brothers, and make them fly into Neustria. But they shall stir up the tusky boar, and returning in a fleet shall encounter with the fox; who at the beginning of the fight shall feign herself dead, and move the boar to compassion. Then shall the boar approach her carcass, and standing over her, shall breathe upon her face and eyes. But she, not forgetting her cunning, shall bite his left foot, and pluck it off from his body. Then shall she leap upon him, and snatch away his right ear and tail, and hide herself in the caverns of the mountains.

Therefore shall the deluded boar require the wolf and bear to restore him his members; who, as soon as they shall enter into the cause, shall promise two feet of the fox, together with the ear and tail, and of these they shall make up the members of a hog. With this he shall be satisfied, and expect the promised restitution. In the meantime shall the fox descend from the mountains, and change herself into a wolf, and under pretense of holding a conference with the boar, she shall go to him, and craftily devour him. After that she shall transform herself into a boar, and feigning a loss of some members, shall wait for her brothers; but as soon as they are come, she shall suddenly kill them with her tusks, and shall be crowned with the head of a lion. In her days shall a serpent be brought forth, which shall be a destroyer of mankind. With its length it shall encompass London, and devour all that pass by it.

The mountain ox shall take the head of a wolf, and whiten his teeth in the Severn. He shall gather to him the flocks of Albania and Cambria, which shall drink the river Thames dry. The ass shall call the goat with the long beard, and shall borrow his shape. Therefore shall the mountain ox be incensed, and having called the wolf, shall become a horned bull against them. In the exercise of his cruelty he shall devour their flesh and bones, but shall be burned upon the top of Urian. The ashes of his funeral-pyre shall be turned into swans, that shall swim on dry ground as on a river. They shall devour fishes in fishes, and swallow up men in men. But when old age shall come upon them, they shall become sea-wolves, and practice their frauds in the deep. They shall drown ships, and collect no small quantity of silver.

The Thames shall again flow, and assembling together the rivers, shall pass beyond the bounds of its channel. It shall cover the adjacent cities, and overturn the mountains that oppose its course. Being full of deceit and wickedness, it shall make use of the fountain Galabes. Hence shall arise factions provoking the Venedotians to war. The oaks of the forest shall meet together, and encounter the rocks of the Gewisseans. A raven shall attend with the kites, and devour the carcasses of the slain. An owl shall build her nest upon the walls of Gloucester, and in her nest shall be brought forth an ass. The serpent of Malvernia shall bring him up, and put him upon many fraudulent practices. Having taken the crown, he shall ascend on high, and frighten the people of the country with his hideous braying. In his days shall the Pachaian mountains tremble, and the provinces be deprived of their woods.

For there shall come a worm with a fiery breath, and with the vapor it sends forth shall burn up the trees. Out of it shall proceed seven lions deformed with the heads of goats. With the stench of their nostrils they shall corrupt women, and make wives turn common prostitutes. The father shall not know his own son, because they shall grow wanton like brute beasts. Then shall come the giant of wickedness, and terrify all with the sharpness of his eyes. Against him shall arise the dragon of Worcester, and shall endeavor to banish him. But in the engagement the dragon shall be worsted, and oppressed by the wickedness of the conqueror. For he shall mount upon the dragon, and putting off his garment shall sit upon him naked. The dragon shall bear him up on high, and beat his naked rider with his tail erected. Upon this the giant rousing up his whole strength, shall break his jaws with his sword. At last the dragon shall fold itself up under its tail, and die of poison. After him shall succeed the boar of Totness, and oppress the people with grievous tyranny. Gloucester shall send forth a lion, and shall disturb him in his cruelty, in several battles. He shall trample him under his feet, and terrify him with open jaws. At last the lion shall quarrel with the kingdom, and get upon the backs of the nobility.

A bull shall come into the quarrel, and strike the lion with his right foot. He shall drive him through all the inns in the kingdom, but shall break his horns against the walls of Oxford. The fox of Kaerdubalem shall take revenge on the lion, and destroy him entirely with her teeth. She shall be encompassed by the adder of Lincoln, who with a horrible hiss shall give notice of his presence to a multitude of dragons. Then shall the dragons encounter, and tear one another to pieces. The winged shall oppress that which wants wings, and fasten its claws into the poisonous cheeks. Others shall come into the quarrel, and kill one another. A fifth shall succeed those that are slain, and by various stratagems shall destroy the rest. He shall get upon the back of one with his sword, and sever his head from his body. Then throwing off his garment, he shall get upon another, and put his right and left hand upon his tail. Thus being naked shall he overcome him, whom when clothed he was not able to deal with. The rest he shall gall in their flight, and drive them round the kingdom. Upon this shall come a roaring lion dreadful for his monstrous cruelty. Fifteen parts shall he reduce to one, and shall alone possess the people.

The giant of the snow white color shall shine, and cause the white people to flourish. Pleasures shall effeminate the princes, and they shall suddenly be changed into beasts. Among them shall arise a lion swelled with human gore. Under him shall a reaper be placed in the standing corn, who, while he is reaping, shall be oppressed by him. A charioteer of York shall appease them, and having banished his lord, shall mount upon the chariot which he shall drive. With his sword unsheathed shall he threaten the East, and fill the tracks of his wheels with blood. Afterward he shall become a sea-fish, who, being roused up with the hissing of a serpent, shall engender with him. From hence shall be produced three thundering bulls, who having eaten up their pastures shall be turned into trees. The first shall carry a whip of vipers, and turn his back upon the next. He shall endeavor to snatch away the whip, but shall be taken by the last. They shall turn away their faces from one another, till they have thrown away the poisoned cup. To him shall succeed a husbandman of Albania, at whose back shall be a serpent. He shall be employed in plowing the ground, that the country may become white with corn. The serpent shall endeavor to diffuse his poison, in order to blast the harvest. A grievous mortality shall sweep away the people, and the walls of cities shall be made desolate.

There shall be given for a remedy the city of Claudius, which shall interpose the nurse of the scourger. For she shall bear a dose of medicine, and in a short time the island shall be restored. Then shall two successively sway the sceptre, whom a horned dragon shall serve. One shall come in armor, and shall ride upon a flying serpent. He shall sit upon his back with his naked body, and cast his right hand upon his tail. With his cry shall the seas be moved, and he shall strike terror into the second. The second therefore shall enter into confederacy with the lion; but a quarrel happening, they shall encounter one another. They shall distress one another, but the courage of the beast shall gain the advantage. Then shall come one with a drum, and appease the rage of the lion. Therefore shall the people of the kingdom be at peace, and provoke the lion to a dose of physic. In his established seat he shall adjust the weights, but shall stretch out his hands into Albania. For which reason the northern provinces shall be grieved, and open the gates of the temples. The sign-bearing wolf shall lead his troops, and surround Cornwall with his tail. He shall be opposed by a soldier in a chariot, who shall transform that people into a boar. The boar therefore shall ravage the provinces, but shall hide his head in the depth of Severn. A man shall embrace the lion in wine, and the dazzling brightness of gold shall blind the eyes of beholders. Silver shall whiten in the circumference, and torment several wine presses.

Men shall be drunk with wine, and, regardless of heaven, shall be intent upon the earth. From them shall the stars turn away their faces, and confound their usual course. Corn will wither at their malign aspects; and there shall fall no dew from heaven. The roots and branches will change their places, and the novelty of the thing shall pass for a miracle. The brightness of the sun shall fade at the amber of Mercury, and horror shall seize the beholders. Stilbon of Arcadia shall change his shield; the helmet of Mars shall call Venus. The helmet of Mars shall make a shadow; and the rage of Mercury pass his bounds. Iron Orion shall unsheath his sword: the marine Phoebus shall torment the clouds; Jupiter shall go out of his lawful paths; and Venus forsake her stated lines. The malignity of the star Saturn shall fall down in rain, and slay mankind with a crooked sickle. The twelve houses of the star shall lament the irregular excursions of their guests; and Gemini omit their usual embraces, and call the urn to the fountains. The scales of Libra shall hang obliquely, till Aries puts his crooked horns under them. The tail of Scorpio shall produce lightning, and Cancer quarrel with the Sun. Virgo shall mount upon the back of Sagittarius, and darken her virgin flowers. The chariot of the Moon shall disorder the zodiac, and the Pleiades break forth into weeping. No offices of Janus shall hereafter return, but his gate being shut shall lie hid in the chinks of Ariadne. The seas shall rise up in the twinkling of an eye, and the dust of ancients shall be restored. The winds shall fight together with a dreadful blast, and their sound shall reach the stars.

Chapter XLV
The Stanzas of the Graves - Englynion Y Beddau

Collected in the Peniarth MS. 98B

and in Myvyrian Archaeology

I

Y Bed yn y Gorvynyd a lyuyaf ai luyossyd
Bed ffyrnnal hael vab Hyulyd

II

Bed Guaynuyn gurgoffri rhung lluvan a llyfni
Gur oed ef guir y neb ni rodri

III

Bed Guydion ap Donn ym Morva Dinlleu
Dan vain dyveillion
Garanauc y geiffyl Meinon

IV

Neut am dinau cwm waithvudic anwaith
Wr clot ior gwaith uudic
Aruynaul gedaul gredic

V

Guedy meirch a seirch crychraun
A guaur a gueuyr uniawn
Am dinon rythych dros odre on
Pen hard Lonan llaw estron

VI

Guedy seirch a meirch melyn
A gawr a gwaewawr gurthryn
Am dineu rhych bych dros odreon
Pen hard Llovan llaw ysgyn

VII

Bed Llovan llaw divo
Yn ar ro Venai yn y gwna ton tolo
Bed Dylan yn Llan Veuno
Bed Llovan llaw divo
Un ar ei o Venei odidauc ai guypo
Namyn Duw a mi heno

VIII

Bed Panna vab yt
Yg gorthir Arvon dan ei oer uervt
Bed Cynon yn Reon Ryt

IX

Bed llew llaw gyffes
Dan achles mor cyn divot y Armes
Gur oed ef gualioc Mei Ormes

X

Pan dyvu Benbych ae beuyl ar Afon ar wawci
Arvauc y unni llas Agen ap Yvrgi
O lias Ager yn Aber Brangoni
Car canhwyliaith hed-ar luoed y taith
Bed Tedel Tydawen yng guarthaf brynn
Arien eny gwna ton tolo
Bed Dylan yn llan Veuno

XI

Eic len don drom dra thywayt
Am vecici Dysgyrnin disgyffedawt
Aches trwm Anghures pechwawt

XII

Bed ylidyr muynvawr ynglau
Mawr nwyedus fawt brydus briodawr
Guenefwr gwr gwrd i gaur.

XIII

Y Bed yngorthir Nanllau
Ny uyr neb y gynneddfeu
Mabon vab Madron glau

XIV

Bed An ap llian ymnewais
Vynyd lluagor llew Emreis
Prif ddewin merdin Emreis

XV

Uwch law ryd y Garw vaen ryde
Y mae bedd Hun ap Alun a Dyve

Translation Notes

XIII

The grave in the upland of Nanllau;
His story no one knows.
Mabon the son of Modron the sincere.

XIV

The grave of the nun's son on Newais:
Mountain of battle, Llew [lion of] Emrys,
Chief Magician, Myrddin Emrys

Chapter XLVI The Rites of Awen - High Magic of the Pheryllt

Adapted by Myrddin Cerrig,

Bard of the Twelfth Chair

High magic of the Pheryllt and Druids concentrates on light work aligned to "radiance" of the Three Rays of Awen. Managing personal Calen (Light Centres and Light Shields) [see Chapter IX] and other magic involves using Rites of Awen to activate this personal awareness - an awareness of the Rays of Universal Power consciously directed by the Druid. Although frequently translated as "alchemists" and "metalsmithers", it may be that the name Pheryllt stems from the *pher-syllu,* literally to "gaze at lights" - making them light, fire and star gazers. This light work, gleaned from the pages of Barddas, Pherylt and other revivals is called simply: The Rites of Awen.

The Triad of Awen

(Hermetic Version)

Instructions for this basic version from the Hermetic vein of mystics invokes the threefold Divine (or unspeakable) name attributed to the Rays of Awen is the Gnostic threefold name: IAO. Alternatively, the threefold name used in other Bardic Druid interpretations is derived from the threefold name given in the Barddas coelbren lore: OIW or OIU. It is believed that these utterances, sounds or vibrations possess all of the power of the universe when used properly.

Face the northern direction. Call down the Radiance in the form of the Silver Ray, feeling and seeing it descend upon you and to the left as you intone the sound "I" (or "ee"). Raise your arms as you inhale the tone and bring them down to your sides as you exhale or intone the sound, using your arms to draw or pull down the air (ray). Do this with the Middle Ray (Crystal Ray) descending through you with the sound "A" (or "ah"), and the Gold Ray upon you and down to the right with the utterance "O" ("oh"). Some Druids invoke "Awen" as "ah-oo-een."

The Three Pillars of Light

(Hughes Version)

From left to right, the first vowel, O, is pronounced as a long oh sound. It arises and resonates from the top of the lungs and the lower throat. It is attributed one of the three functions of *awen* – to understand the truth. The second vowel is I and is pronounced a long ee sound. It arises and resonates high in the throat and at the back of the mouth. It is attributed he second primary function of *awen* – to love the truth. The third vowel is W and is pronounced as an oo sound. It resonates at the mid and front sections of the mouth, then transfers through the pallet into the nasal region. It is attributed the third primary function of *awen* – to maintain truth.

The Three Rays of Light

(Greer Version)

The sign made by these three lines or cuttings, / | \ , is the emblem of the Three Rays of Light that brought the world into being, and they form the holy sign of the Druids. Each ray has a name: the left-hand ray is Grwon (virtue), and to it is assigned the quality of knowledge; the right-hand ray is Plennydd (light), and to it is assigned the quality of power; and the central ray is Alawn (harmony), and to it is assigned the quality of peace. Knowledge, power, and peace are therefore manifest in and called forth by this sign.

The Inner Temple of Merlyn

A personal rite to cleanse the inner temple and as a preparatory ritual for AWEN light work in the Druidic tradition.

1.

Sit comfortably, hands and feet not crossing.

2.

Visualize an atmosphere of white cleansing energy.

3.

Begin inhaling it into your body.

4.

Allow it to wash through you.

5.

Now breathe in clear air.

6.

As you breathe in clear air, see and feel it pushing out the impurities, the cleansing air is purified.

7.

These impurities fall to your feet and are pushed into the ground.

8.

Perform the Rite of the Three Rays of Awen.

9.

Intone: Yr Awen a ganf - or dwfn y dygaf.

> (Urr ah-wehn a GAN-av - oh-rr dOO-vun uh DUG-av)
> The Awen I sing - from the deep I bring it.
> I am washed clean in radiance of Awen.

10.

Visualize the white light energy returning around you.

11.

Feel and see it perform a protective aura around your body, beginning with the head and moving down. You are now prepared for Awen radiance light work.

The Golden Radiance of Awen

Energy of the Golden Ray of AWEN can bring golden blessings. To attain this, you must vibrate the energy you seek to attract - like forces attract like forces. To attract a golden life, use the rays of Awen to attract and project golden light rays.

1.

Activate the Inner Temple of Merlyn

2.

With eyes open, see golden light ray energy all around you.

3.

Hold this imagery for at least three minutes and then inhale the energy.

4.

Allow it to wash through your entire being.

5.

Intone: I am filled by the golden rays of Awen - the Rays and I are one. I make them a part of myself - so mote it be.

6.

Vibrate the golden light ray energy into your auric field.

7.

Practice this many times daily for optimum results.

Chapter XLVII The Truth Against the World

Verses by Myrddin Cerrig

Bard of the Twelfth Chair

The Personal Quest for Truth

Truth is the essence of life. Truth is the unseen power that governs all things. Truth is the key to unlocking the secrets of the universe. But in the material realm, truth becomes subjective in experience as no two people appear to share the same truth. It is through the understanding of our 'personal truth' that we might better understand the nature of ourselves and why we think, feel and act the way we do.

It is written that if you try to understand the universe, you will discover nothing at all, but seek to understand the self and there alone lies the Great Key to the mysteries of all creation.

Know Thyself

The wise instruct us many times to: know thyself – and those two simple words have meaning of utmost importance here. What he meant was that by understanding human nature, all else that could be desired to know, would fall into place.

What many Druids today do not grasp is that before one seeks to know about trees, rocks, animals and other worlds, that they should first come to know themselves. Humans are like a collage of what could be labeled mind, body and spirit, which are simultaneously connected and separate.

Science vs. Spirit

Contemporary systems of science do not really understand the multifaceted aspects of humans because science is only programmed with the ability to establish physical and mundane basis for phenomenon and existence. For science, man is only a brain; the mind is essentially nonexistent.

The brain is programmed to be a construct limited to the physical reality of existence. The mind, on the contrary, is not a physical form and is full of unlimited potentiality. It is only through Truth that we are able to unlock the unlimited power of the mind. Because of conditioning, the thirst for the quest for the Truth, and the ability to perceive it clearly, can be lost with age.

Ineffable Truth

I point out here semantic differences between "Truth" and "truth." There are "truths" all around us - but they are composed by man, built upon the language structure and definitions entangled together to provide arbitrary meanings.

In youth, a child has yet to be conformed to this semantic level of truth and it is at this point that they might be unconditionally brought to recognize reality self-honestly for the remainder of their life.

Perfect Balance

The path to the Truth is not necessarily one that is focused on perfect balance of forces in the material world - in fact, on a physical level this idea of perfect balance can never be attained.

A Druidical doctrine exists that explains that the human spirit needs a 'constructive imbalance' to grow, whereas true 'balance' is actually 'static' and promotes stagnation of energy.

When the time comes for you to be 'perfectly balanced' you will not be able, or have need to, exist in the physical world, which is everything but static and unchanging. All manifestation is in some state of imperfection on a spiritual "level" - being fragmented from the ALL into a condensed material existence.

Semantic Issues on the Quest

One step often missed on the quest for truth is that one is even forced to analyze what "Truth" means. How can you know you have found the Truth if you don't know what it is? Likewise, how can you quest for something you don't know? We must determine what is true and how we can know it to be true.

Can we turn to a man-made "artificial" knowledge to distinguish the truth? No, because it is the man-made truths that limit us in our programming and place barriers on what we are capable of understanding socially.

Seek and Ye shall Find

Many believe knowledge can only be gained through direct physical and personal experiences - but we also find that this is not the case.

It is said that Truth can be found in the unity of 'experiencing, studying and knowing' all things, but the Truth may not be found in any one of those three things.

Truth may be gained or at least brought closer to your reach through what Socrates called "Right Action" and philosophers and mystics often refer to as the "Right Way." This is living in accordance with the natural forces of the universe and by one's true and self-honest intuition.

"Men have always gone to their graves preaching their own truths; yet the sun still rises."

We must understand that "beliefs" will come and go, religions will open and shut, civilizations will rise and fall but the ineffable Truth of All Thing will remain unchanged.

Social Programming

Holding on to tightly to man-made truths will cancel out what is real because this type of artificial truth programming seeks immediate dominance, but will fade, leaving its believer in "darkness" trying to grasp on whatever will hold them. Another man-made truth program will be there to replace the first and so on.

Ritualism

Many interpret the search for truth, or this type of philosophy or Druidry as a magic - and in many ways it is , but 'practical magic' and ritualism is merely an 'outward' expression of the 'inner' search for "Truth," or at least they should be. So, in order to gain a 'peaceful' environment we must radiate peace from within - like attracts like.

The Tri-Force

The methodology of questing for Truth as a tri-force is existent in doctrinal lore of the Ancient Druidic Council - which sought all Truth in Knowledge as comprised of three aspects: Strength, Wisdom and Compassion.

To attempt to reach the Truth while on the physical plane is to stand on a ladder delicately balanced and composed of many far-reaching aspects. Skip one step, and you fall backwards. Misinterpret your foundation, and your ladder will not balance. Seek the false truths, and your ladder will be left leaning against the sky with nothing of substance to hold it upright.

and when the student is ready,
the teacher shall appear.

Here endeth the book of pheryllt

Bibliography

The following manuscripts/books were consulted for support or confirmation during development of this Book of Pheryllt allegorical facsimile as a credible Druidical source book companion and anthology reference of original and antiquated writings prepared for modern times. Selections from some antiquated sources may be adapted for the current volume, whereas more modern sources are cited for clarification, correction and/or comparison.

Black Book of Carmarthen. National Library of Wales, Peniarth MS 1. Wales, 1250.

Book of Ballymote. Royal Irish Academy, MS 23 P-3. Ballymote, 1390-1391.

Book of Taliesin. National Library of Wales, Peniarth MS 2. Wales, 1250.

Red Book of Hergest. Bodleian Library, Oxford, MS 111. Wales, 1385.

Blamires, Steve. *Celtic Tree Mysteries*. Llewellyn, 1997.

Calder, George. *Auraicept na n-Eces: The Scholar's Primer & Ogham Tracts*. Edinburgh, 1917.

Clouter, Gregory. *Lost Zodiac of the Druids*. Vega, 2003.

Conway, D.J. *By Oak, Ash & Thorn*. Llewellyn, 1994.

Conway, D.J. *Celtic Magic*. Llewellyn, 1990.

Davies, Edward. *Mythology and Rites of the British Druids*. J. Booth, 1809.

Duke, Edward. *Druidical Temples of the County of Wilts*. J.R. Smith, 1846.

Flesch, Matthew. *Ogham: Druid Oracle of the Trees*. Dragon Torque, 1997.

Free, Joshua. *Arcanum: Great Magical Arcanum*. Mardukite, 2008.

Free, Joshua. *Book of Druidry*. Mardukite, 2016 (original 2001).

Free, Joshua. *Book of Elven-Faerie.* Mardukite, 2014 (original 2004).

Free, Joshua. *Draconomicon.* Mardukite, 2016 (original 1996).

Free, Joshua. *Pheryllt* (3 Volumes). Mardukite, 2014-2018.

Free, Joshua (Merlyn Stone). *Sorcerer's Handbook.* Mardukite, 2018 (original 1998).

Graves, Robert. *The White Goddess.* Faber & Faber, 1948.

Greer, John Michael. *The Celtic Golden Dawn.* Llewellyn, 2013.

Heselton, Philip. *Magical Guardians.* Capall Bann, 1998.

Hughes, Kristoffer. *The Book of Celtic Magic.* Llewellyn, 2014.

Hughes, Kristoffer. *From the Cauldron Born.* Llewellyn, 2012.

MacCulloch, J.A. *Religion of the Ancient Celts.* T.&T. Clark, 1911.

Monmouth, Geoffrey of. *Historia Regum Britanniae* (History of the Kings of Britain). 1136.

Monmouth, Geoffrey of. *Brut y Brenhinedd* (History of the Kings of Britain). National Library of Wales, Peniarth MS 23C. Wales, 1475.

Monmouth, Geoffrey of. *Prophetiae Merlini* (Prophecies of Merlin). 1135.

Monmouth, Geoffrey of. *Vita Merlini* (The Life of Merlin). 1150.

Monroe, Douglas. *The Deepteachings of Merlyn.* Kima Global, 2011.

Monroe, Douglas. *Lost Books of Merlyn.* Llewellyn, 1998

Monroe, Douglas. *Twenty-One Lessons of Merlyn.* Llewellyn, 1992.

Murray, Liz and Colin. *Celtic Tree Oracle.* St. Martin's Press, 1988.

Nash, David W. *Taliesin -or- The Bards and Druids of Britain.* J.R. Smith, 1858.

Reade, William Winwood. *Veil of Isis -or- Mysteries of the Druids.* C.J. Skeet, 1861.

Sikes, Wirt. *British Goblins: Welsh Folklore, Legends & Traditions*. Sampson & Low, 1880.

Spence, Lewis. *History and Origins of Druidism*. Rider, 1949.

Spence, Lewis. *Mysteries of Britain: Secret Rites & Traditions*. Fisher, Knight & Co., 1905.

Toland, John. *History of Celtic Religion and Learning: Containing an Account of the Druids*. Letters to Lord Molesworth, 1726 (reprinted by Lackington, Allen & Co.).

Toland, John. *History of the Druids: A New Edition*. J. Watt, 1814.

Vere, Nicholas de. *Dragon Legacy*. The Book Tree, 2004.

Williams ab Ithel, Edward/John (Iolo Morganwg) and Llywelyn Sion. *Barddas*. Longman, 1862.

Williams, Edward (Iolo Morganwg), Owen Jones and William Pughe. *Myvyrian Archaeology: Ancient Manuscripts of Wales* (3 Volumes). Gwyneddigion Society, 1801-1807.

Williams, Taliesin (ed.). *Iolo Manuscripts: A Selection of Ancient Welsh Manuscripts*. Longman, 1848.

Wright, Dudley. *Druidism: The Ancient Faith of Britain*. Ed. J. Burrow, 1924.

Index

A

Abred 42-43, 213

Annwn 26-27, 42, 45, 99, 189, 241, 263, 266-268, 286, 300-307

Arthur 18, 28, 72, 75, 103, 139, 150, 157, 265-266, 268, 301-307, 344, 347 348

Avalon 34, 246, 265, 294

B

Ballymote 16, 172, 188-189, 191, 193, 195, 197, 243, 245, 249

Bard 5, 13-14, 18, 21-24, 26-27, 31-34, 38, 46-48, 50-51, 54, 56, 58, 62-65, 69, 71, 74, 77, 80, 87, 103, 106, 108, 116, 121, 125, 135-136, 143, 148, 151, 155, 160-165, 172, 228, 232, 247, 259, 284, 286-289, 291, 293, 296, 301, 305, 310-312, 314, 321, 323, 324, 358-359, 361, 363, 365-367, 388, 392

Barddas 15-16, 18, 42, 44, 164, 388

Beltane 92, 96-97, 199, 219, 236, 270-273

C

Cabala 24, 42-44, 189, 202, 301

Cad Goddeu 13, 15, 143, 145, 147, 149-151, 153, 155, 157, 159, 189, 265, 300

Calen 109, 124, 165-166, 168, 170, 388

Ceridwen 18, 30, 103-107, 295, 300-301

Charm of Making 16

Ceugent 42, 44, 166

Chakra 108-109, 301

Charm of Making 15, 114

Crane Bag 169, 243, 245

D

Dragon 14-16, 17-18, 27, 94, 96, 100, 108-109, 111, 113-114, 117-118, 121, 126, 128, 132-133, 135-139, 139, 169, 221-222, 239, 264, 266, 268, 288, 324, 338-339, 342-343, 368-369, 371, 373, 374-376, 382-383

E

Egg 166, 261, 278, 290, 291, 293-295, 353, 380

Egyptian 29, 31, 137-139, 278, 281, 307

G

Gorsedd 9, 22-23, 25, 46-49, 92

Grail 95, 285, 301, 306

Gwynedd 42-44, 78, 166, 286, 358

I

Imbolc 92, 95, 97, 219, 267, 313

K

Keridwen 287-289, 294, 305

Kundalini 108

L

Ley line 108-109

Lughnassadh 92, 96, 98, 220, 268, 270

Lugnasad 274

M

Mabinogion 15, 129, 285-286, 300, 305

Menw 23, 68, 96

Merkaba 111

Merlin 139, 305, 325-333, 336, 340, 344-345, 349, 352, 354-355, 369-371, 374

Merlyn 11, 14, 17, 73, 75, 78, 139, 207, 223, 276-277, 279, 281, 283, 325, 327, 329, 331, 333, 335, 337, 339, 341, 343, 345, 347, 349, 351, 353, 355, 357, 368-369, 371, 373-375, 377, 379, 381, 383, 390-391

Myrddin 5, 15, 17, 29, 34, 51, 87, 108, 125, 135, 139, 143, 160, 165, 188, 197, 202, 207, 209, 213, 216, 224, 228, 232, 236, 238, 243, 249, 257, 269, 276, 284, 290, 296, 300, 315, 321, 323, 325, 358-359, 361-365, 367-368, 374, 387-388, 392

O

Ovate 38, 46-50, 293

Ovydd 33, 54

Oxford 18, 106, 133, 265, 288, 356, 382

S

Samhain 92, 96, 98, 207, 220, 236, 268-270, 274

Starfire 109-110, 246

Stonehenge 139, 209, 278-279, 282

T

Taliesin 15, 18, 28, 67, 73, 103, 105-107, 143, 266, 268, 285, 287, 289, 293, 295, 300-301, 306, 308-309, 311-315, 317, 319-320, 339-340, 344-345, 350, 355

V

Vortigern 339, 345, 347, 368-374

W

Wales 17, 28, 75, 106, 137, 265, 271, 285-286, 288, 292, 308, 321, 325, 337, 347

Welsh 14-16, 24, 30, 100, 137-138, 263, 270, 284-285, 287-289, 291-294, 301, 323, 325, 337, 345, 356

About the Author

Joshua Free has been involved with practical Earth magic since he was 12, starting with his first initiation into Pheryllt Druidism in the mid-1990's as Merlyn Stone. At that time, he was once the youngest initiate ever of the Order of Bards, Ovates & Druids (OBOD) in England, before leaving to exclusively pursue a Druidic apprenticeship with Douglas Monroe, and is now Bard of the Twelfth Chair at New Forest Centre for Magickal Studies.

Joshua Free

Best known publicly as a prodigious mystic, prolific author and founder of the modern Mardukite movement (in 2008) and its *Necronomicon Anunnaki Bible,* Mr. Free has actually spent his lifetime exploring Druid histories, mysteries and lore - much of it collected here in his realization of *The Book of Pheryllt.*

An Invitation

We, the publisher, trust that you enjoyed this book and invite you to visit our web site www.us.kimabooks.com for more instructive reading. We especially recommend:

The Deepteachings of Merlyn

This is the concluding chapter in the best selling Merlyn trilogy by Douglas Monroe. This is the final quest for the deeper secrets of the druids and contains a wealth of deep research, all of which is relevant to modern practice in today's world.

ISBN: 978-1-920533-06-9

It is available from the Kima Global Publishers web site http://bit.ly/2NFPw9O

or from Amazon https://amzn.to/2N8Smoj

CPSIA information can be obtained
at www.ICGtesting.com
Printed in the USA
BVHW032236020820
585292BV00064B/14

9 781928 234364